GARFIELD
GOES HOG WILD

BY JIM DAVIS

Ballantine Books ● New York

Hudson Area Public Library
PO Box 461
Hudson, IL 61748

A Ballantine Books Trade Paperback Original

Copyright © 2020 by PAWS, Inc. All Rights Reserved. "GARFIELD" and the GARFIELD characters are trademarks of PAWS, Inc. NICKELODEON is a Trademark of Viacom International, Inc. Based on the Garfield® characters created by Jim Davis.

Published in the United States by Ballantine Books, an imprint of Random House, a division of Penguin Random House LLC, New York.

BALLANTINE and the HOUSE colophon are registered trademarks of Penguin Random House LLC.

All of the comics in this work have been previously published.

ISBN 978-0-593-15642-1
Ebook ISBN 978-0-593-15643-8

Printed in China on acid-free paper

randomhousebooks.com

9 8 7 6 5 4 3 2 1

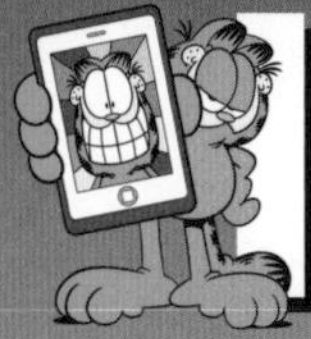

IT'S ALL ABOUT MEME

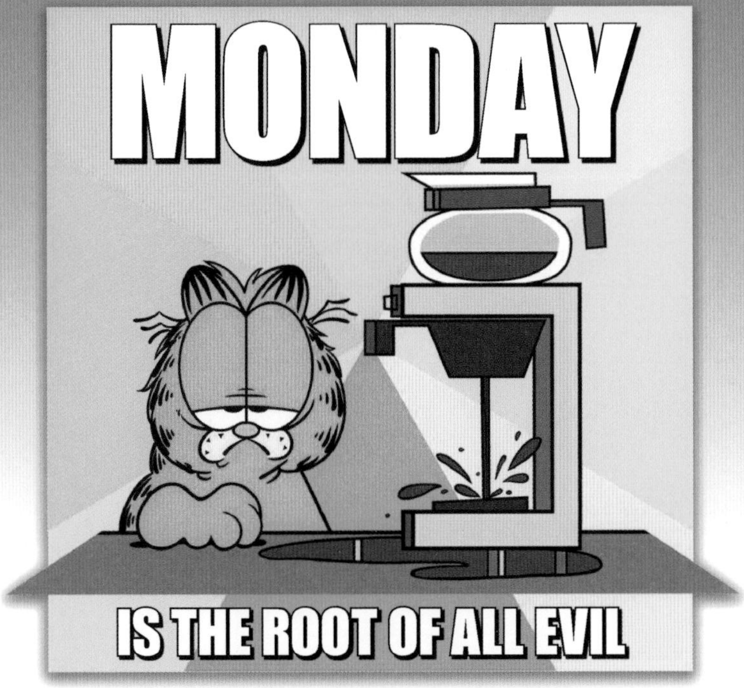
MONDAY
IS THE ROOT OF ALL EVIL

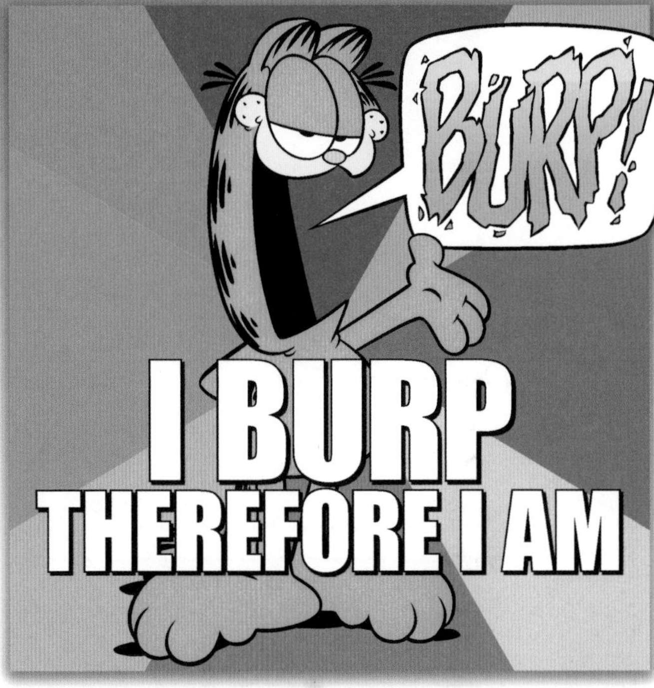
BURP!
I BURP
THEREFORE I AM

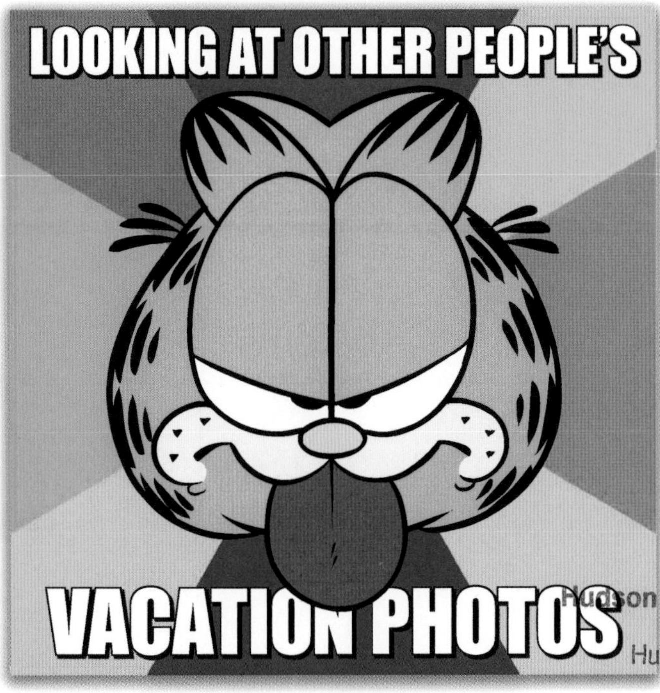
LOOKING AT OTHER PEOPLE'S
VACATION PHOTOS

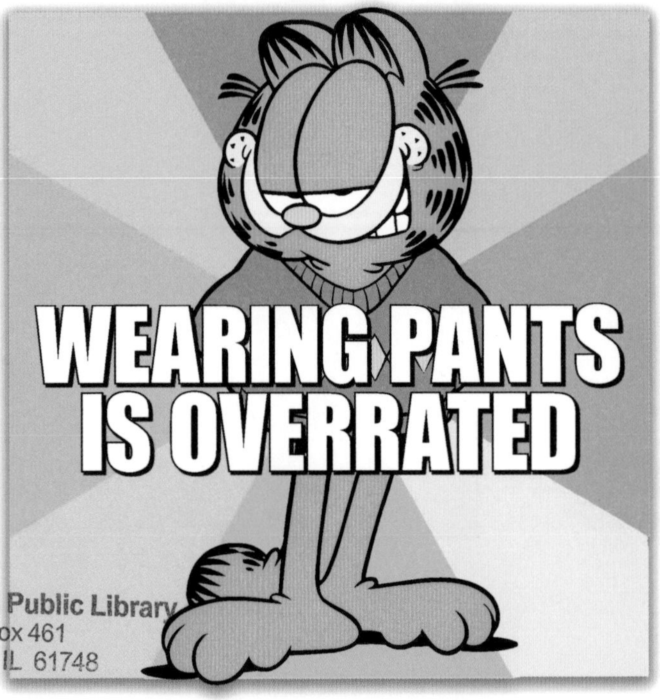
WEARING PANTS
IS OVERRATED

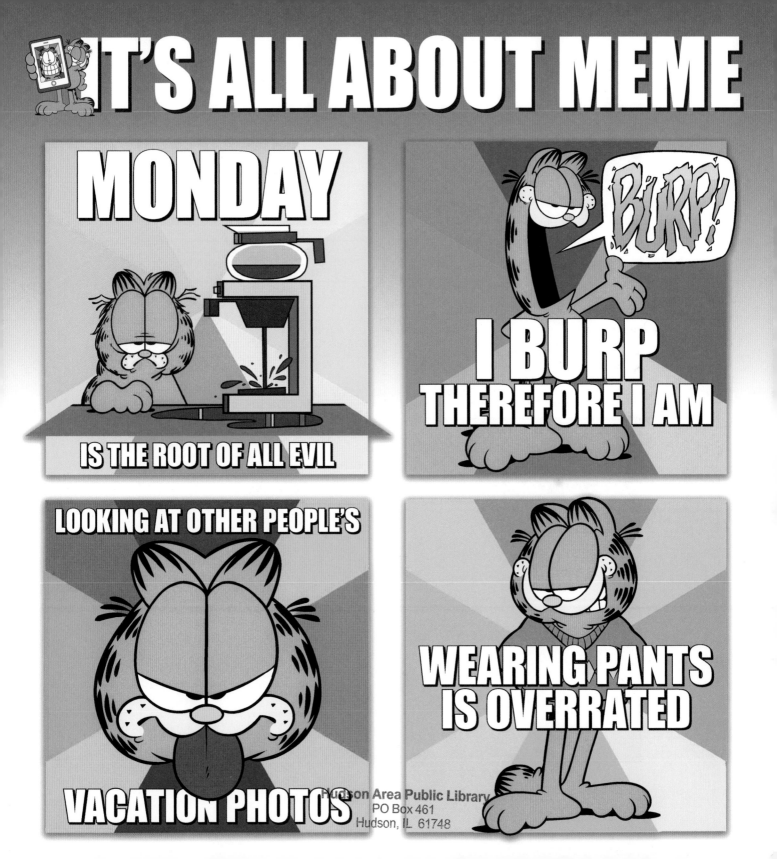

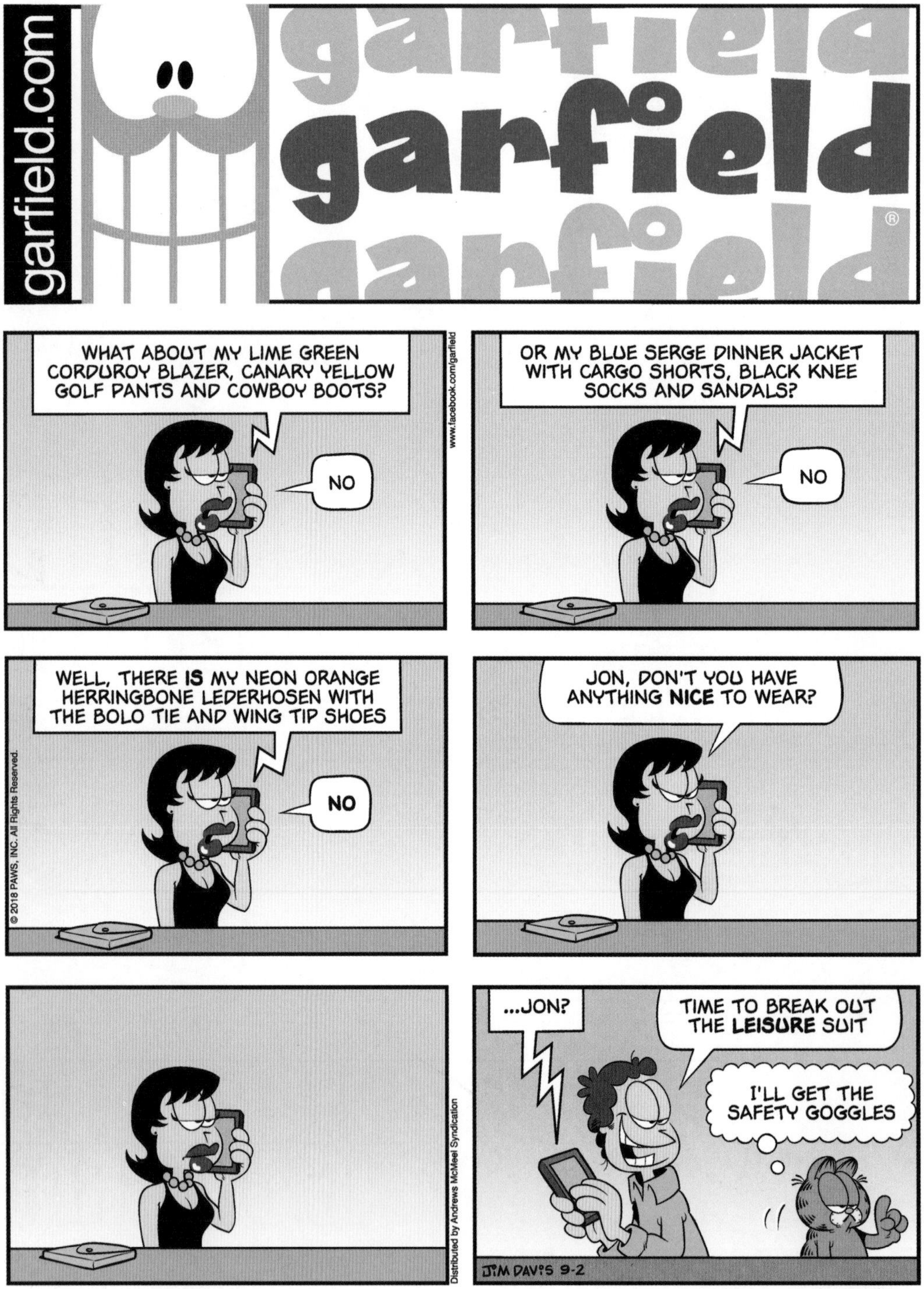
garfield.com
garfield
garfield
garfield
WHAT ABOUT MY LIME GREEN CORDUROY BLAZER, CANARY YELLOW GOLF PANTS AND COWBOY BOOTS?
NO
www.facebook.com/garfield
OR MY BLUE SERGE DINNER JACKET WITH CARGO SHORTS, BLACK KNEE SOCKS AND SANDALS?
NO
WELL, THERE **IS** MY NEON ORANGE HERRINGBONE LEDERHOSEN WITH THE BOLO TIE AND WING TIP SHOES
NO
© 2018 PAWS, INC. All Rights Reserved.
JON, DON'T YOU HAVE ANYTHING **NICE** TO WEAR?
Distributed by Andrews McMeel Syndication
...JON?
TIME TO BREAK OUT THE **LEISURE** SUIT
I'LL GET THE SAFETY GOGGLES
JIM DAVIS 9-2

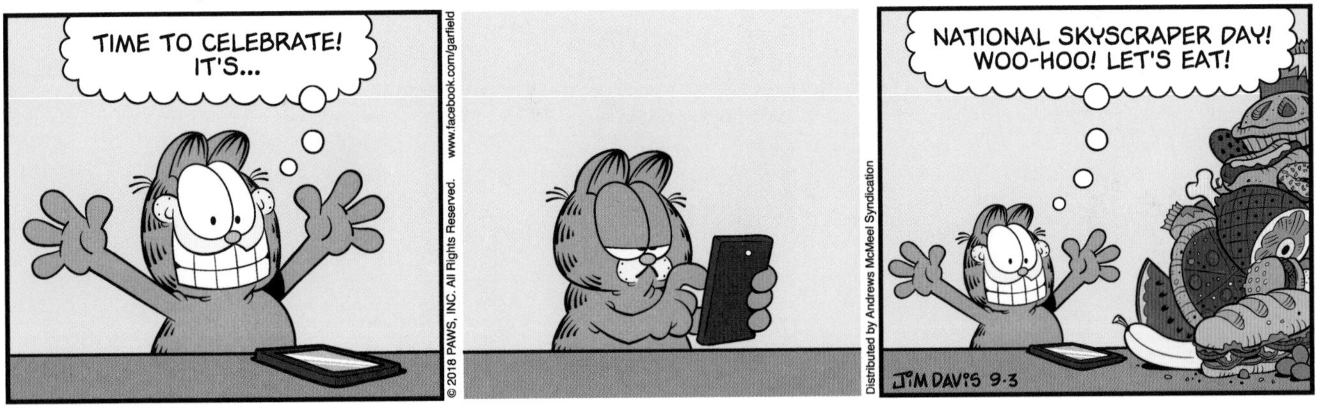
TIME TO CELEBRATE! IT'S...
© 2018 PAWS, INC. All Rights Reserved. www.facebook.com/garfield
NATIONAL SKYSCRAPER DAY! WOO-HOO! LET'S EAT!
Distributed by Andrews McMeel Syndication
JIM DAVIS 9-3

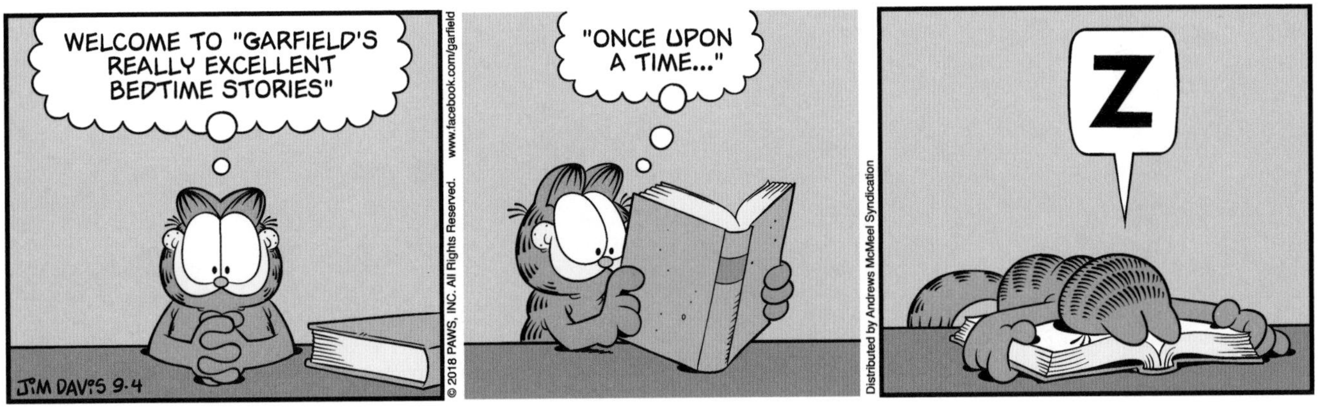
WELCOME TO "GARFIELD'S REALLY EXCELLENT BEDTIME STORIES"
JIM DAVIS 9-4
© 2018 PAWS, INC. All Rights Reserved. www.facebook.com/garfield
"ONCE UPON A TIME..."
Distributed by Andrews McMeel Syndication
Z

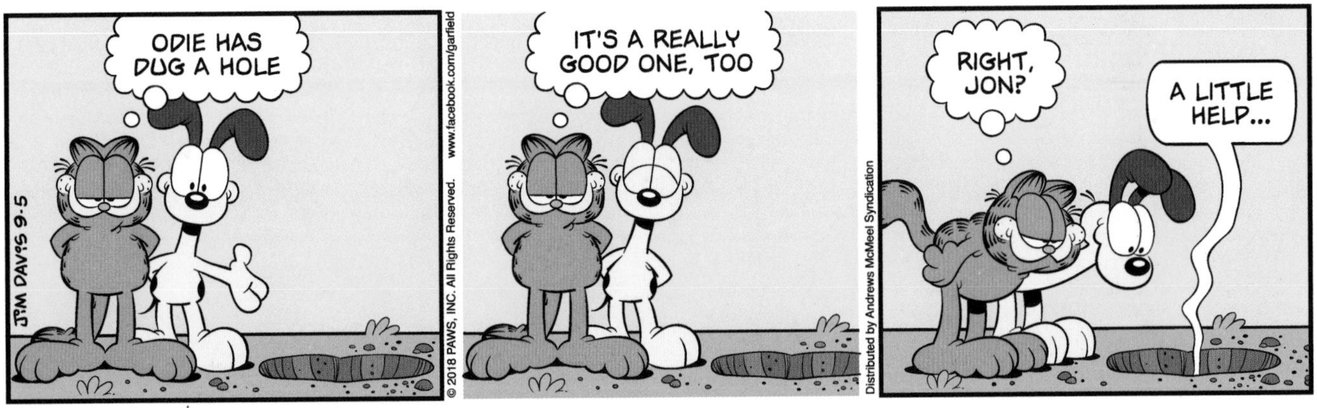
ODIE HAS DUG A HOLE
JIM DAVIS 9-5
© 2018 PAWS, INC. All Rights Reserved. www.facebook.com/garfield
IT'S A REALLY GOOD ONE, TOO
Distributed by Andrews McMeel Syndication
RIGHT, JON?
A LITTLE HELP...

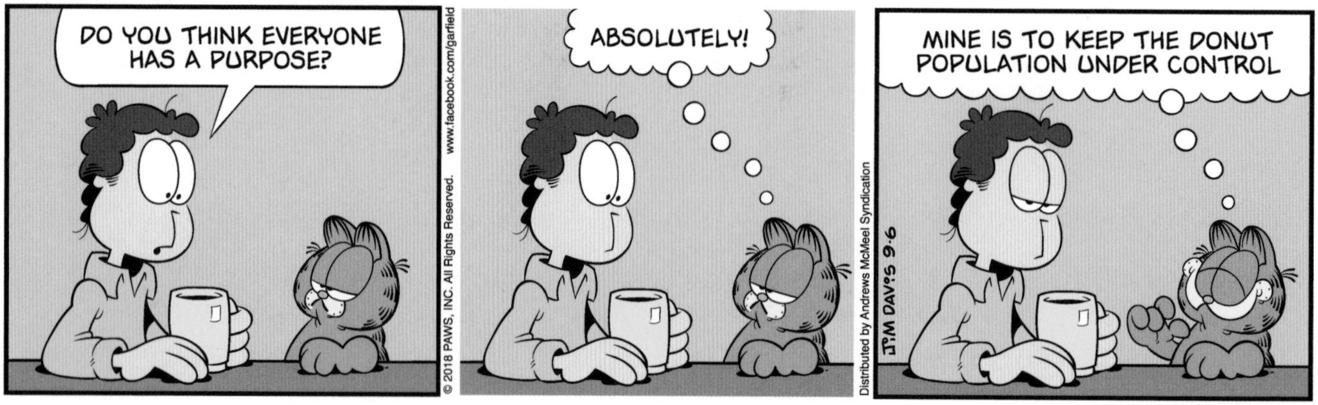
DO YOU THINK EVERYONE HAS A PURPOSE?
ABSOLUTELY!
MINE IS TO KEEP THE DONUT POPULATION UNDER CONTROL
JIM DAVIS 9-6

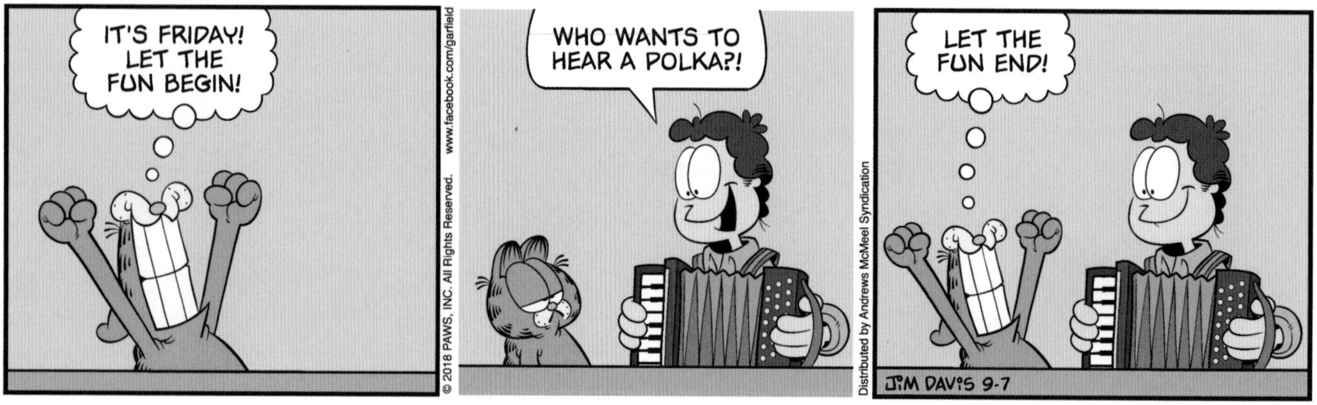
IT'S FRIDAY! LET THE FUN BEGIN!
WHO WANTS TO HEAR A POLKA?!
LET THE FUN END!
JIM DAVIS 9-7

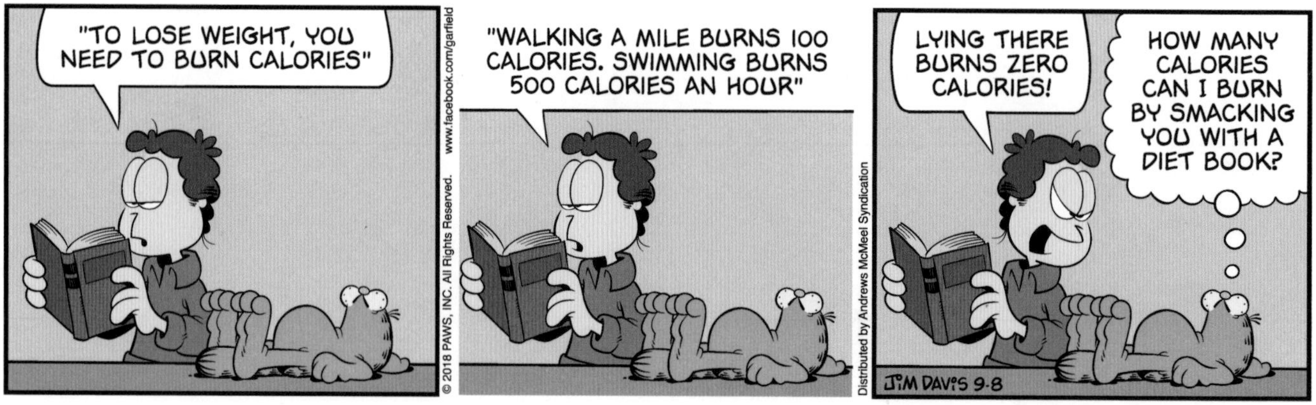
"TO LOSE WEIGHT, YOU NEED TO BURN CALORIES"
"WALKING A MILE BURNS 100 CALORIES. SWIMMING BURNS 500 CALORIES AN HOUR"
LYING THERE BURNS ZERO CALORIES!
HOW MANY CALORIES CAN I BURN BY SMACKING YOU WITH A DIET BOOK?
JIM DAVIS 9-8

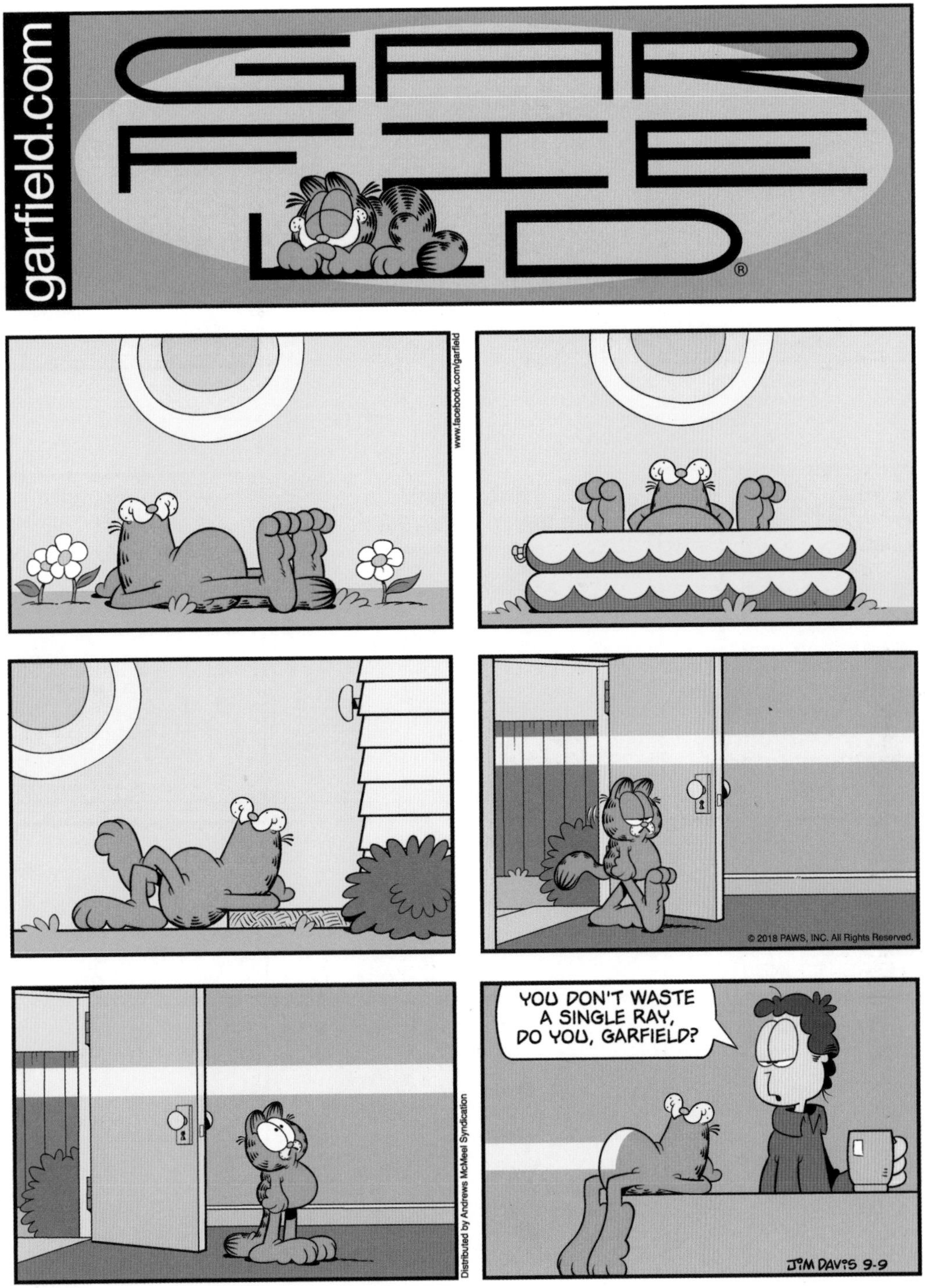
garfield.com
GARFIELD®
www.facebook.com/garfield
© 2018 PAWS, INC. All Rights Reserved.
Distributed by Andrews McMeel Syndication
YOU DON'T WASTE A SINGLE RAY, DO YOU, GARFIELD?
JIM DAVIS 9-9

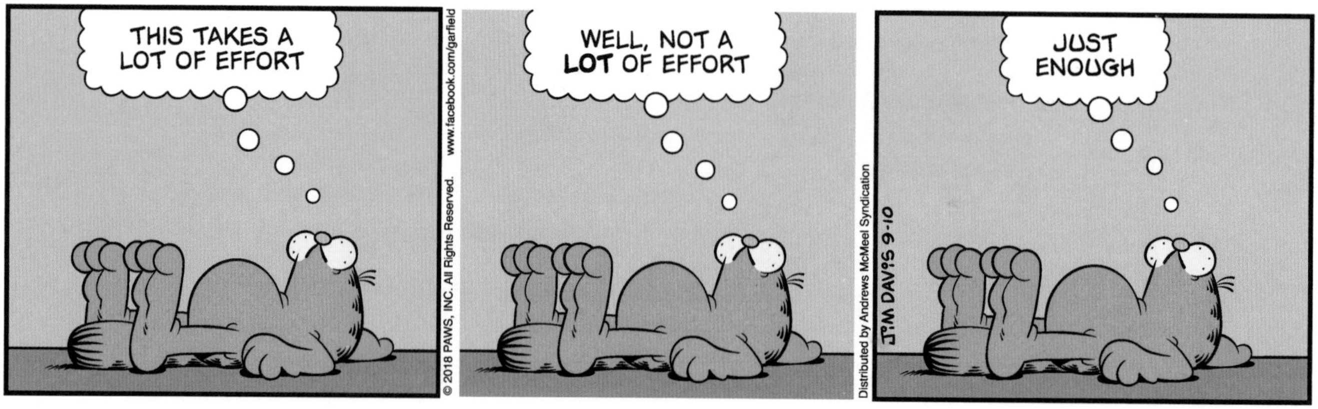
THIS TAKES A LOT OF EFFORT
© 2018 PAWS, INC. All Rights Reserved. www.facebook.com/garfield
WELL, NOT A LOT OF EFFORT
Distributed by Andrews McMeel Syndication
JIM DAVIS 9-10
JUST ENOUGH

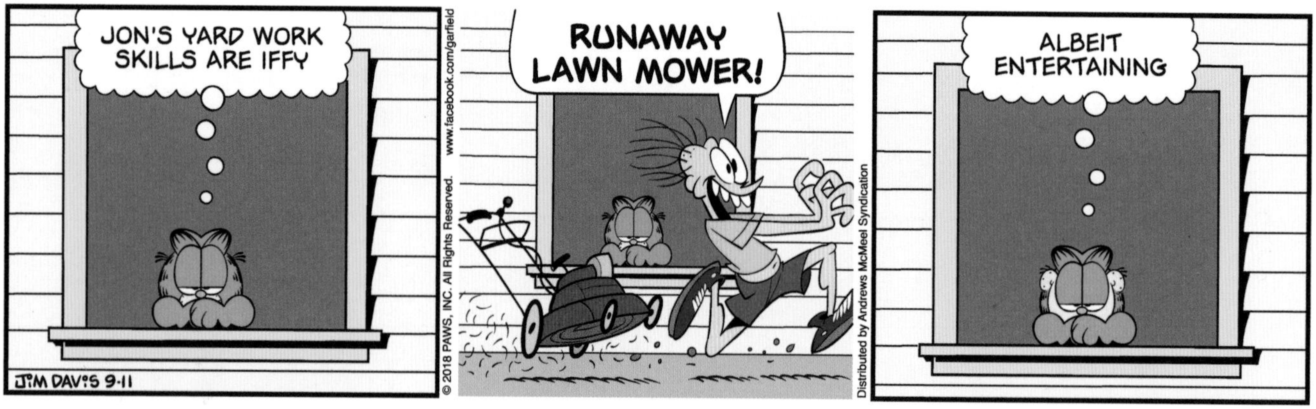
JON'S YARD WORK SKILLS ARE IFFY
JIM DAVIS 9-11
© 2018 PAWS, INC. All Rights Reserved. www.facebook.com/garfield
RUNAWAY LAWN MOWER!
Distributed by Andrews McMeel Syndication
ALBEIT ENTERTAINING

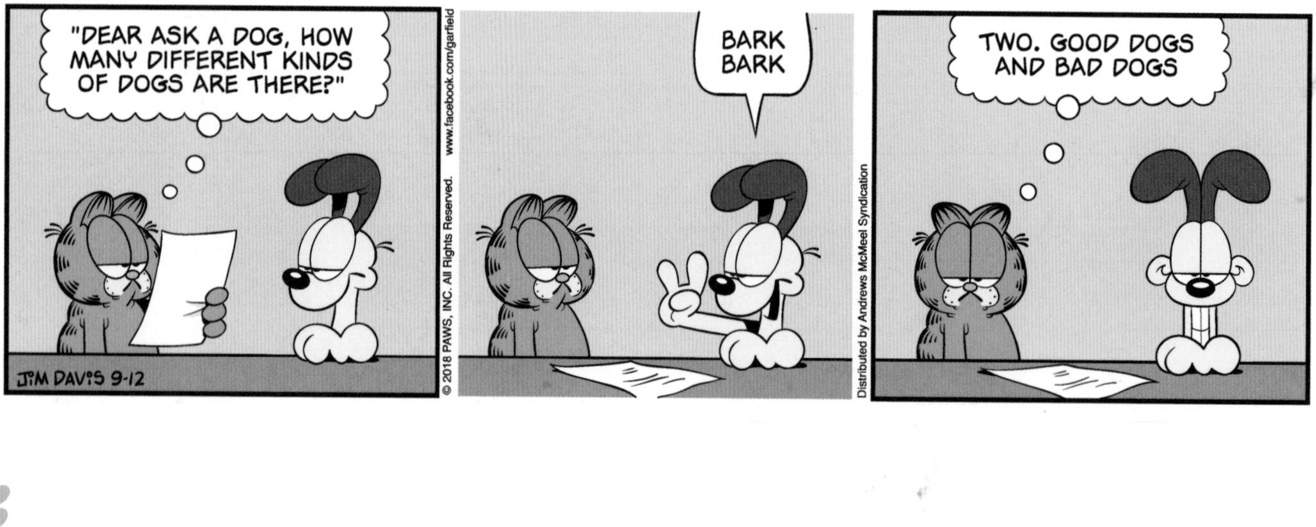
"DEAR ASK A DOG, HOW MANY DIFFERENT KINDS OF DOGS ARE THERE?"
JIM DAVIS 9-12
© 2018 PAWS, INC. All Rights Reserved. www.facebook.com/garfield
BARK BARK
Distributed by Andrews McMeel Syndication
TWO. GOOD DOGS AND BAD DOGS

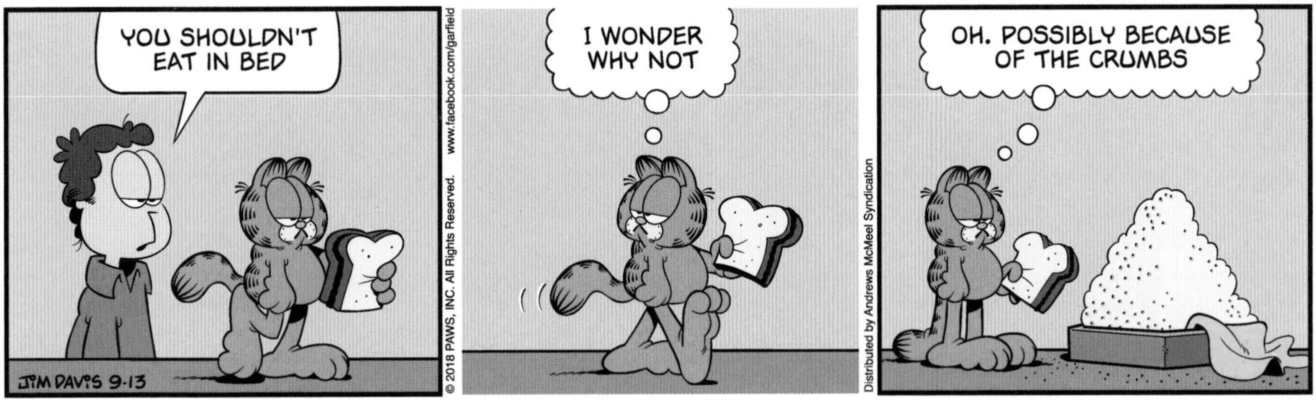
YOU SHOULDN'T EAT IN BED
I WONDER WHY NOT
OH. POSSIBLY BECAUSE OF THE CRUMBS
JIM DAVIS 9-13
© 2018 PAWS, INC. All Rights Reserved. www.facebook.com/garfield
Distributed by Andrews McMeel Syndication

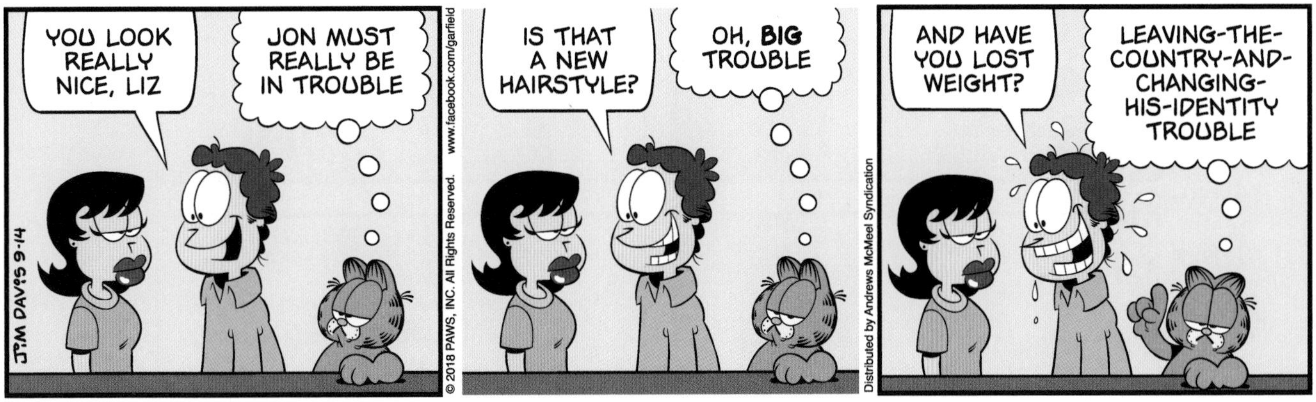
YOU LOOK REALLY NICE, LIZ
JON MUST REALLY BE IN TROUBLE
IS THAT A NEW HAIRSTYLE?
OH, **BIG** TROUBLE
AND HAVE YOU LOST WEIGHT?
LEAVING-THE-COUNTRY-AND-CHANGING-HIS-IDENTITY TROUBLE
JIM DAVIS 9-14
© 2018 PAWS, INC. All Rights Reserved. www.facebook.com/garfield
Distributed by Andrews McMeel Syndication

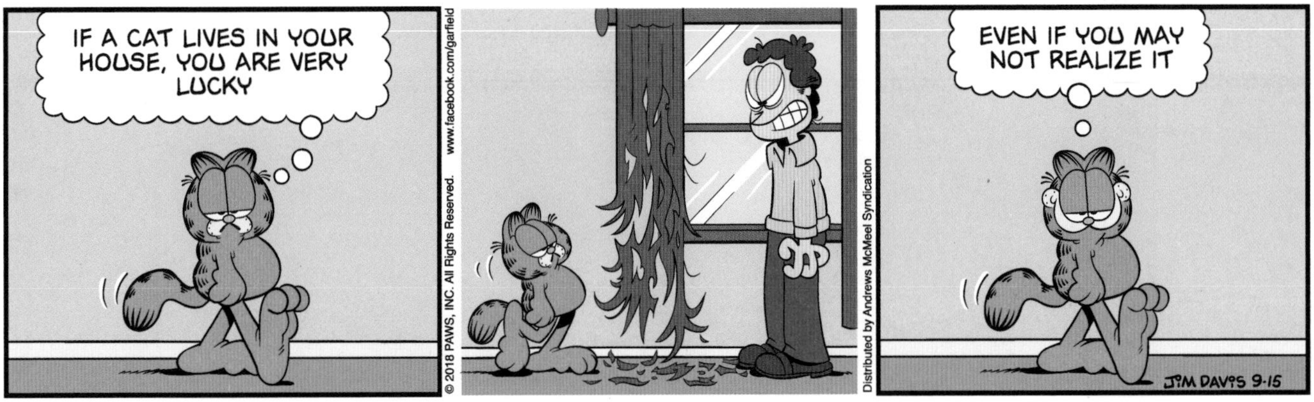
IF A CAT LIVES IN YOUR HOUSE, YOU ARE VERY LUCKY
EVEN IF YOU MAY NOT REALIZE IT
JIM DAVIS 9-15
© 2018 PAWS, INC. All Rights Reserved. www.facebook.com/garfield
Distributed by Andrews McMeel Syndication

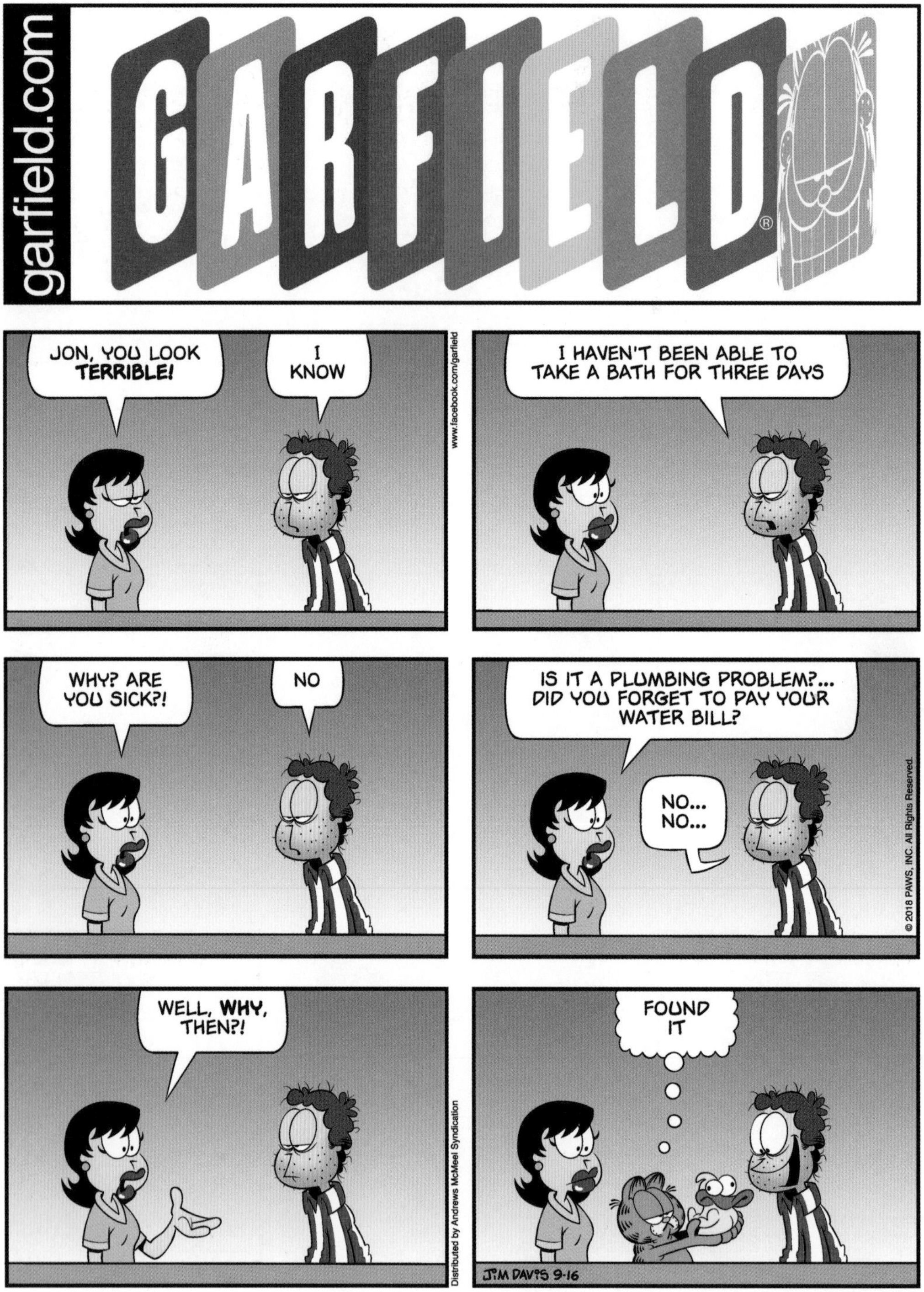
garfield.com
GARFIELD®
JON, YOU LOOK **TERRIBLE!**
I KNOW
www.facebook.com/garfield
I HAVEN'T BEEN ABLE TO TAKE A BATH FOR THREE DAYS
WHY? ARE YOU SICK?!
NO
IS IT A PLUMBING PROBLEM?... DID YOU FORGET TO PAY YOUR WATER BILL?
NO... NO...
© 2018 PAWS, INC. All Rights Reserved.
WELL, **WHY**, THEN?!
Distributed by Andrews McMeel Syndication
FOUND IT
JIM DAVIS 9-16

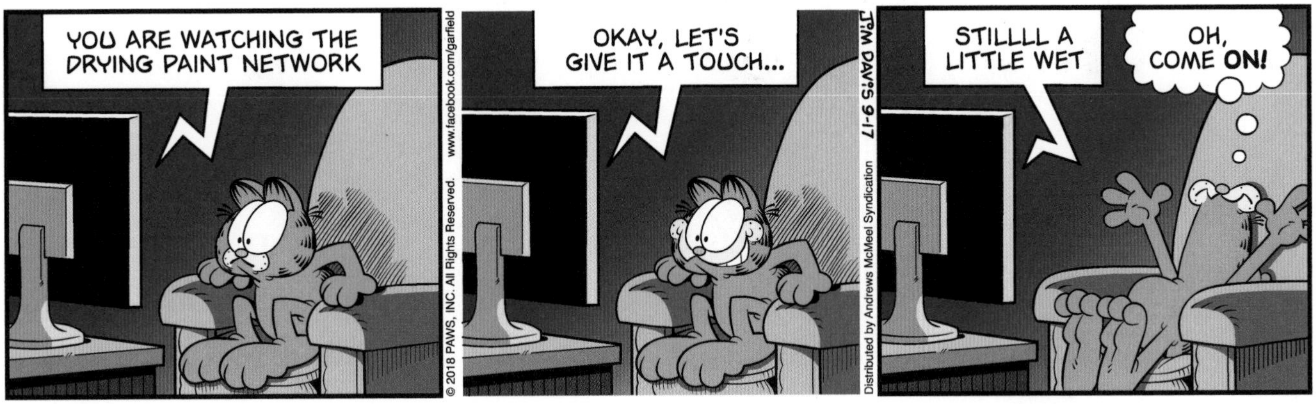
YOU ARE WATCHING THE DRYING PAINT NETWORK
© 2018 PAWS, INC. All Rights Reserved. www.facebook.com/garfield
OKAY, LET'S GIVE IT A TOUCH...
JIM DAVIS 9-17
Distributed by Andrews McMeel Syndication
STILLLLL A LITTLE WET
OH, COME ON!

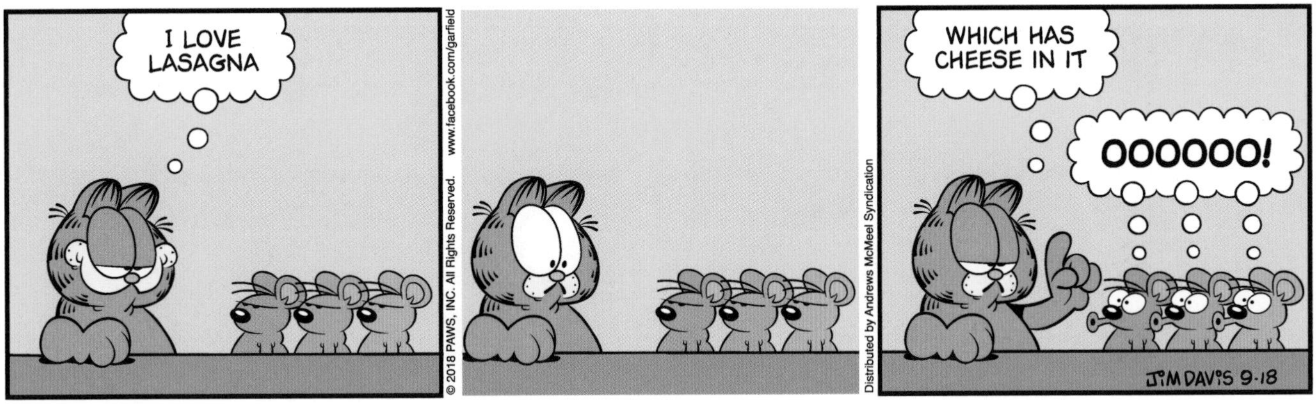
I LOVE LASAGNA
© 2018 PAWS, INC. All Rights Reserved. www.facebook.com/garfield
Distributed by Andrews McMeel Syndication
WHICH HAS CHEESE IN IT
OOOOOO!
JIM DAVIS 9-18

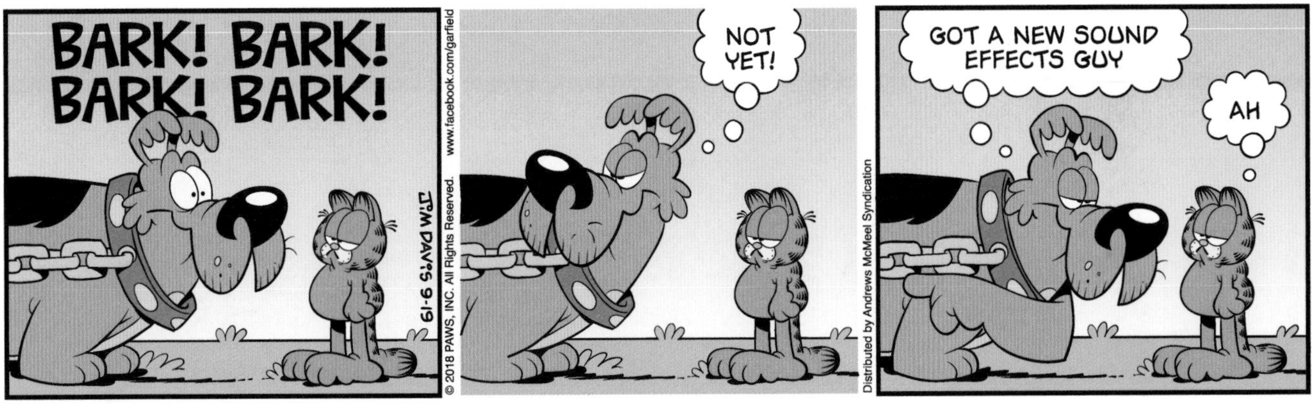
BARK! BARK! BARK! BARK!
JIM DAVIS 9-19
© 2018 PAWS, INC. All Rights Reserved. www.facebook.com/garfield
NOT YET!
Distributed by Andrews McMeel Syndication
GOT A NEW SOUND EFFECTS GUY
AH

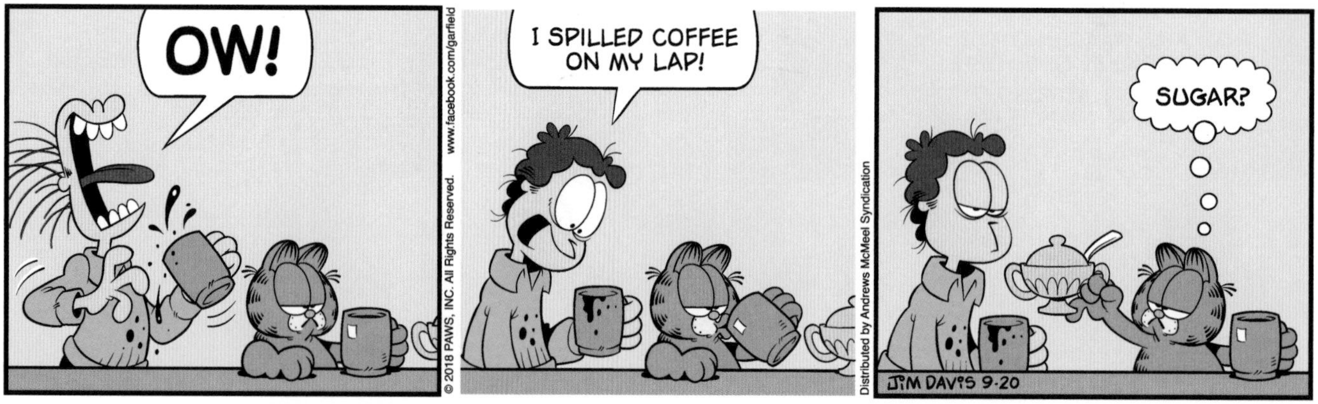
OW!
I SPILLED COFFEE ON MY LAP!
SUGAR?
© 2018 PAWS, INC. All Rights Reserved. www.facebook.com/garfield
Distributed by Andrews McMeel Syndication
JIM DAVIS 9-20

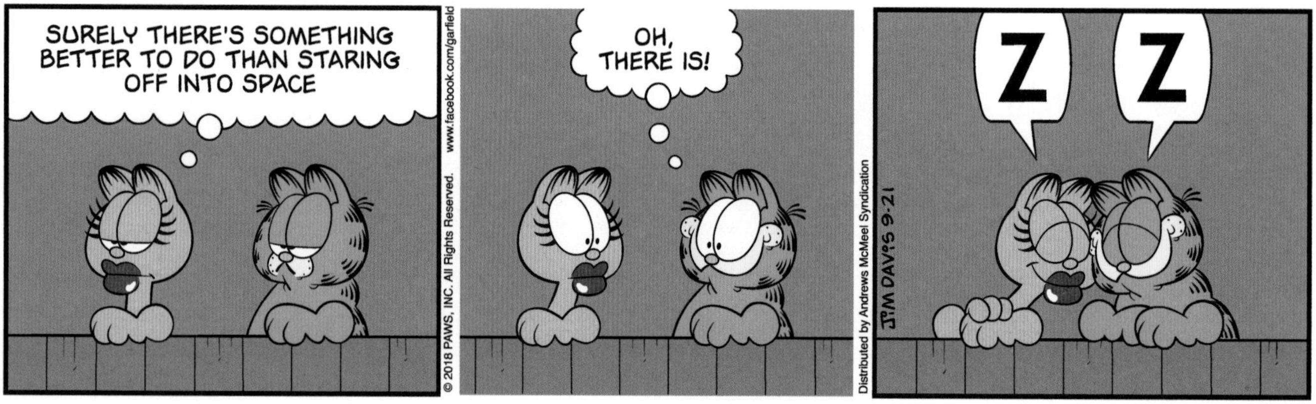
SURELY THERE'S SOMETHING BETTER TO DO THAN STARING OFF INTO SPACE
OH, THERE IS!
Z
Z
© 2018 PAWS, INC. All Rights Reserved. www.facebook.com/garfield
Distributed by Andrews McMeel Syndication
JIM DAVIS 9-21

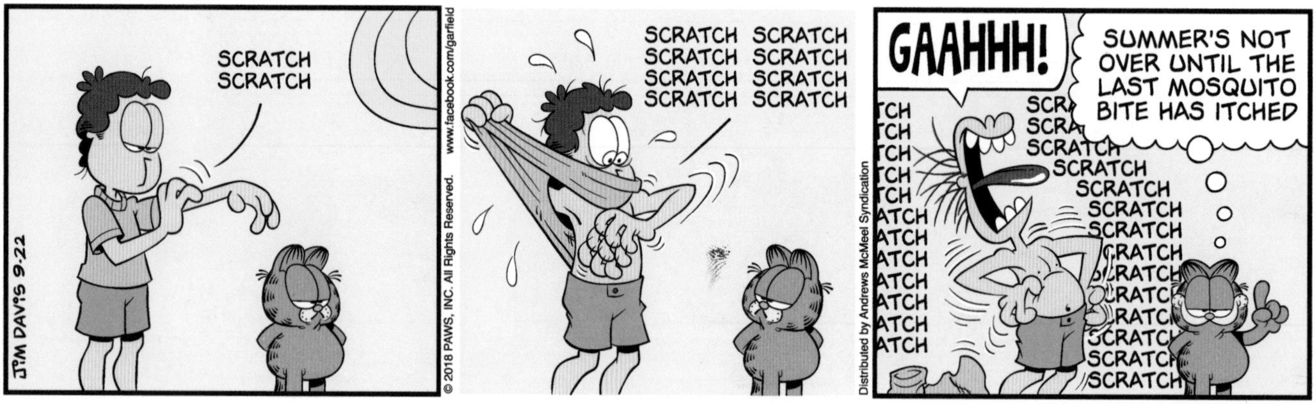
SCRATCH SCRATCH
SCRATCH SCRATCH SCRATCH SCRATCH SCRATCH SCRATCH SCRATCH SCRATCH
GAAHHH!
SCRATCH
SUMMER'S NOT OVER UNTIL THE LAST MOSQUITO BITE HAS ITCHED
© 2018 PAWS, INC. All Rights Reserved. www.facebook.com/garfield
Distributed by Andrews McMeel Syndication
JIM DAVIS 9-22

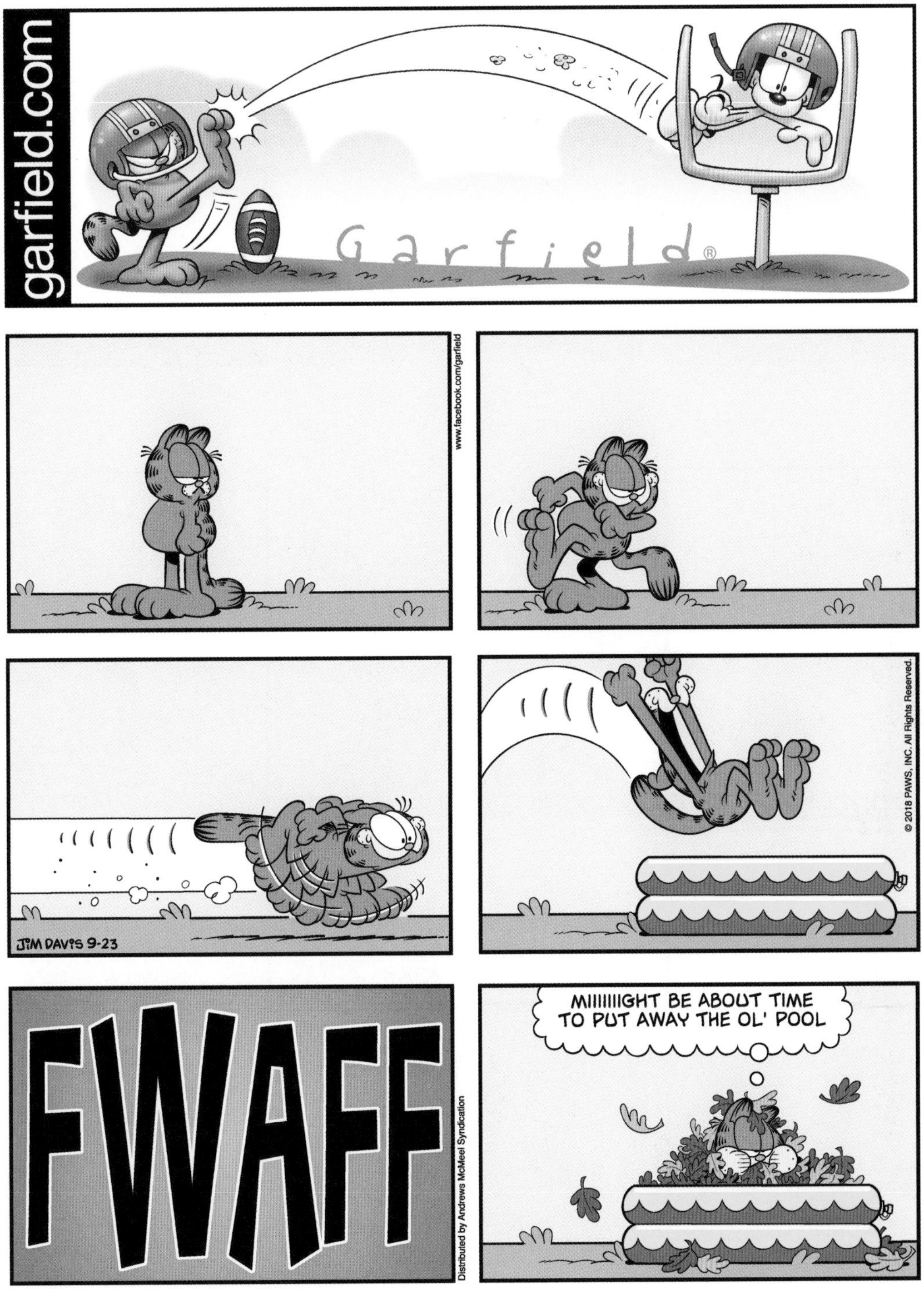
garfield.com
Garfield®
www.facebook.com/garfield
JIM DAVIS 9-23
© 2018 PAWS, INC. All Rights Reserved.
FWAFF
Distributed by Andrews McMeel Syndication
MIIIIIIIGHT BE ABOUT TIME TO PUT AWAY THE OL' POOL

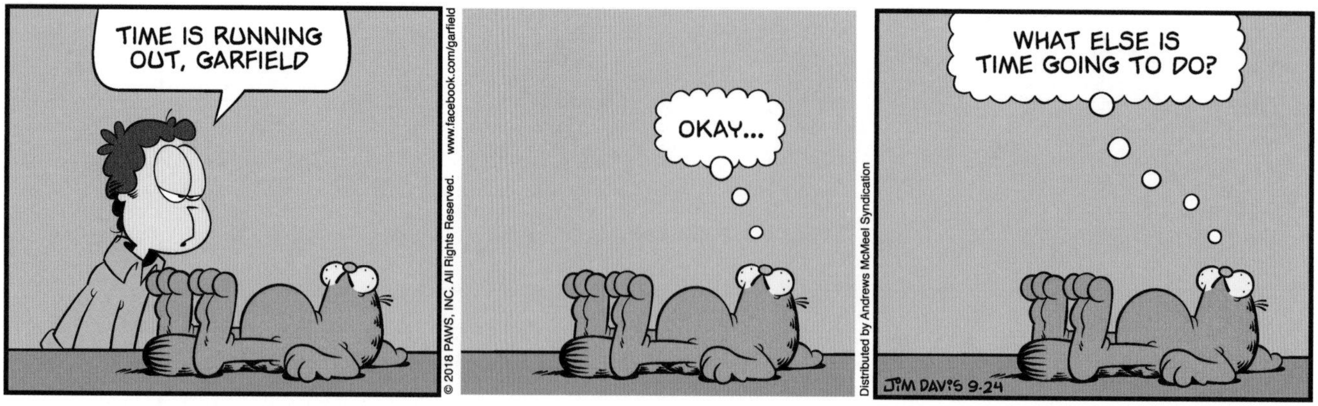
TIME IS RUNNING OUT, GARFIELD
OKAY...
WHAT ELSE IS TIME GOING TO DO?
JIM DAVIS 9-24
© 2018 PAWS, INC. All Rights Reserved. www.facebook.com/garfield
Distributed by Andrews McMeel Syndication

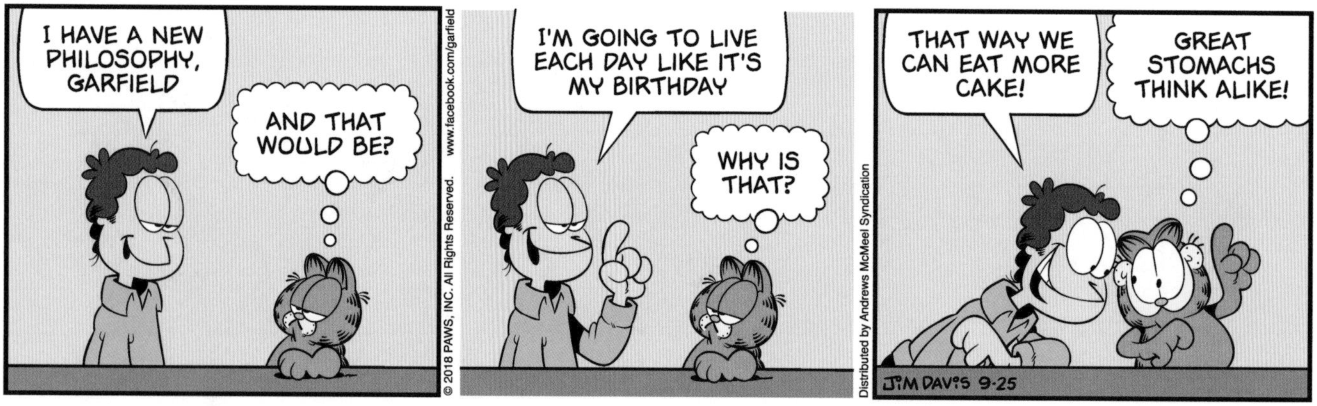
I HAVE A NEW PHILOSOPHY, GARFIELD
AND THAT WOULD BE?
I'M GOING TO LIVE EACH DAY LIKE IT'S MY BIRTHDAY
WHY IS THAT?
THAT WAY WE CAN EAT MORE CAKE!
GREAT STOMACHS THINK ALIKE!
JIM DAVIS 9-25
© 2018 PAWS, INC. All Rights Reserved. www.facebook.com/garfield
Distributed by Andrews McMeel Syndication

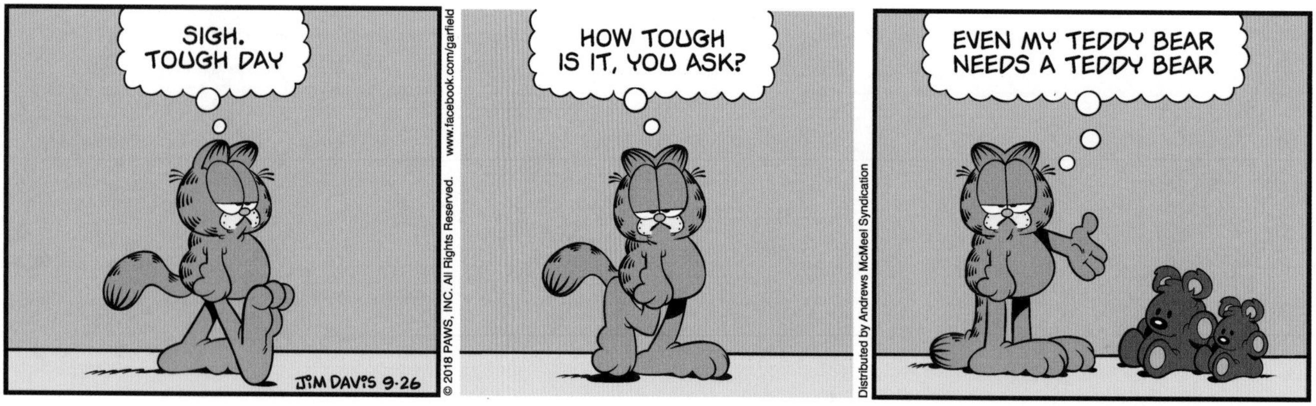
SIGH. TOUGH DAY
JIM DAVIS 9-26
HOW TOUGH IS IT, YOU ASK?
EVEN MY TEDDY BEAR NEEDS A TEDDY BEAR
© 2018 PAWS, INC. All Rights Reserved. www.facebook.com/garfield
Distributed by Andrews McMeel Syndication

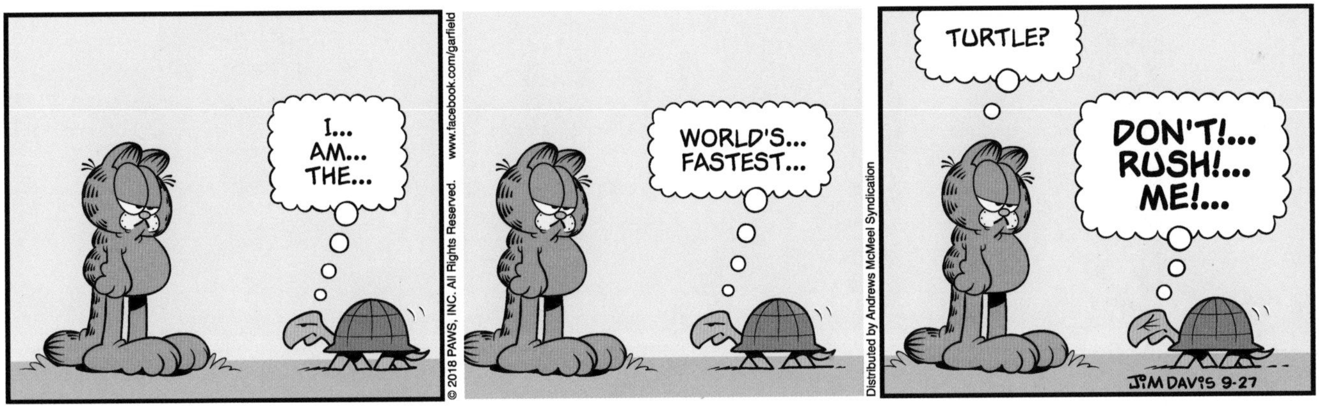
I... AM... THE...
WORLD'S... FASTEST...
TURTLE?
DON'T!... RUSH!... ME!...
JIM DAVIS 9-27
© 2018 PAWS, INC. All Rights Reserved. www.facebook.com/garfield
Distributed by Andrews McMeel Syndication

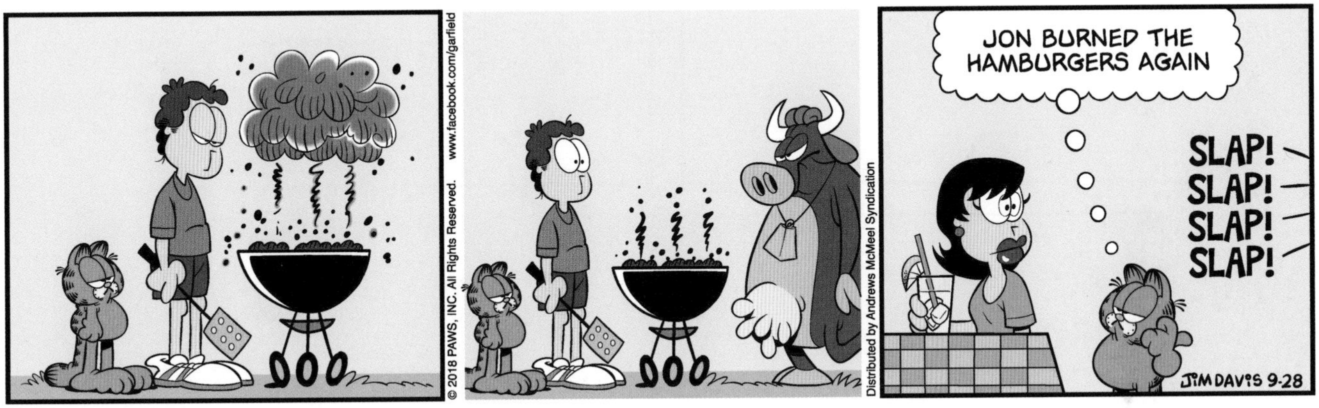
JON BURNED THE HAMBURGERS AGAIN
SLAP! SLAP! SLAP! SLAP!
JIM DAVIS 9-28
© 2018 PAWS, INC. All Rights Reserved. www.facebook.com/garfield
Distributed by Andrews McMeel Syndication

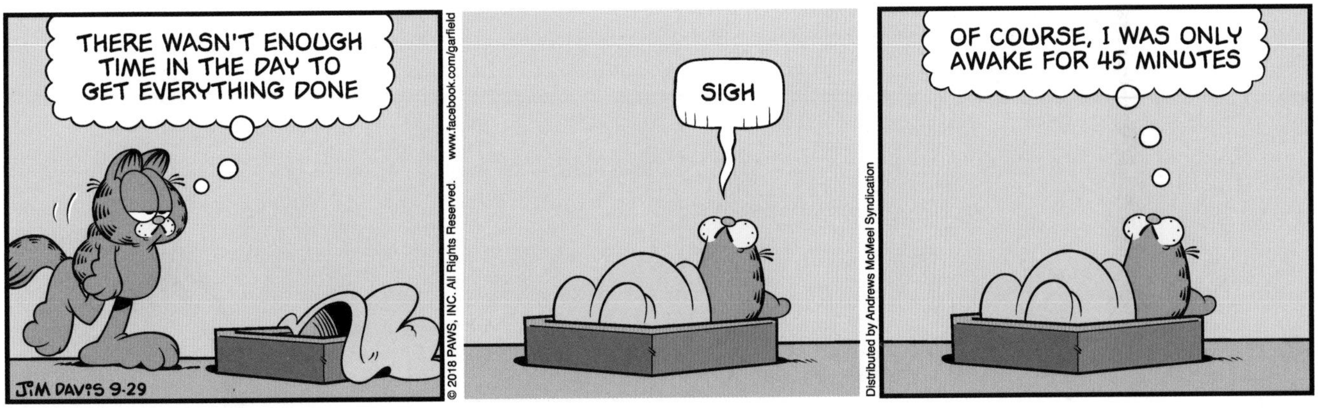
THERE WASN'T ENOUGH TIME IN THE DAY TO GET EVERYTHING DONE
JIM DAVIS 9-29
SIGH
OF COURSE, I WAS ONLY AWAKE FOR 45 MINUTES
© 2018 PAWS, INC. All Rights Reserved. www.facebook.com/garfield
Distributed by Andrews McMeel Syndication

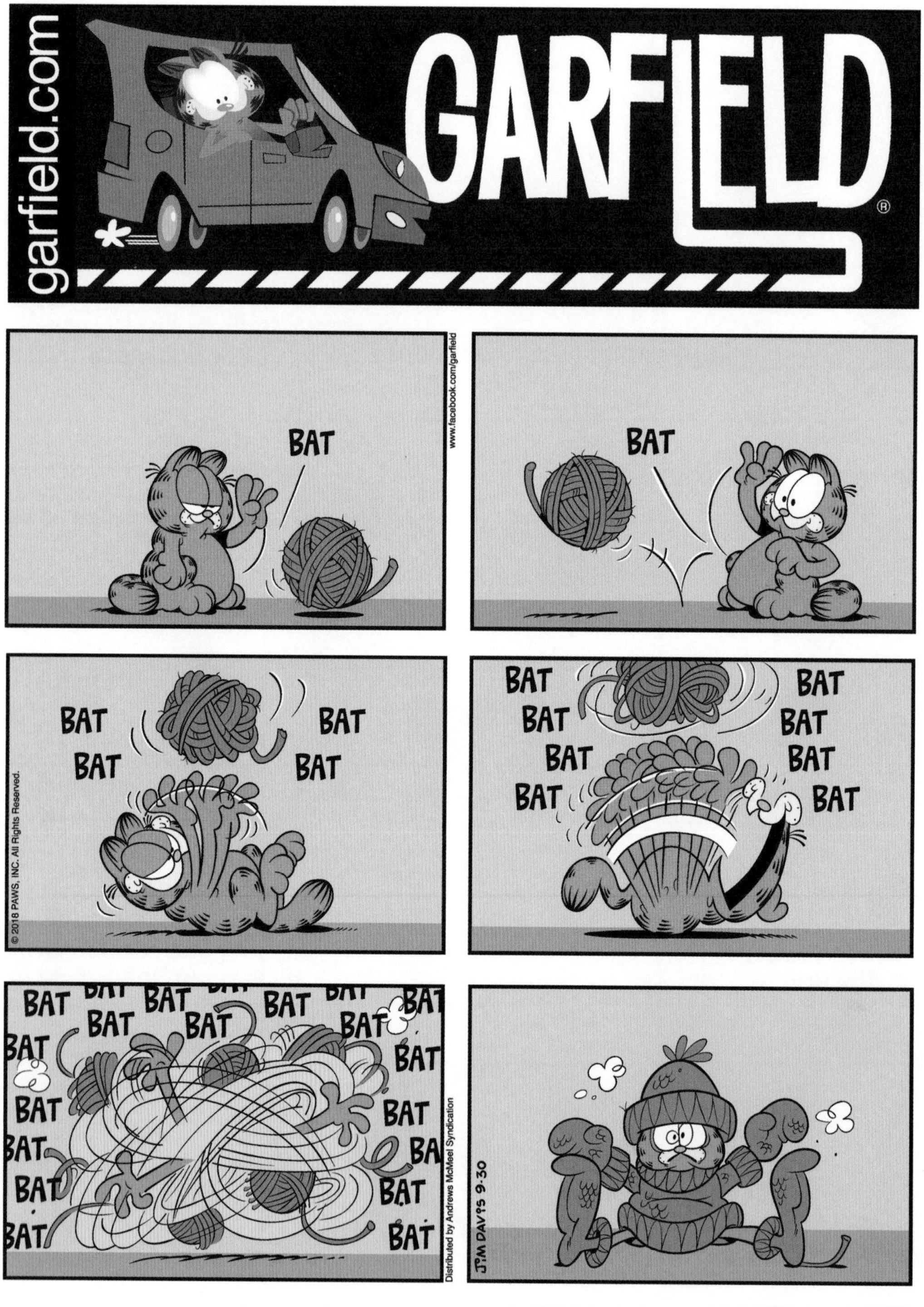
garfield.com
GARFIELD®
www.facebook.com/garfield
BAT
BAT
BAT
BAT
BAT
BAT
© 2018 PAWS, INC. All Rights Reserved.
BAT
BAT
BAT
BAT
BAT
BAT
BAT
BAT
BAT BAT BAT BAT BAT BAT
BAT BAT BAT BAT
BAT
BAT
BAT
BAT
BAT
Distributed by Andrews McMeel Syndication
JIM DAVIS 9-30

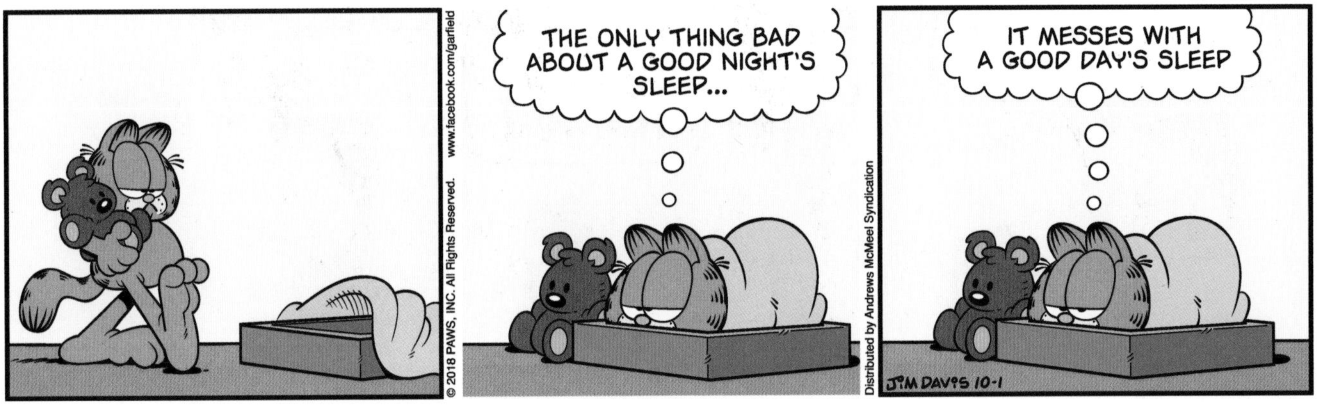
THE ONLY THING BAD ABOUT A GOOD NIGHT'S SLEEP...
IT MESSES WITH A GOOD DAY'S SLEEP
© 2018 PAWS, INC. All Rights Reserved. www.facebook.com/garfield
Distributed by Andrews McMeel Syndication
JIM DAVIS 10-1

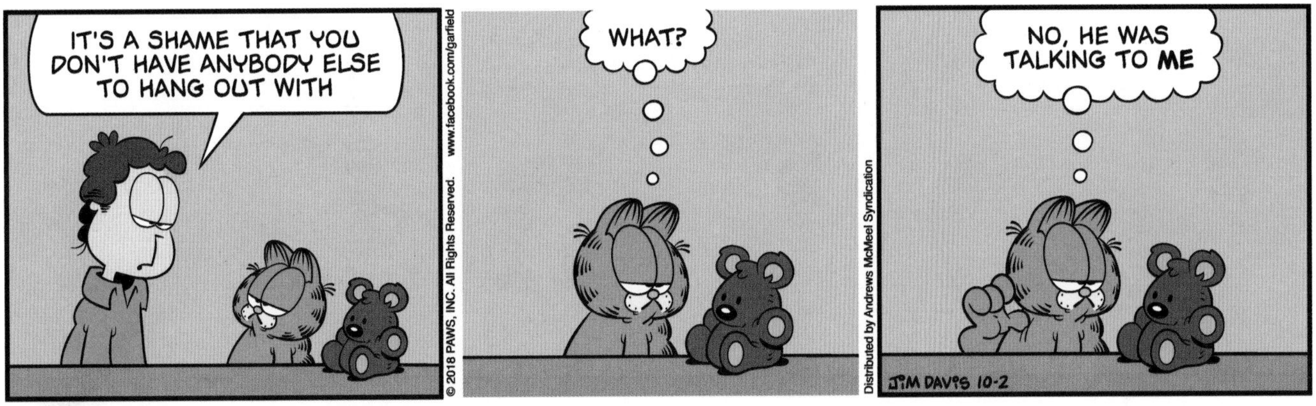
IT'S A SHAME THAT YOU DON'T HAVE ANYBODY ELSE TO HANG OUT WITH
WHAT?
NO, HE WAS TALKING TO **ME**
© 2018 PAWS, INC. All Rights Reserved. www.facebook.com/garfield
Distributed by Andrews McMeel Syndication
JIM DAVIS 10-2

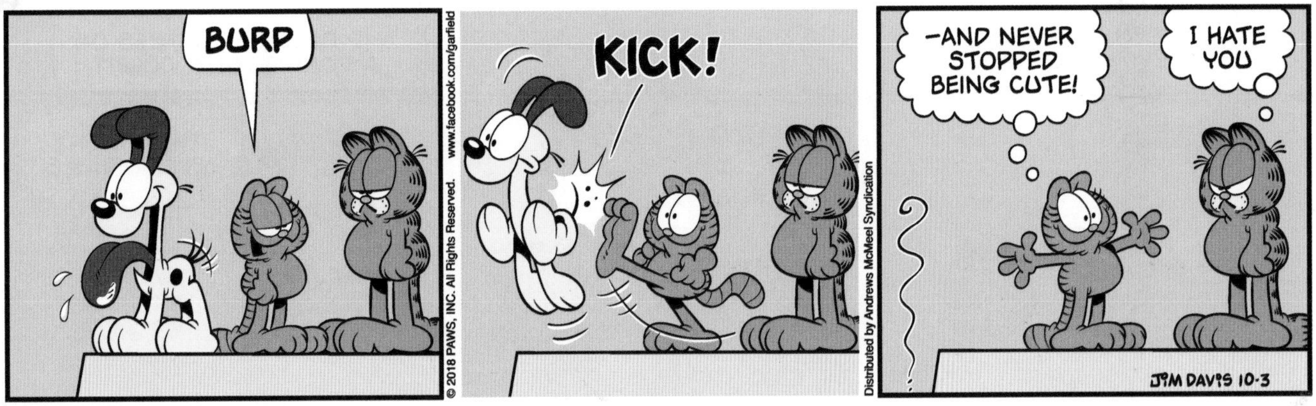
BURP
KICK!
–AND NEVER STOPPED BEING CUTE!
I HATE YOU
© 2018 PAWS, INC. All Rights Reserved. www.facebook.com/garfield
Distributed by Andrews McMeel Syndication
JIM DAVIS 10-3

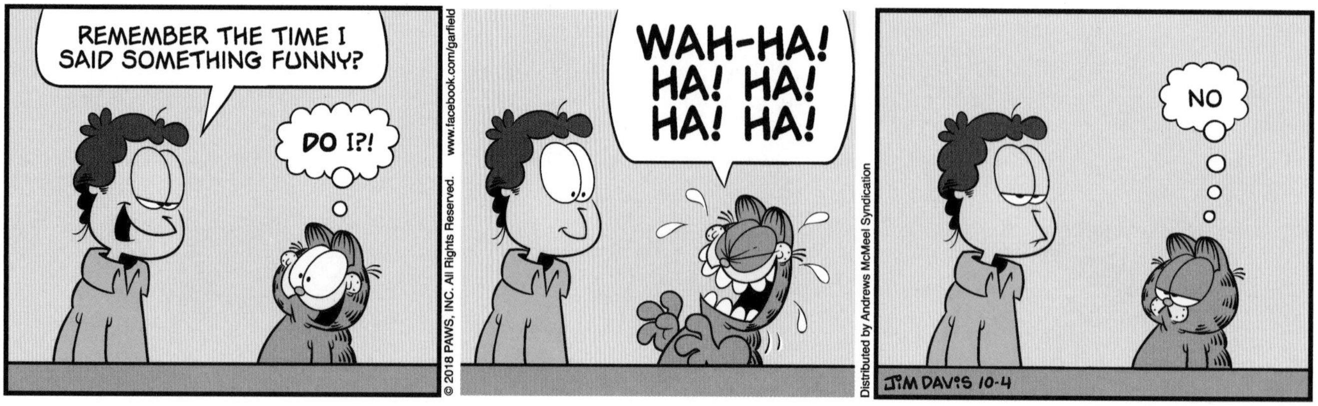
REMEMBER THE TIME I SAID SOMETHING FUNNY?
DO I?!
© 2018 PAWS, INC. All Rights Reserved. www.facebook.com/garfield
WAH-HA! HA! HA! HA! HA!
Distributed by Andrews McMeel Syndication
NO
JIM DAVIS 10-4

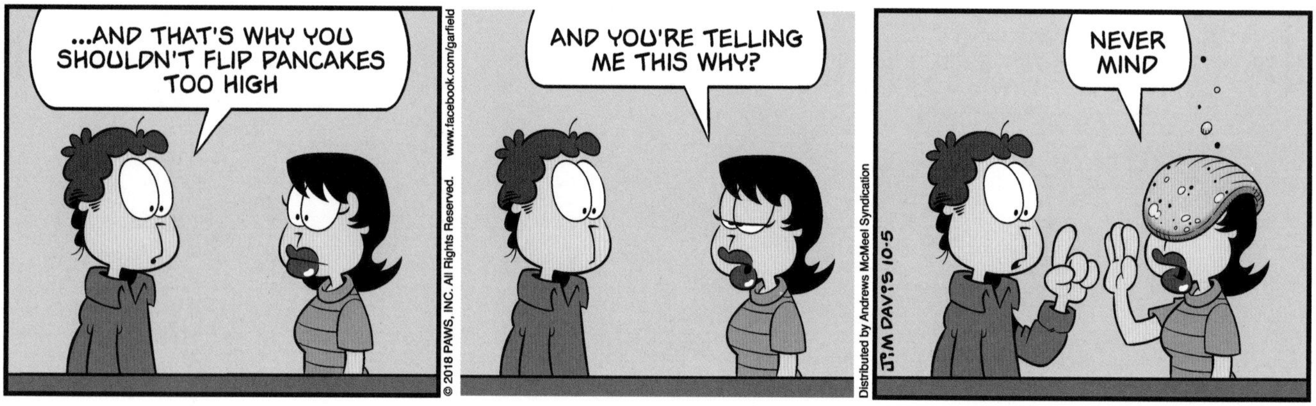
...AND THAT'S WHY YOU SHOULDN'T FLIP PANCAKES TOO HIGH
© 2018 PAWS, INC. All Rights Reserved. www.facebook.com/garfield
AND YOU'RE TELLING ME THIS WHY?
Distributed by Andrews McMeel Syndication
JIM DAVIS 10-5
NEVER MIND

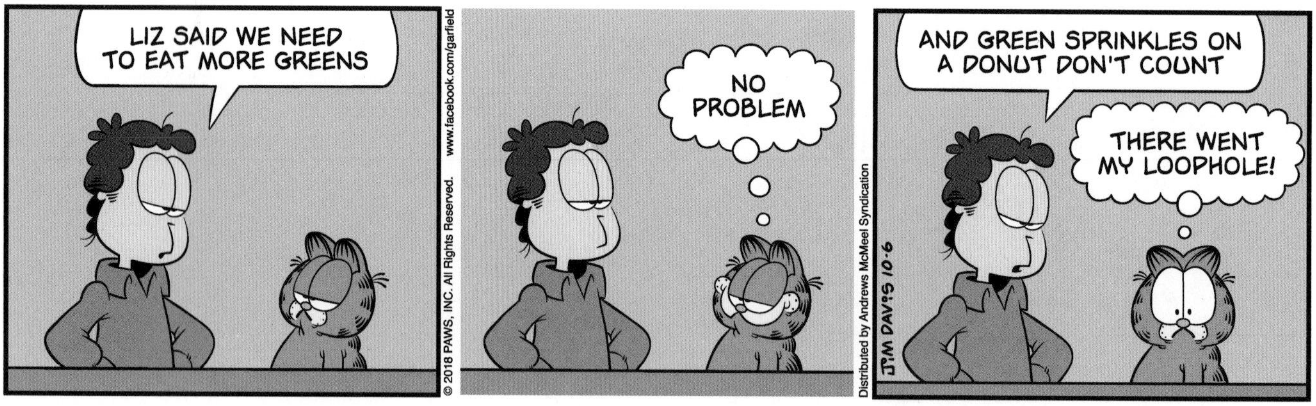
LIZ SAID WE NEED TO EAT MORE GREENS
© 2018 PAWS, INC. All Rights Reserved. www.facebook.com/garfield
NO PROBLEM
Distributed by Andrews McMeel Syndication
JIM DAVIS 10-6
AND GREEN SPRINKLES ON A DONUT DON'T COUNT
THERE WENT MY LOOPHOLE!

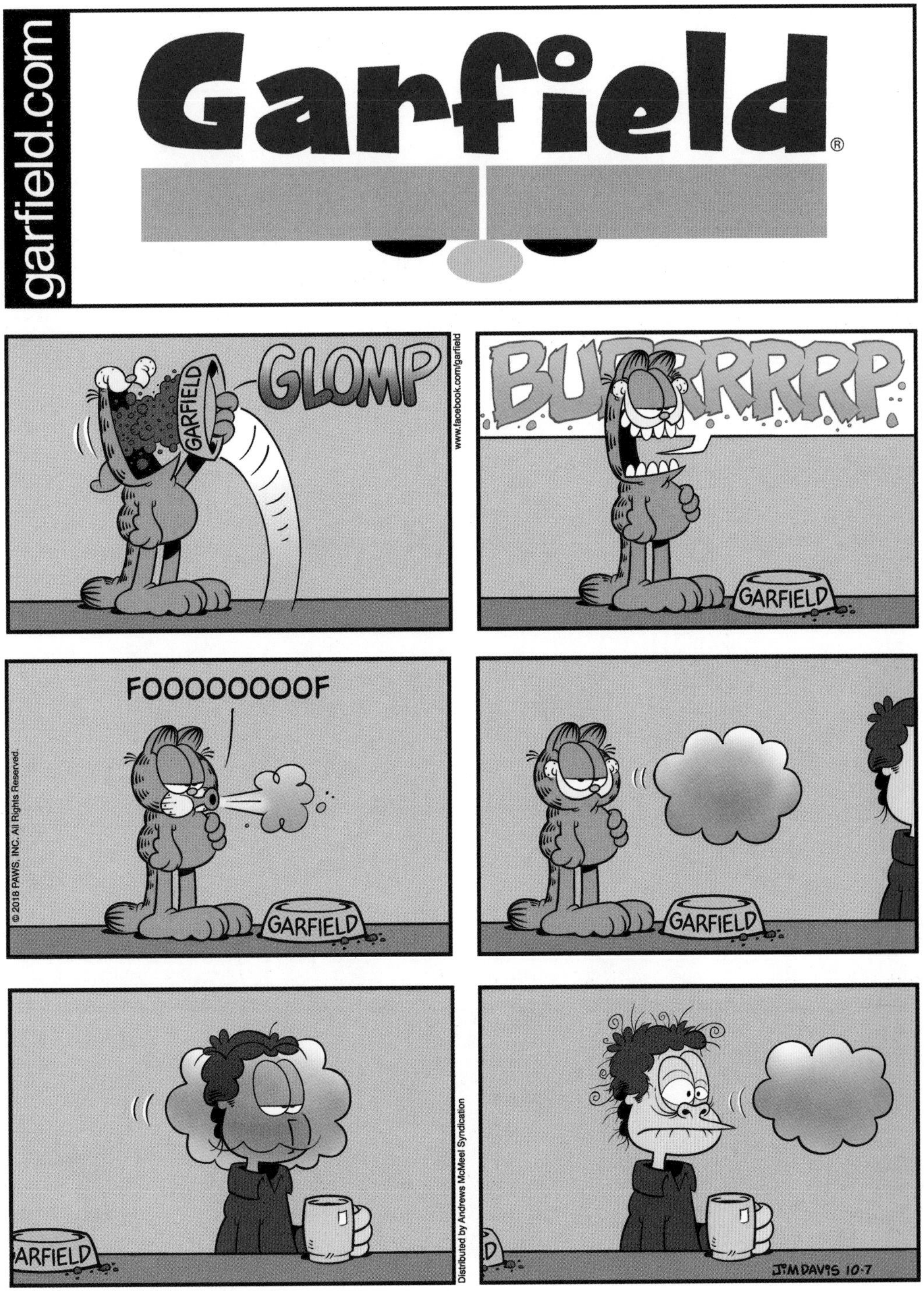

garfield.com
Garfield®
GLOMP
GARFIELD
www.facebook.com/garfield
BU RRRRRP
GARFIELD
FOOOOOOOOF
© 2018 PAWS, INC. All Rights Reserved.
GARFIELD
GARFIELD
ARFIELD
Distributed by Andrews McMeel Syndication
D
JIM DAVIS 10-7

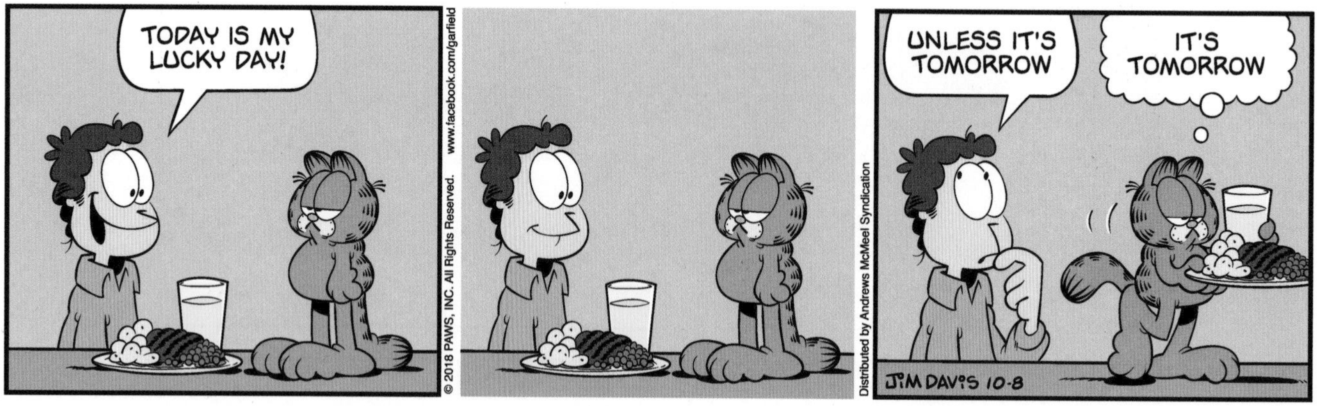
TODAY IS MY LUCKY DAY!
UNLESS IT'S TOMORROW
IT'S TOMORROW
© 2018 PAWS, INC. All Rights Reserved. www.facebook.com/garfield
Distributed by Andrews McMeel Syndication
JIM DAVIS 10-8

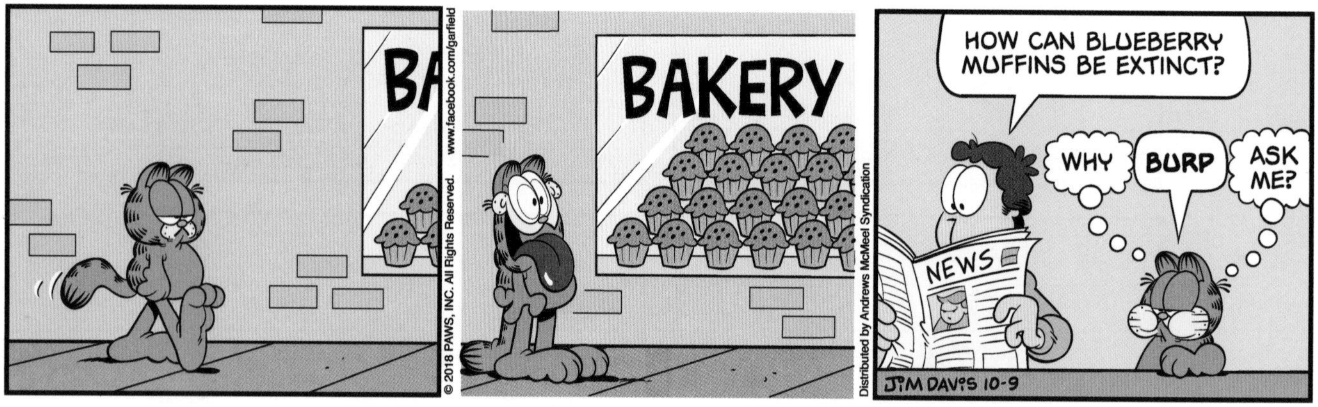
BAKERY
HOW CAN BLUEBERRY MUFFINS BE EXTINCT?
WHY
BURP
ASK ME?
NEWS
© 2018 PAWS, INC. All Rights Reserved. www.facebook.com/garfield
Distributed by Andrews McMeel Syndication
JIM DAVIS 10-9

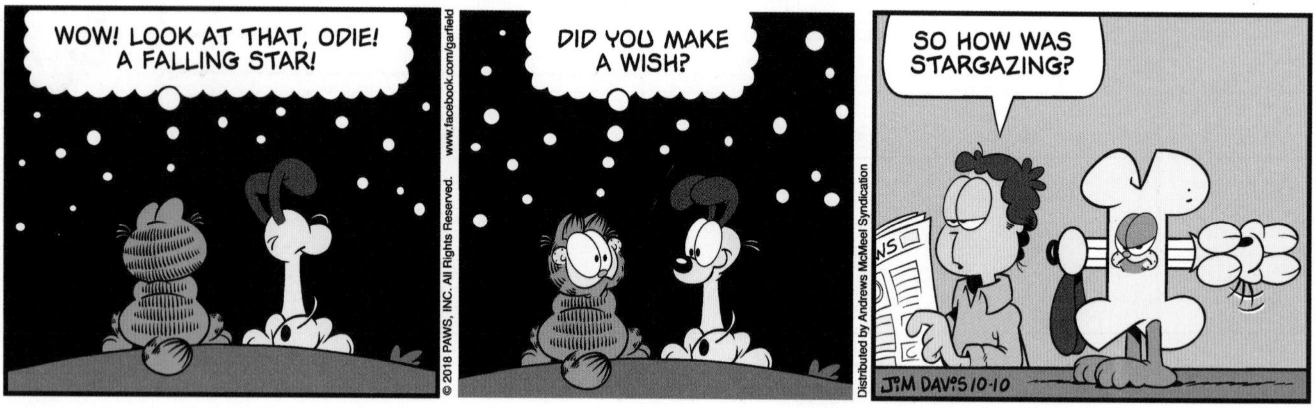
WOW! LOOK AT THAT, ODIE! A FALLING STAR!
DID YOU MAKE A WISH?
SO HOW WAS STARGAZING?
© 2018 PAWS, INC. All Rights Reserved. www.facebook.com/garfield
Distributed by Andrews McMeel Syndication
JIM DAVIS 10-10

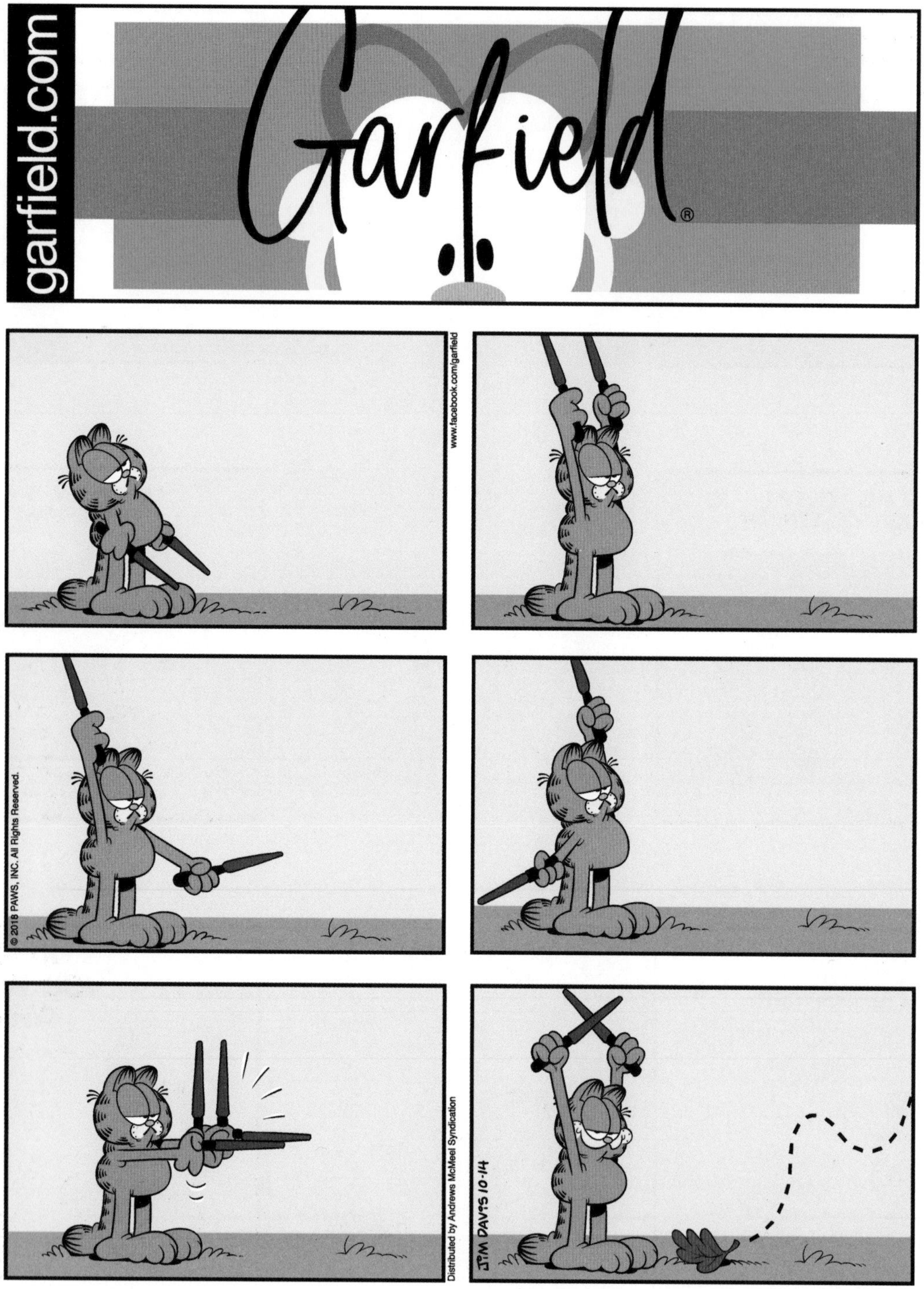
garfield.com
Garfield
www.facebook.com/garfield
© 2018 PAWS, INC. All Rights Reserved.
Distributed by Andrews McMeel Syndication
JIM DAVIS 10-14

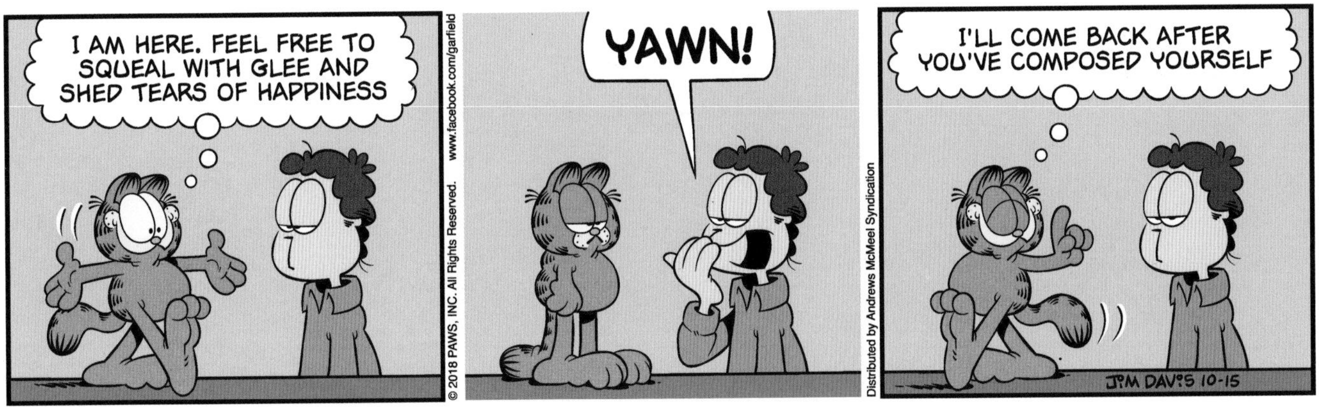
I AM HERE. FEEL FREE TO SQUEAL WITH GLEE AND SHED TEARS OF HAPPINESS
YAWN!
I'LL COME BACK AFTER YOU'VE COMPOSED YOURSELF
JIM DAVIS 10-15
© 2018 PAWS, INC. All Rights Reserved. www.facebook.com/garfield
Distributed by Andrews McMeel Syndication

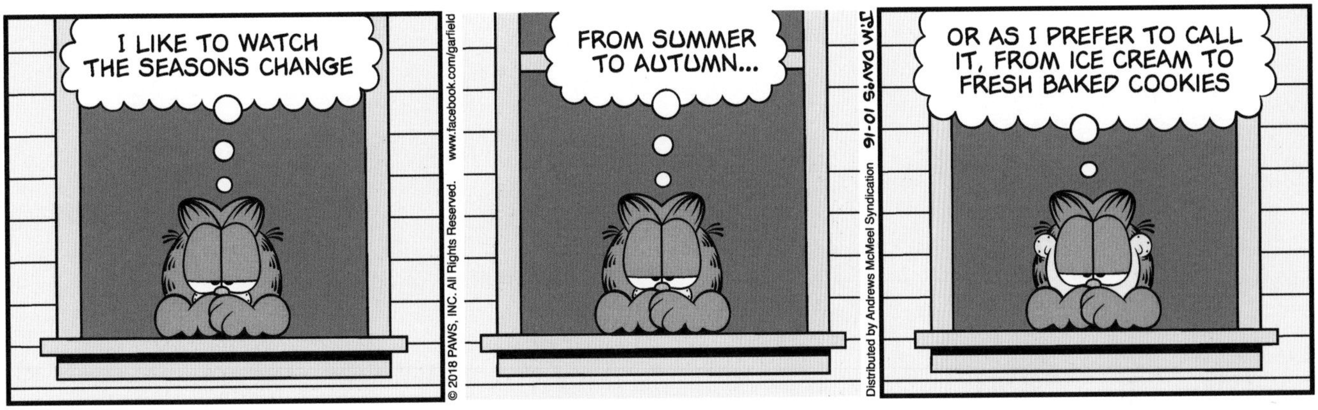
I LIKE TO WATCH THE SEASONS CHANGE
FROM SUMMER TO AUTUMN...
OR AS I PREFER TO CALL IT, FROM ICE CREAM TO FRESH BAKED COOKIES
JIM DAVIS 10-16
© 2018 PAWS, INC. All Rights Reserved. www.facebook.com/garfield
Distributed by Andrews McMeel Syndication

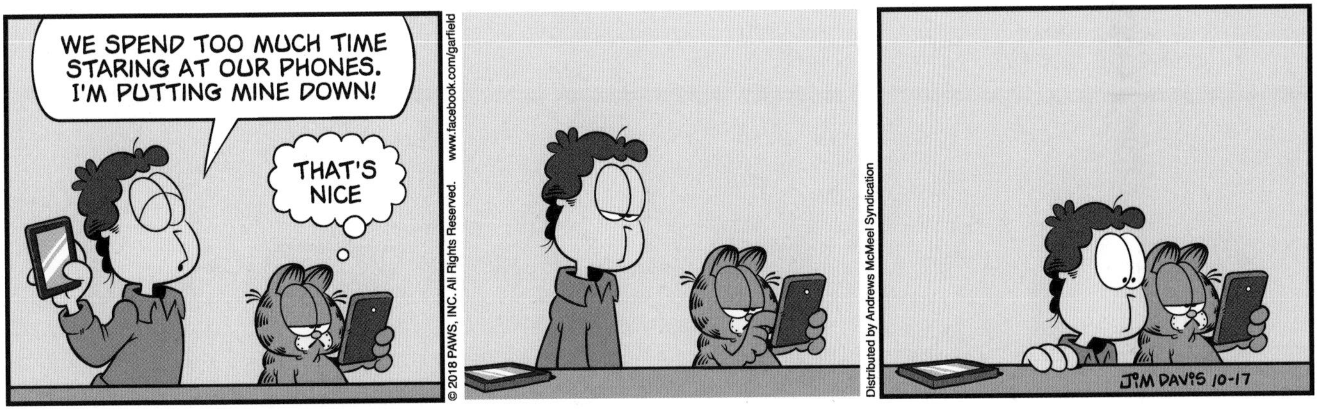
WE SPEND TOO MUCH TIME STARING AT OUR PHONES. I'M PUTTING MINE DOWN!
THAT'S NICE
JIM DAVIS 10-17
© 2018 PAWS, INC. All Rights Reserved. www.facebook.com/garfield
Distributed by Andrews McMeel Syndication

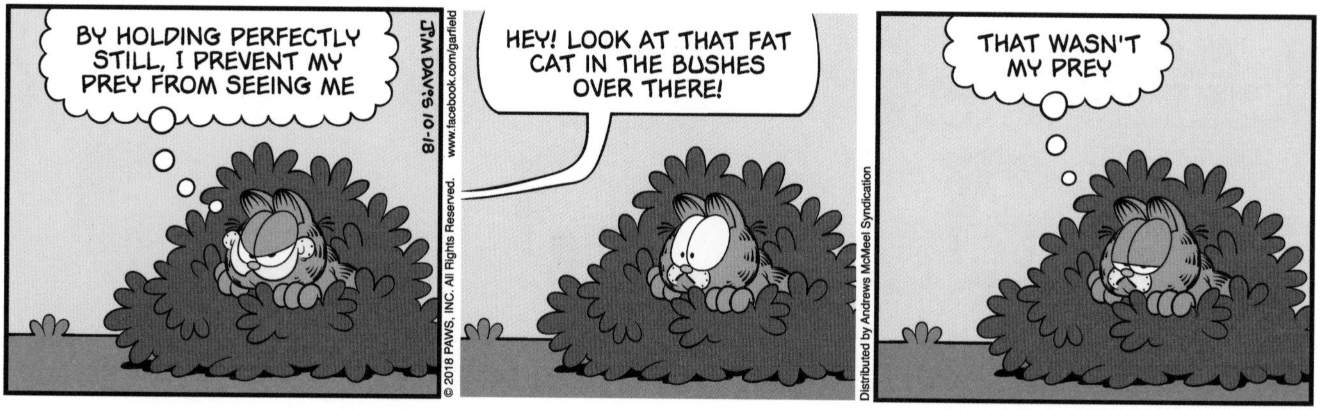
BY HOLDING PERFECTLY STILL, I PREVENT MY PREY FROM SEEING ME
HEY! LOOK AT THAT FAT CAT IN THE BUSHES OVER THERE!
THAT WASN'T MY PREY
JIM DAVIS 10-18

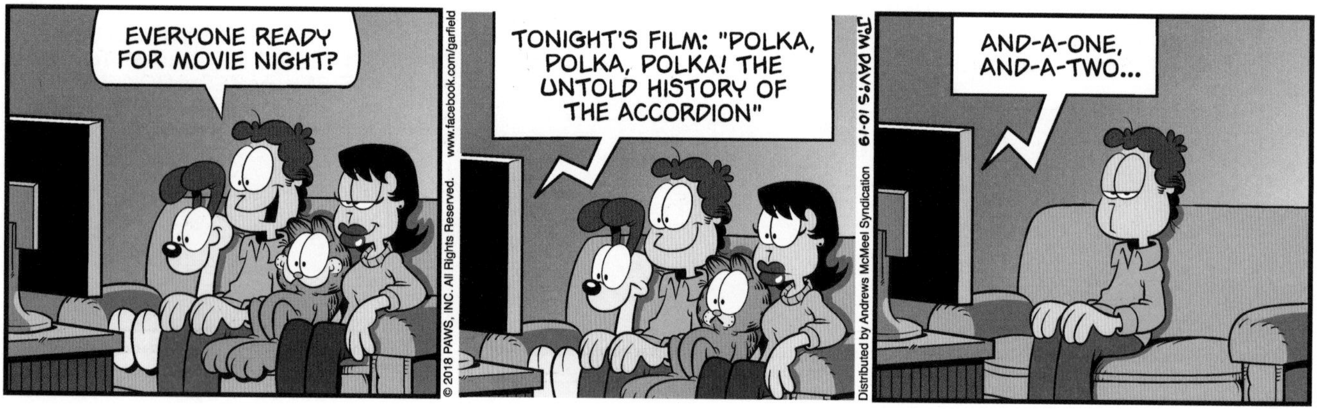
EVERYONE READY FOR MOVIE NIGHT?
TONIGHT'S FILM: "POLKA, POLKA, POLKA! THE UNTOLD HISTORY OF THE ACCORDION"
AND-A-ONE, AND-A-TWO...
JIM DAVIS 10-19

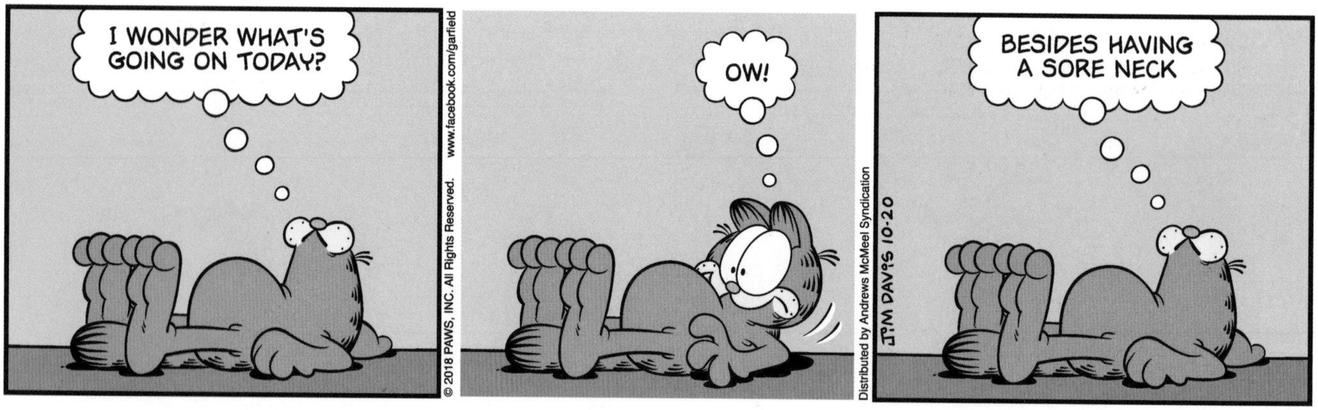
I WONDER WHAT'S GOING ON TODAY?
OW!
BESIDES HAVING A SORE NECK
JIM DAVIS 10-20

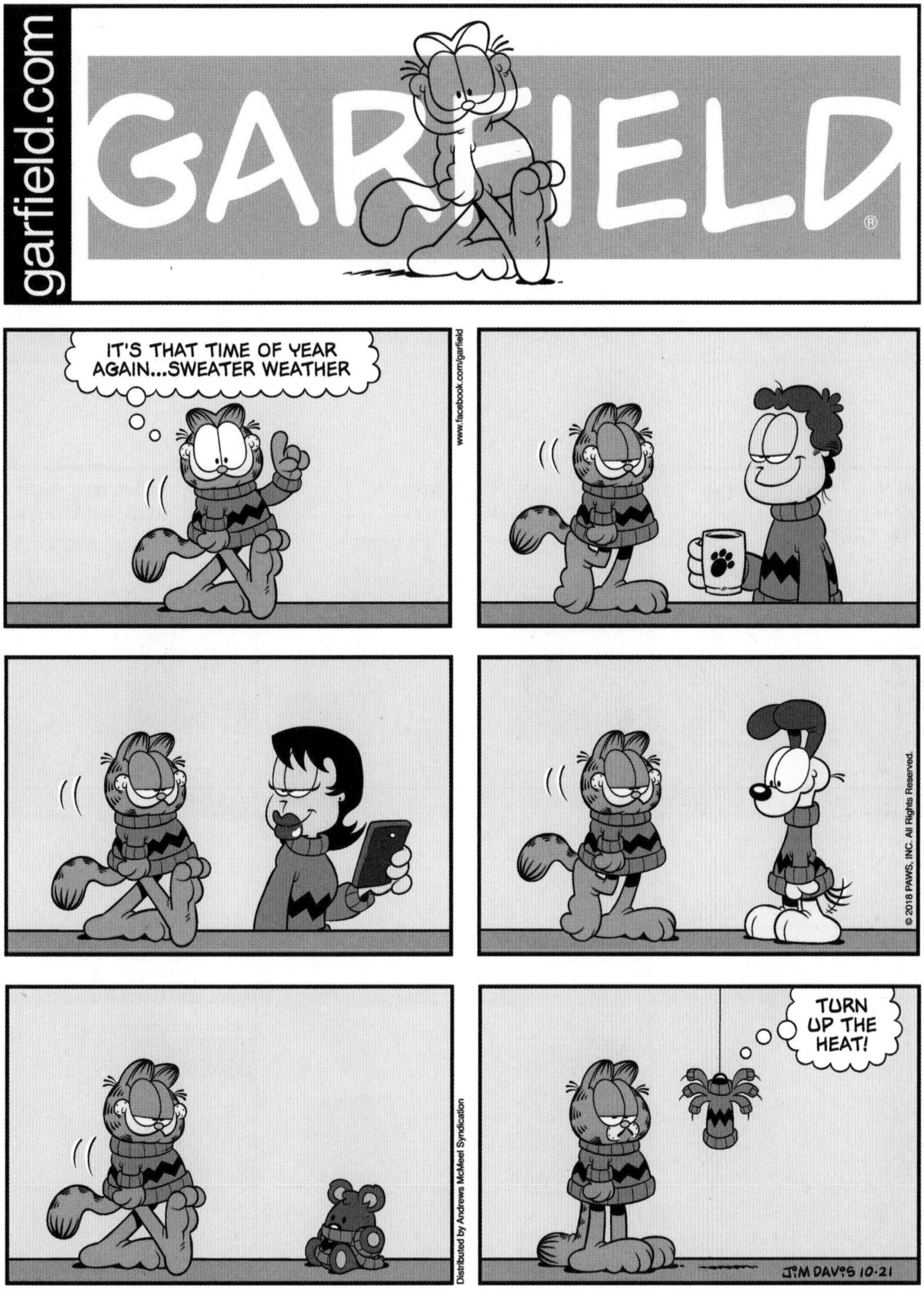
garfield.com
GARFIELD
IT'S THAT TIME OF YEAR AGAIN...SWEATER WEATHER
www.facebook.com/garfield
© 2018 PAWS, INC. All Rights Reserved.
Distributed by Andrews McMeel Syndication
TURN UP THE HEAT!
JIM DAVIS 10-21

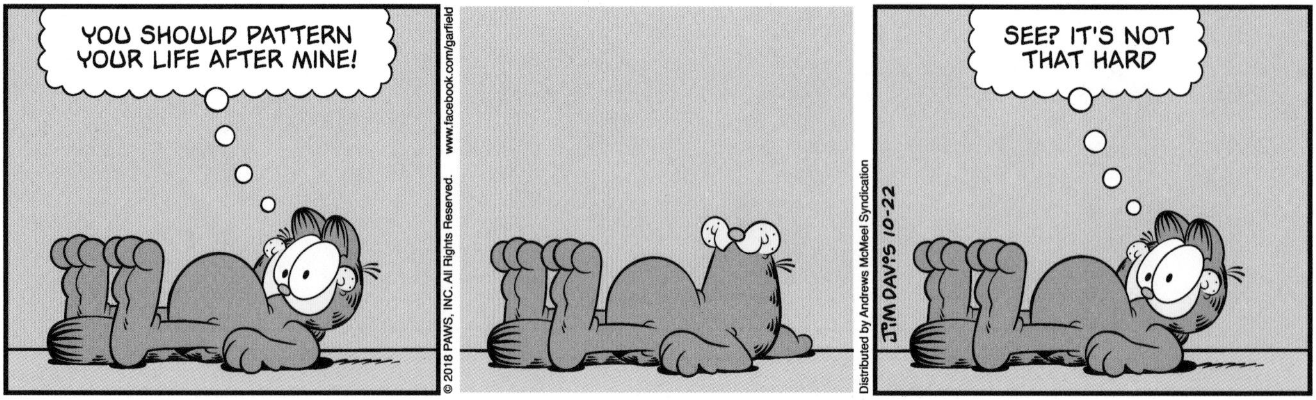
YOU SHOULD PATTERN YOUR LIFE AFTER MINE!
© 2018 PAWS, INC. All Rights Reserved. www.facebook.com/garfield
Distributed by Andrews McMeel Syndication
JIM DAVIS 10-22
SEE? IT'S NOT THAT HARD

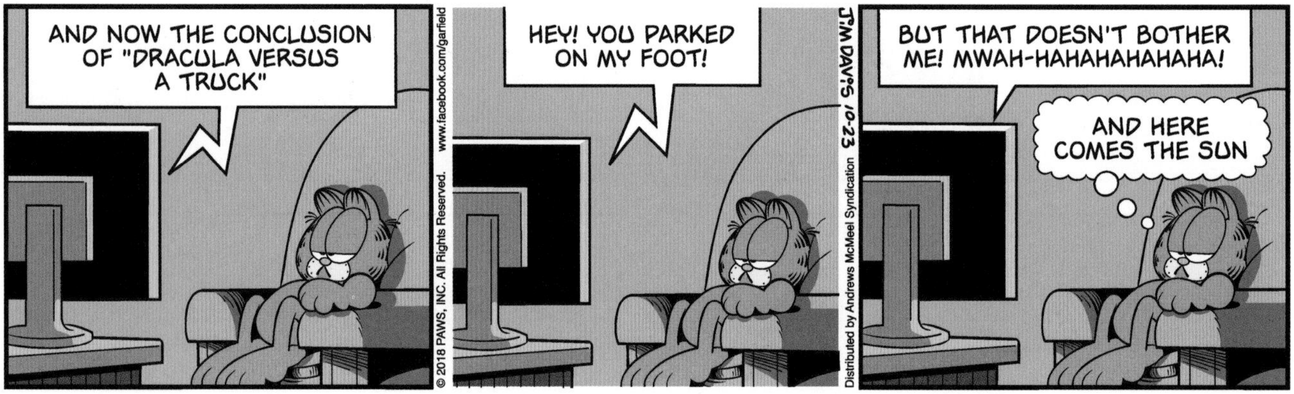
AND NOW THE CONCLUSION OF "DRACULA VERSUS A TRUCK"
© 2018 PAWS, INC. All Rights Reserved. www.facebook.com/garfield
HEY! YOU PARKED ON MY FOOT!
JIM DAVIS 10-23
Distributed by Andrews McMeel Syndication
BUT THAT DOESN'T BOTHER ME! MWAH-HAHAHAHAHAHA!
AND HERE COMES THE SUN

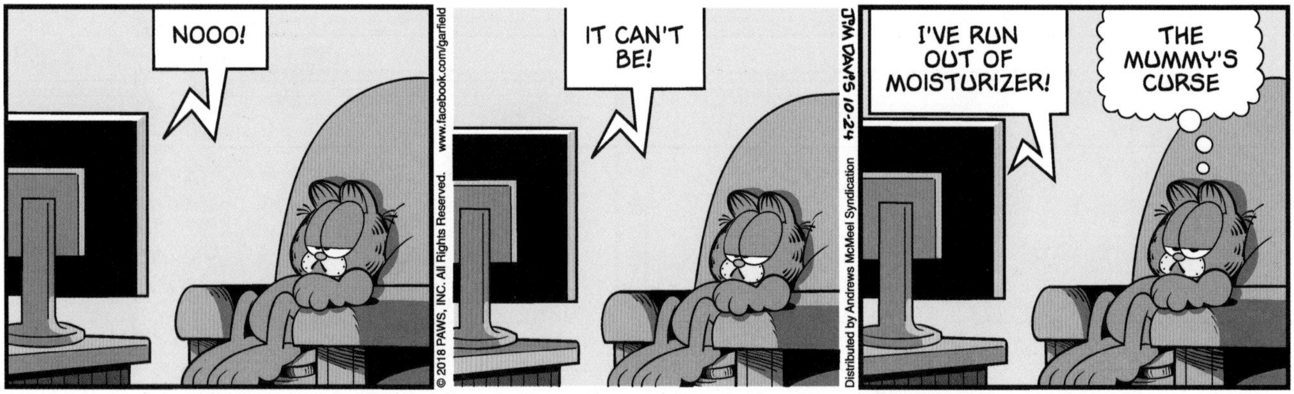
NOOO!
© 2018 PAWS, INC. All Rights Reserved. www.facebook.com/garfield
IT CAN'T BE!
JIM DAVIS 10-24
Distributed by Andrews McMeel Syndication
I'VE RUN OUT OF MOISTURIZER!
THE MUMMY'S CURSE

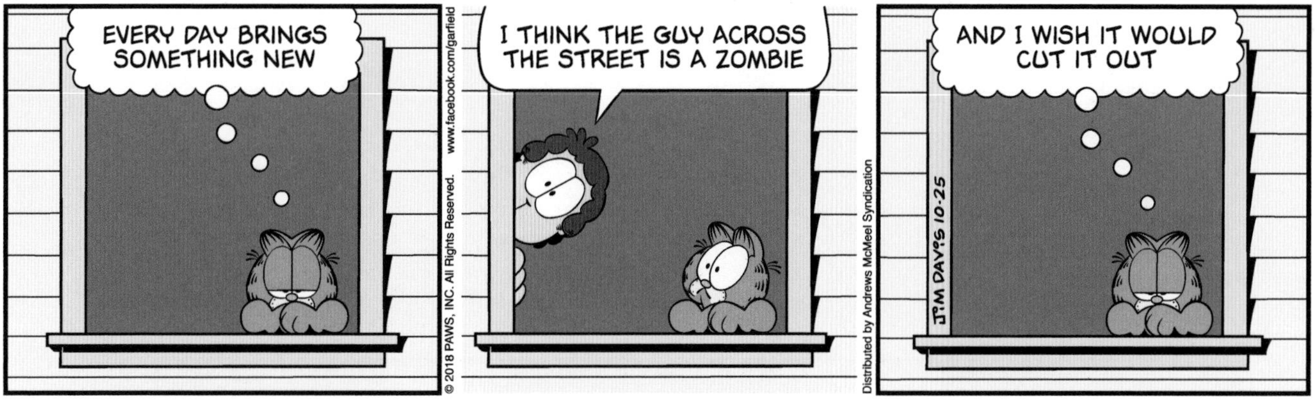
EVERY DAY BRINGS SOMETHING NEW
I THINK THE GUY ACROSS THE STREET IS A ZOMBIE
AND I WISH IT WOULD CUT IT OUT
JIM DAVIS 10-25
© 2018 PAWS, INC. All Rights Reserved. www.facebook.com/garfield
Distributed by Andrews McMeel Syndication

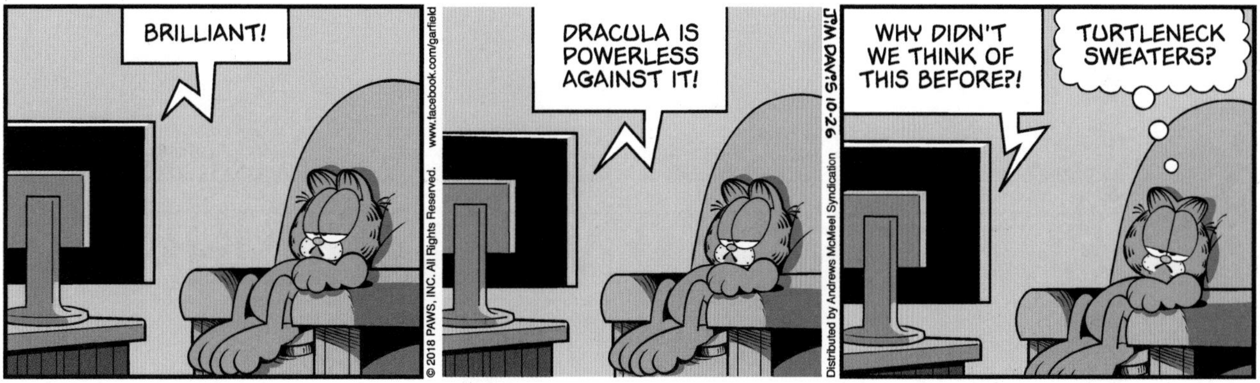
BRILLIANT!
DRACULA IS POWERLESS AGAINST IT!
WHY DIDN'T WE THINK OF THIS BEFORE?!
TURTLENECK SWEATERS?
JIM DAVIS 10-26
© 2018 PAWS, INC. All Rights Reserved. www.facebook.com/garfield
Distributed by Andrews McMeel Syndication

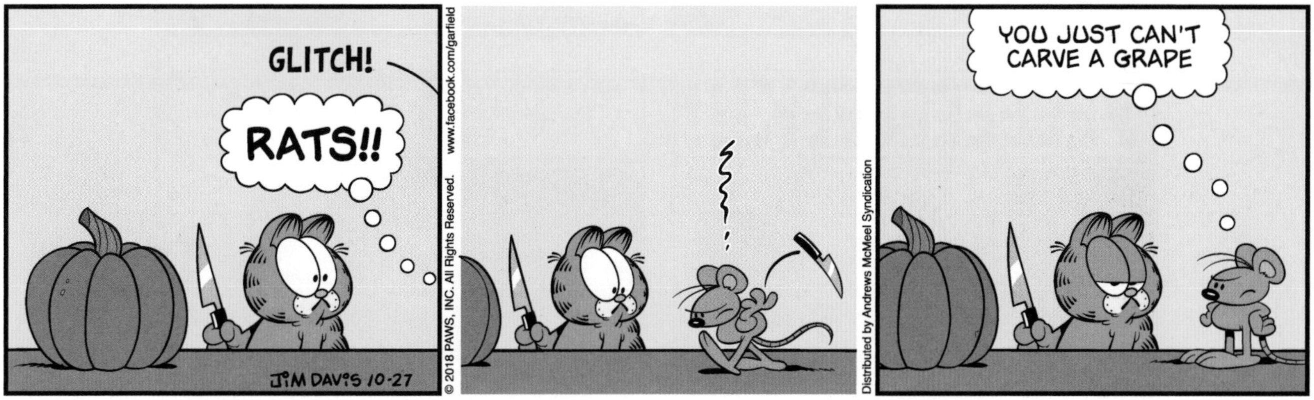
GLITCH!
RATS!!
YOU JUST CAN'T CARVE A GRAPE
JIM DAVIS 10-27
© 2018 PAWS, INC. All Rights Reserved. www.facebook.com/garfield
Distributed by Andrews McMeel Syndication

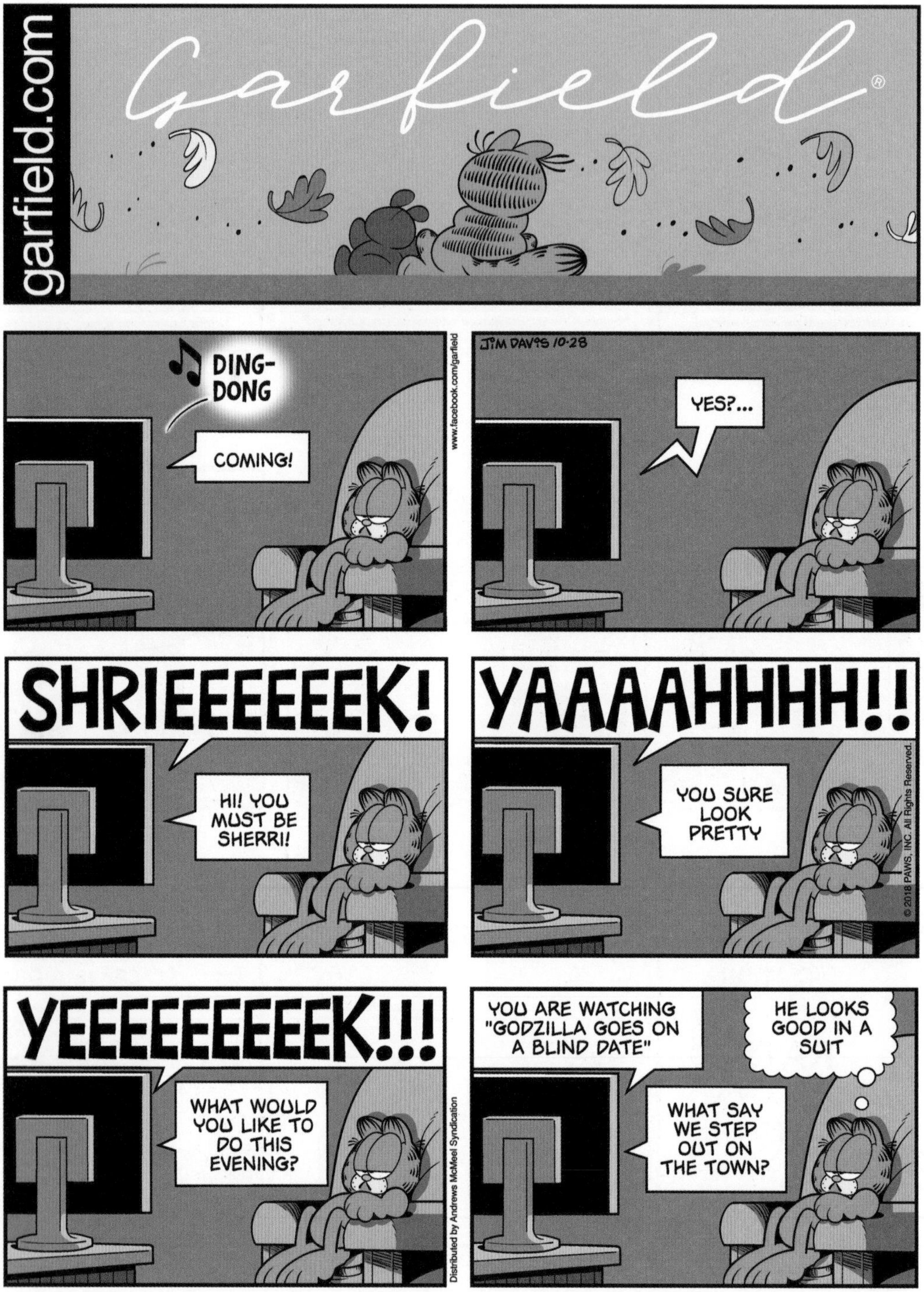
garfield.com
Garfield
DING-DONG
COMING!
www.facebook.com/garfield
JIM DAVIS 10-28
YES?...
SHRIEEEEEEK!
HI! YOU MUST BE SHERRI!
YAAAAHHHH!!
YOU SURE LOOK PRETTY
© 2018 PAWS, INC. All Rights Reserved.
YEEEEEEEEEK!!!
WHAT WOULD YOU LIKE TO DO THIS EVENING?
Distributed by Andrews McMeel Syndication
YOU ARE WATCHING "GODZILLA GOES ON A BLIND DATE"
HE LOOKS GOOD IN A SUIT
WHAT SAY WE STEP OUT ON THE TOWN?

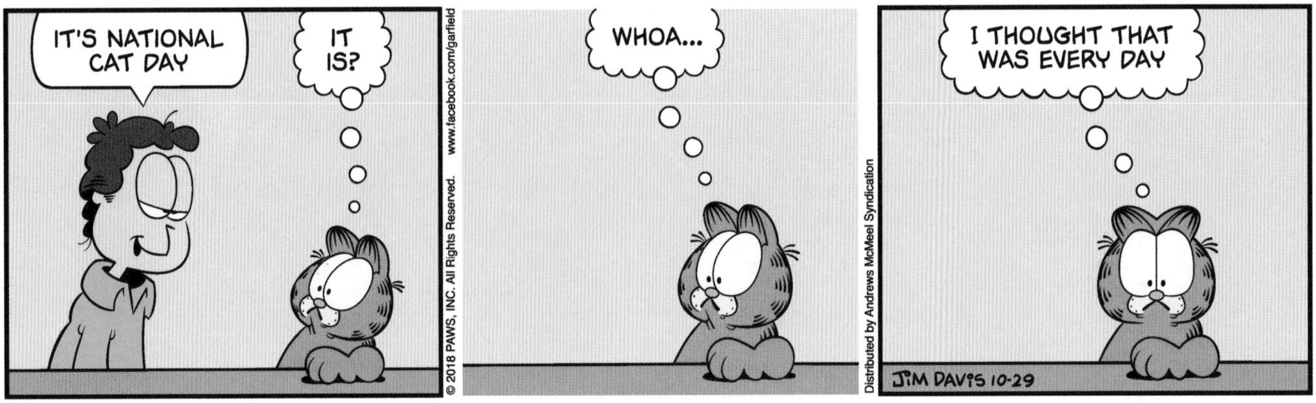
IT'S NATIONAL CAT DAY
IT IS?
WHOA...
I THOUGHT THAT WAS EVERY DAY
JIM DAVIS 10-29
© 2018 PAWS, INC. All Rights Reserved. www.facebook.com/garfield
Distributed by Andrews McMeel Syndication

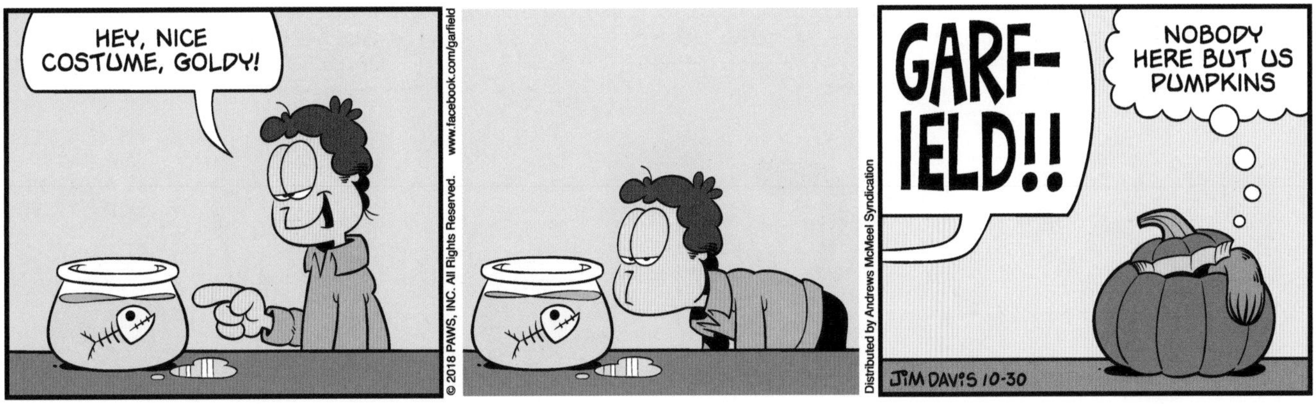
HEY, NICE COSTUME, GOLDY!
GARF-IELD!!
NOBODY HERE BUT US PUMPKINS
JIM DAVIS 10-30
© 2018 PAWS, INC. All Rights Reserved. www.facebook.com/garfield
Distributed by Andrews McMeel Syndication

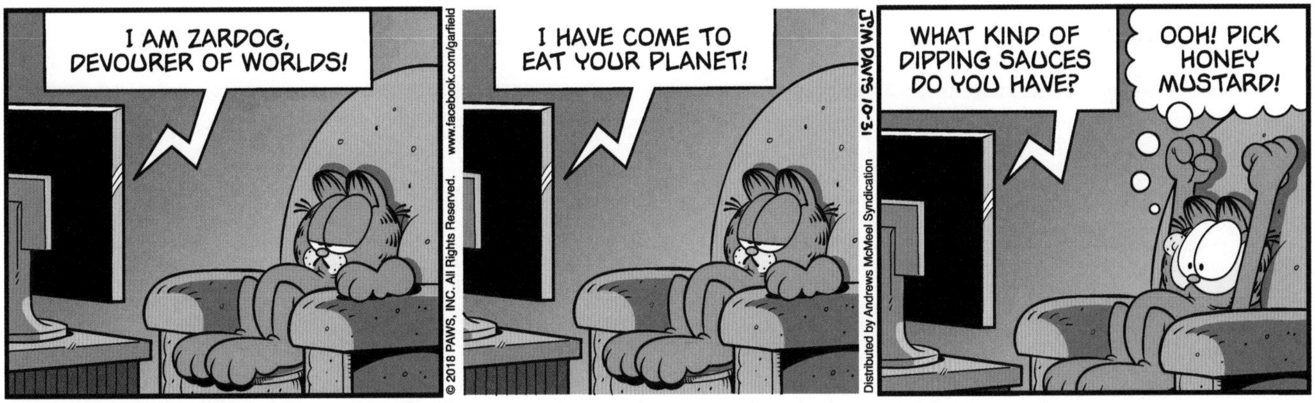
I AM ZARDOG, DEVOURER OF WORLDS!
I HAVE COME TO EAT YOUR PLANET!
WHAT KIND OF DIPPING SAUCES DO YOU HAVE?
OOH! PICK HONEY MUSTARD!
JIM DAVIS 10-31
© 2018 PAWS, INC. All Rights Reserved. www.facebook.com/garfield
Distributed by Andrews McMeel Syndication

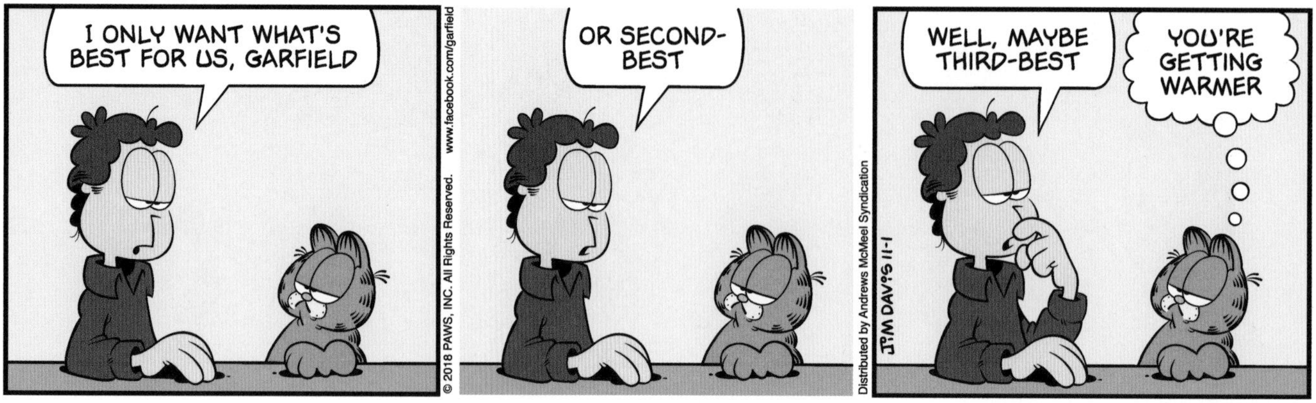
I ONLY WANT WHAT'S BEST FOR US, GARFIELD
OR SECOND-BEST
WELL, MAYBE THIRD-BEST
YOU'RE GETTING WARMER
JIM DAVIS 11-1
© 2018 PAWS, INC. All Rights Reserved. www.facebook.com/garfield
Distributed by Andrews McMeel Syndication

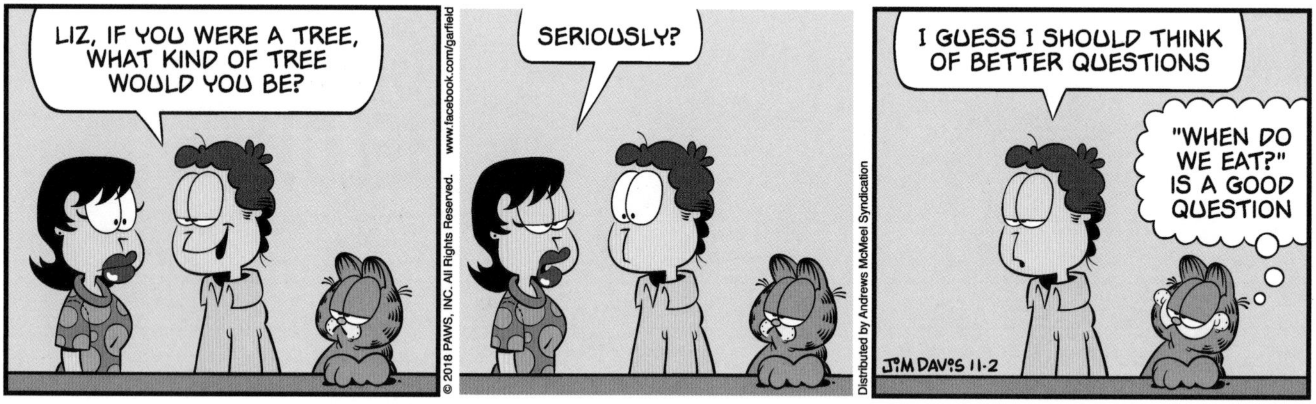
LIZ, IF YOU WERE A TREE, WHAT KIND OF TREE WOULD YOU BE?
SERIOUSLY?
I GUESS I SHOULD THINK OF BETTER QUESTIONS
"WHEN DO WE EAT?" IS A GOOD QUESTION
JIM DAVIS 11-2
© 2018 PAWS, INC. All Rights Reserved. www.facebook.com/garfield
Distributed by Andrews McMeel Syndication

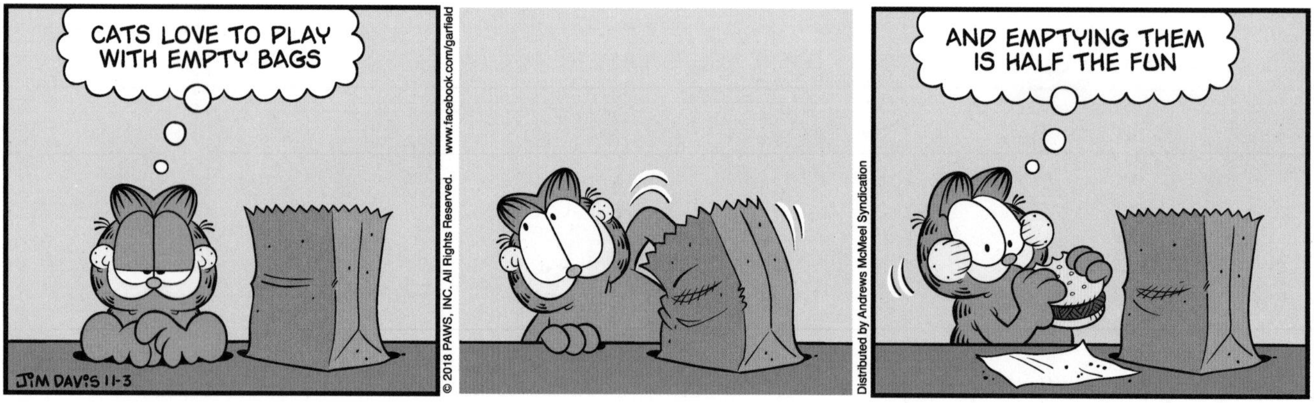
CATS LOVE TO PLAY WITH EMPTY BAGS
JIM DAVIS 11-3
AND EMPTYING THEM IS HALF THE FUN
© 2018 PAWS, INC. All Rights Reserved. www.facebook.com/garfield
Distributed by Andrews McMeel Syndication

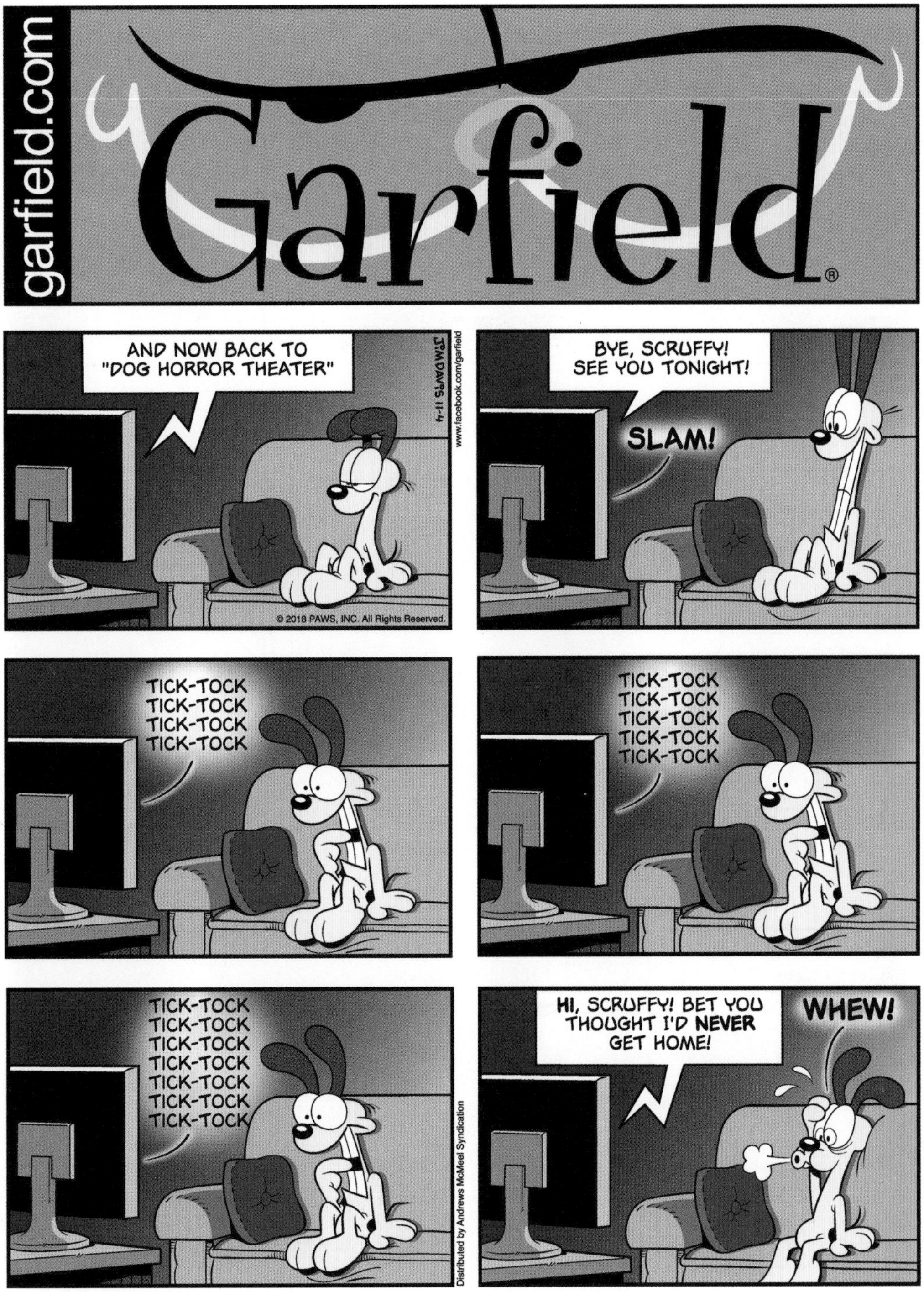
garfield.com
Garfield®
AND NOW BACK TO "DOG HORROR THEATER"
JIM DAVIS 11-4
www.facebook.com/garfield
© 2018 PAWS, INC. All Rights Reserved.
BYE, SCRUFFY! SEE YOU TONIGHT!
SLAM!
TICK-TOCK TICK-TOCK TICK-TOCK TICK-TOCK
TICK-TOCK TICK-TOCK TICK-TOCK TICK-TOCK TICK-TOCK
TICK-TOCK TICK-TOCK TICK-TOCK TICK-TOCK TICK-TOCK TICK-TOCK TICK-TOCK
Distributed by Andrews McMeel Syndication
HI, SCRUFFY! BET YOU THOUGHT I'D NEVER GET HOME!
WHEW!

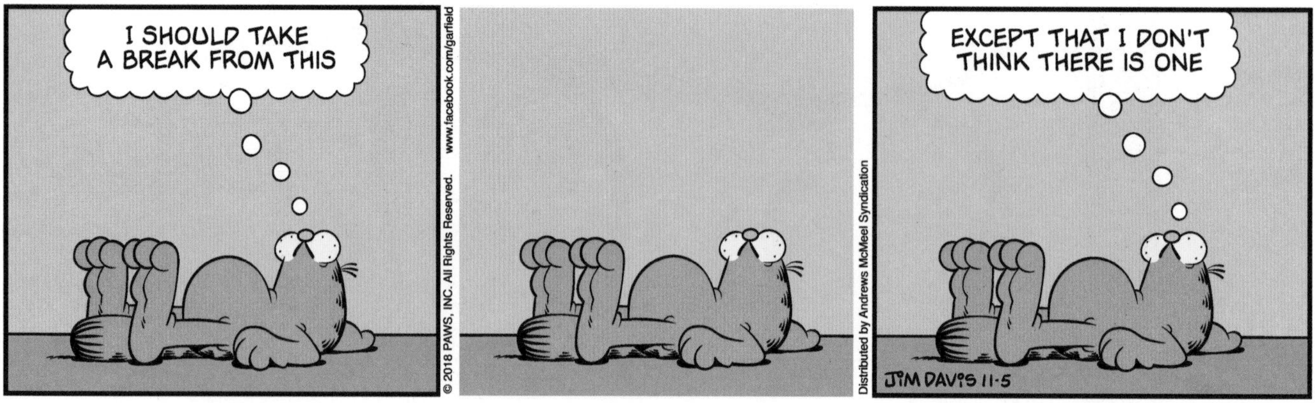
I SHOULD TAKE A BREAK FROM THIS
EXCEPT THAT I DON'T THINK THERE IS ONE
JIM DAVIS 11-5

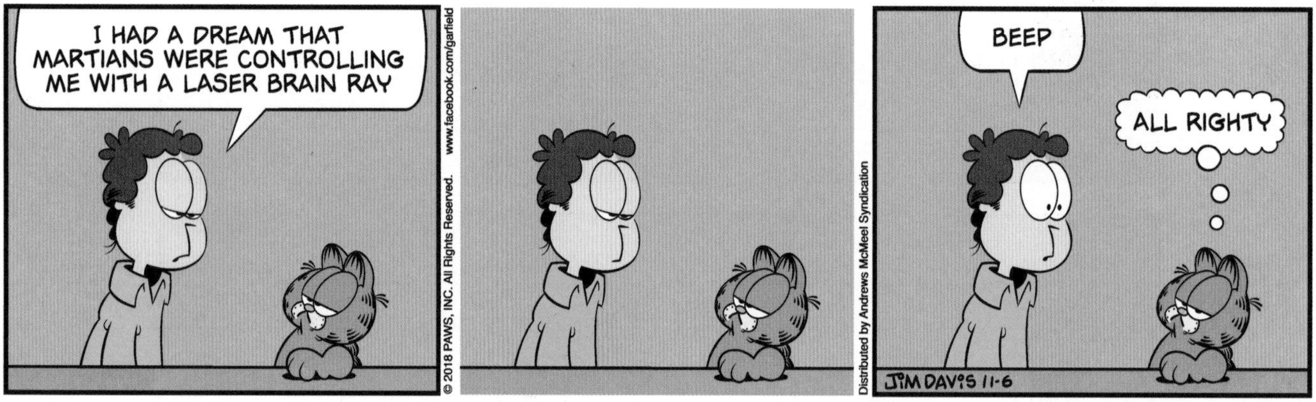
I HAD A DREAM THAT MARTIANS WERE CONTROLLING ME WITH A LASER BRAIN RAY
BEEP
ALL RIGHTY
JIM DAVIS 11-6

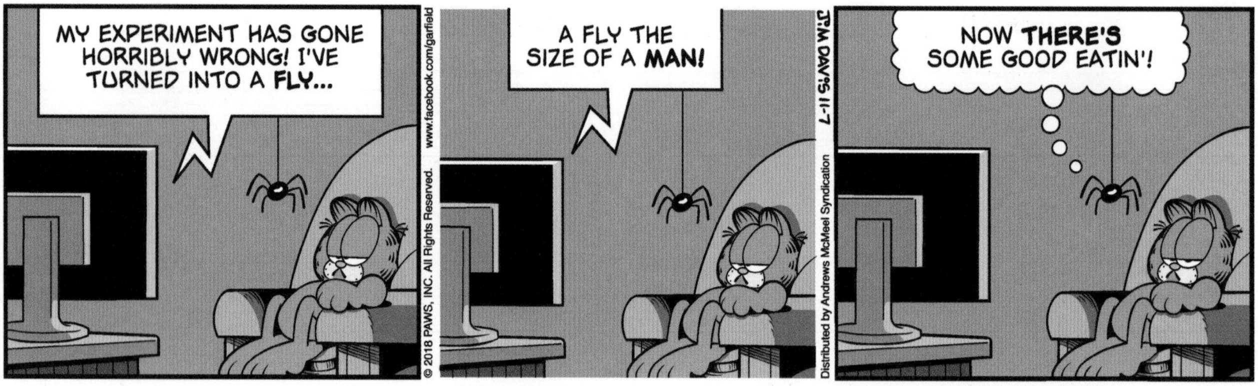
MY EXPERIMENT HAS GONE HORRIBLY WRONG! I'VE TURNED INTO A FLY...
A FLY THE SIZE OF A MAN!
NOW THERE'S SOME GOOD EATIN'!
JIM DAVIS 11-7

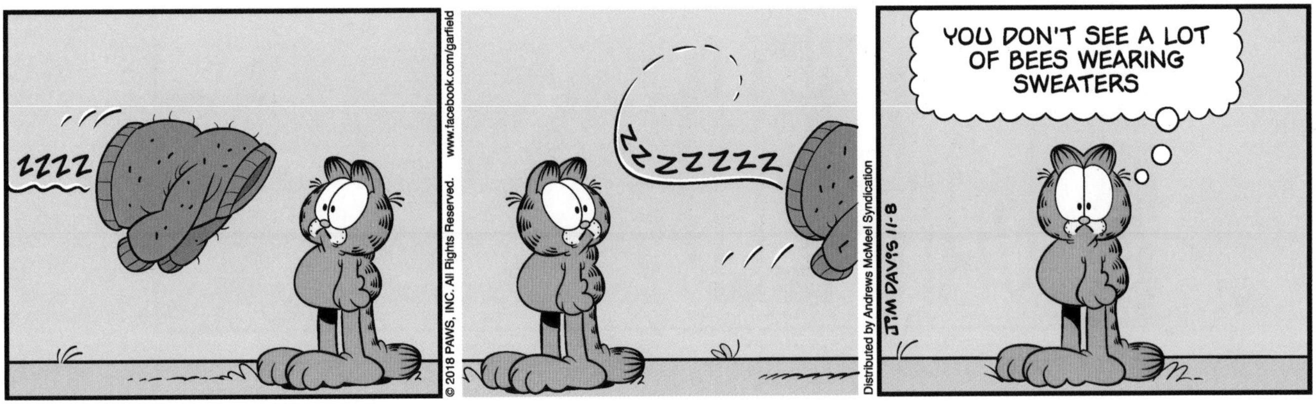
ZZZZ
ZZZZZZZ
YOU DON'T SEE A LOT OF BEES WEARING SWEATERS
© 2018 PAWS, INC. All Rights Reserved. www.facebook.com/garfield
Distributed by Andrews McMeel Syndication
JIM DAVIS 11-8

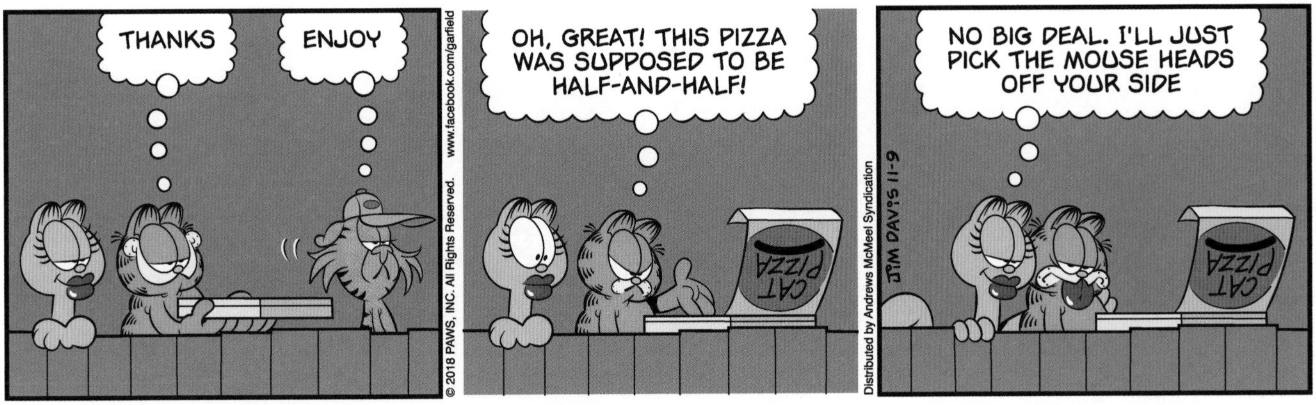
THANKS
ENJOY
OH, GREAT! THIS PIZZA WAS SUPPOSED TO BE HALF-AND-HALF!
NO BIG DEAL. I'LL JUST PICK THE MOUSE HEADS OFF YOUR SIDE
CAT PIZZA
© 2018 PAWS, INC. All Rights Reserved. www.facebook.com/garfield
Distributed by Andrews McMeel Syndication
JIM DAVIS 11-9

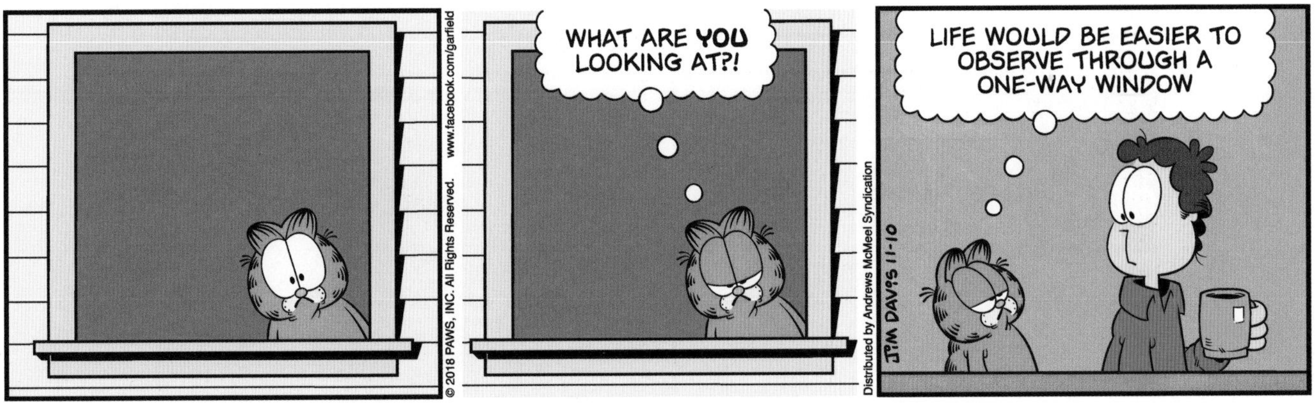
WHAT ARE **YOU** LOOKING AT?!
LIFE WOULD BE EASIER TO OBSERVE THROUGH A ONE-WAY WINDOW
© 2018 PAWS, INC. All Rights Reserved. www.facebook.com/garfield
Distributed by Andrews McMeel Syndication
JIM DAVIS 11-10

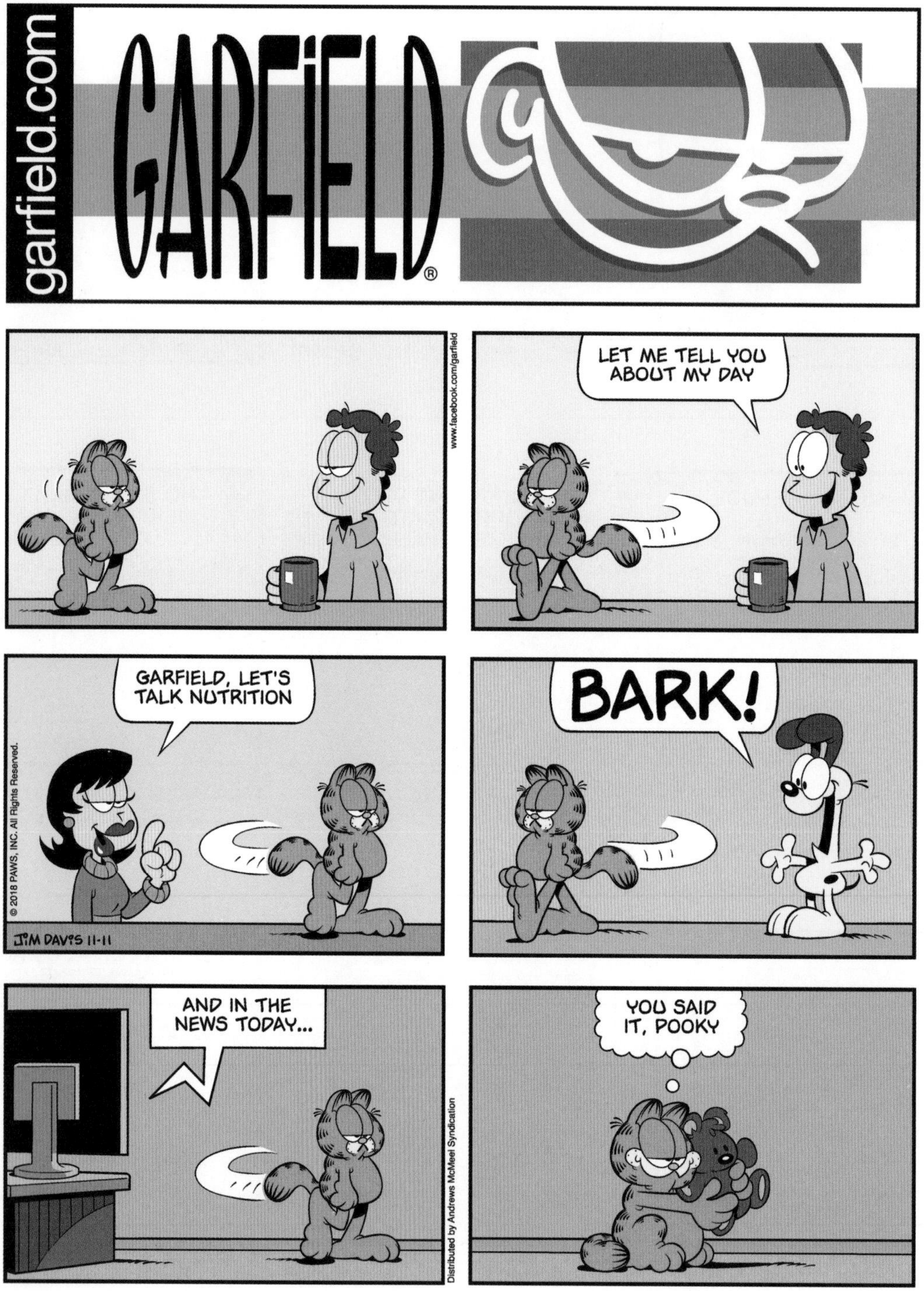
garfield.com
GARFIELD®
www.facebook.com/garfield
LET ME TELL YOU ABOUT MY DAY
GARFIELD, LET'S TALK NUTRITION
© 2018 PAWS, INC. All Rights Reserved.
JIM DAVIS 11-11
BARK!
AND IN THE NEWS TODAY...
Distributed by Andrews McMeel Syndication
YOU SAID IT, POOKY

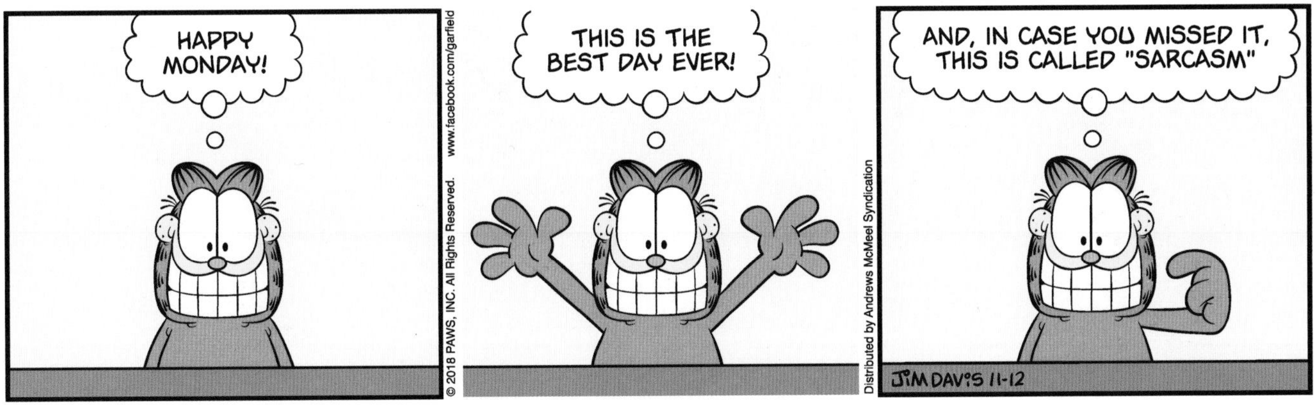
HAPPY MONDAY!
© 2018 PAWS, INC. All Rights Reserved. www.facebook.com/garfield
THIS IS THE BEST DAY EVER!
Distributed by Andrews McMeel Syndication
AND, IN CASE YOU MISSED IT, THIS IS CALLED "SARCASM"
JIM DAVIS 11-12

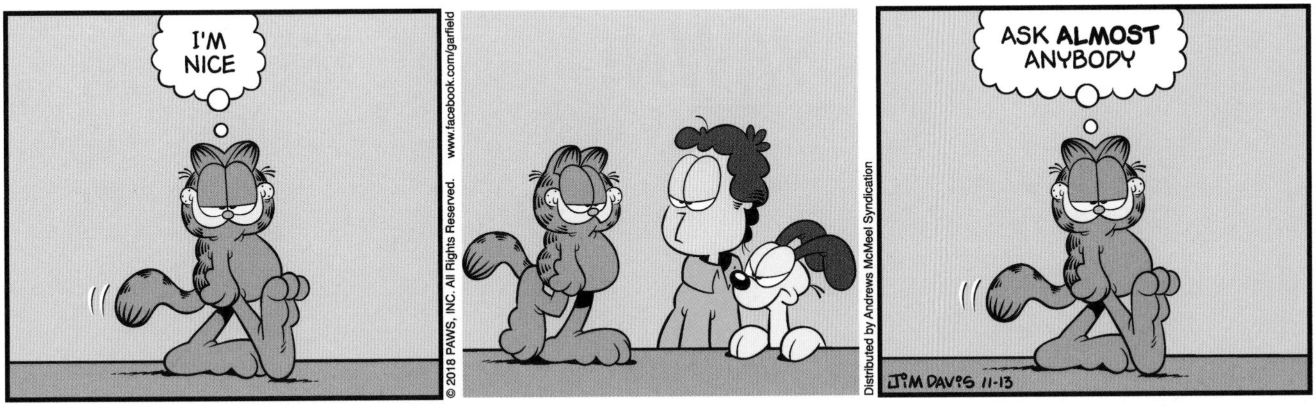
I'M NICE
© 2018 PAWS, INC. All Rights Reserved. www.facebook.com/garfield
Distributed by Andrews McMeel Syndication
ASK **ALMOST** ANYBODY
JIM DAVIS 11-13

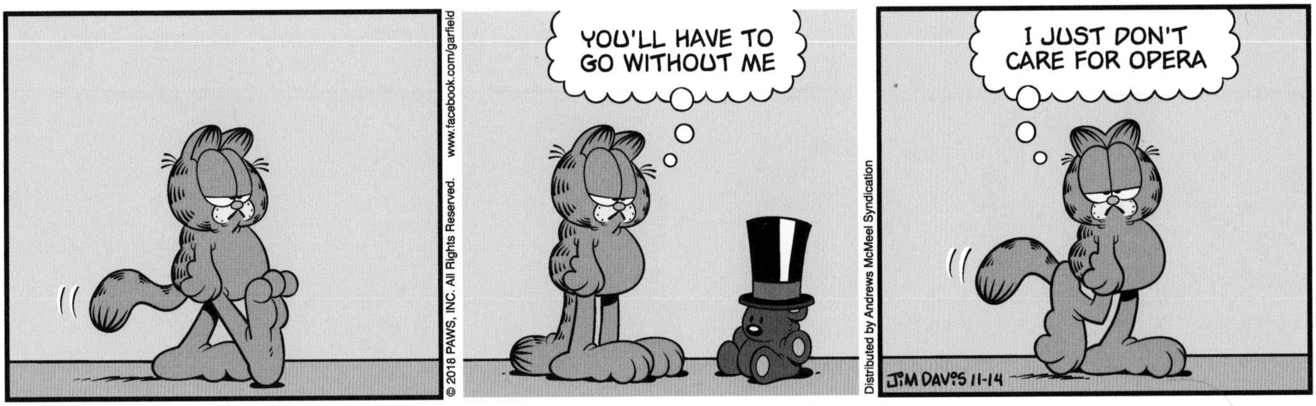
© 2018 PAWS, INC. All Rights Reserved. www.facebook.com/garfield
YOU'LL HAVE TO GO WITHOUT ME
Distributed by Andrews McMeel Syndication
I JUST DON'T CARE FOR OPERA
JIM DAVIS 11-14

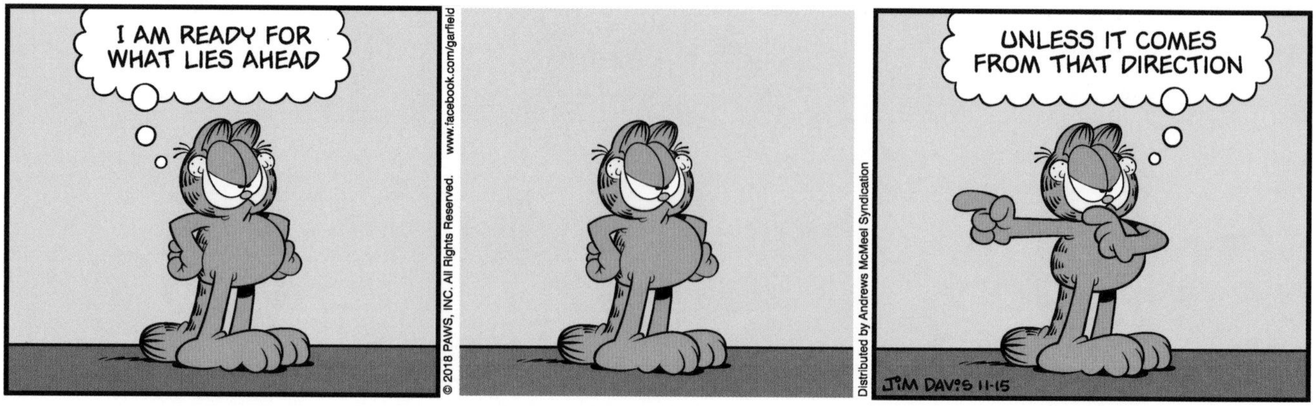
I AM READY FOR WHAT LIES AHEAD
UNLESS IT COMES FROM THAT DIRECTION
© 2018 PAWS, INC. All Rights Reserved. www.facebook.com/garfield
Distributed by Andrews McMeel Syndication
JIM DAVIS 11-15

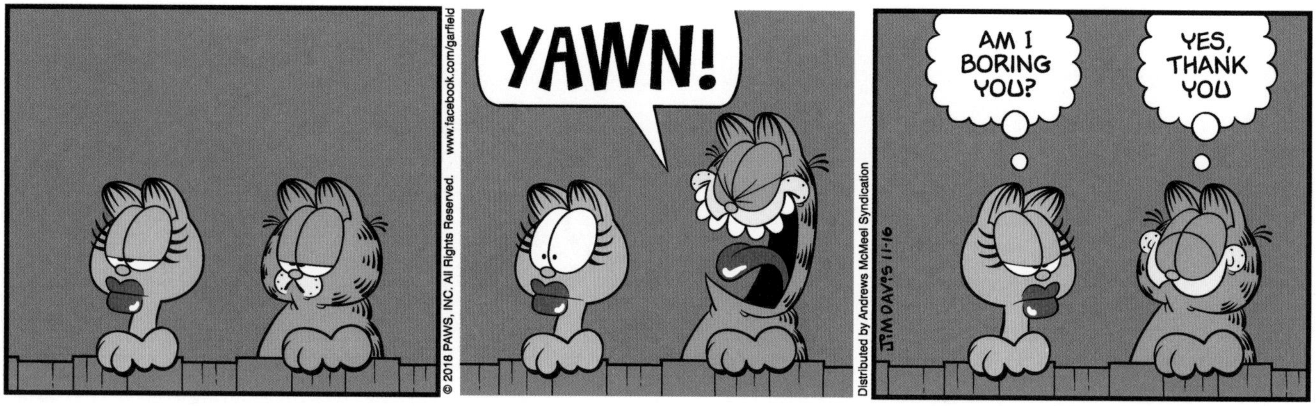
YAWN!
AM I BORING YOU?
YES, THANK YOU
© 2018 PAWS, INC. All Rights Reserved. www.facebook.com/garfield
Distributed by Andrews McMeel Syndication
JIM DAVIS 11-16

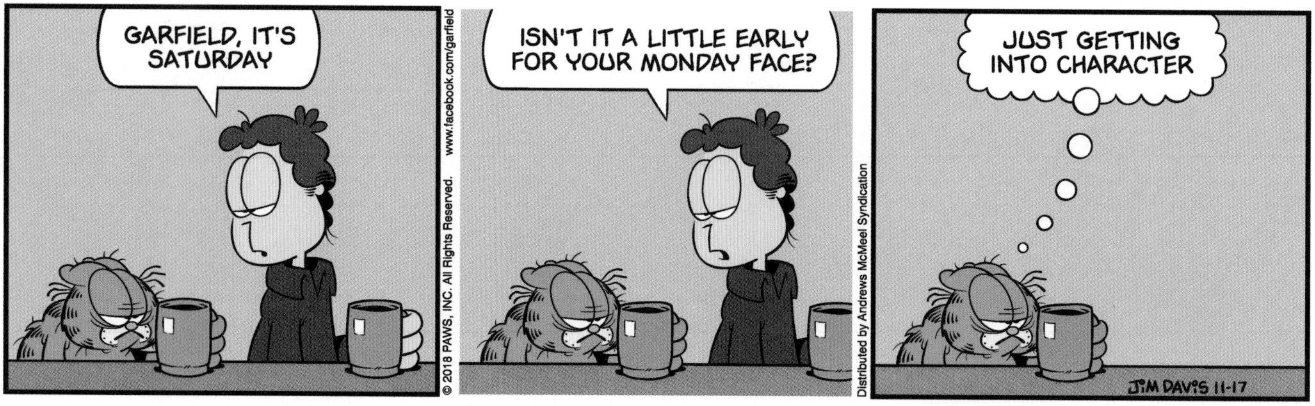
GARFIELD, IT'S SATURDAY
ISN'T IT A LITTLE EARLY FOR YOUR MONDAY FACE?
JUST GETTING INTO CHARACTER
© 2018 PAWS, INC. All Rights Reserved. www.facebook.com/garfield
Distributed by Andrews McMeel Syndication
JIM DAVIS 11-17

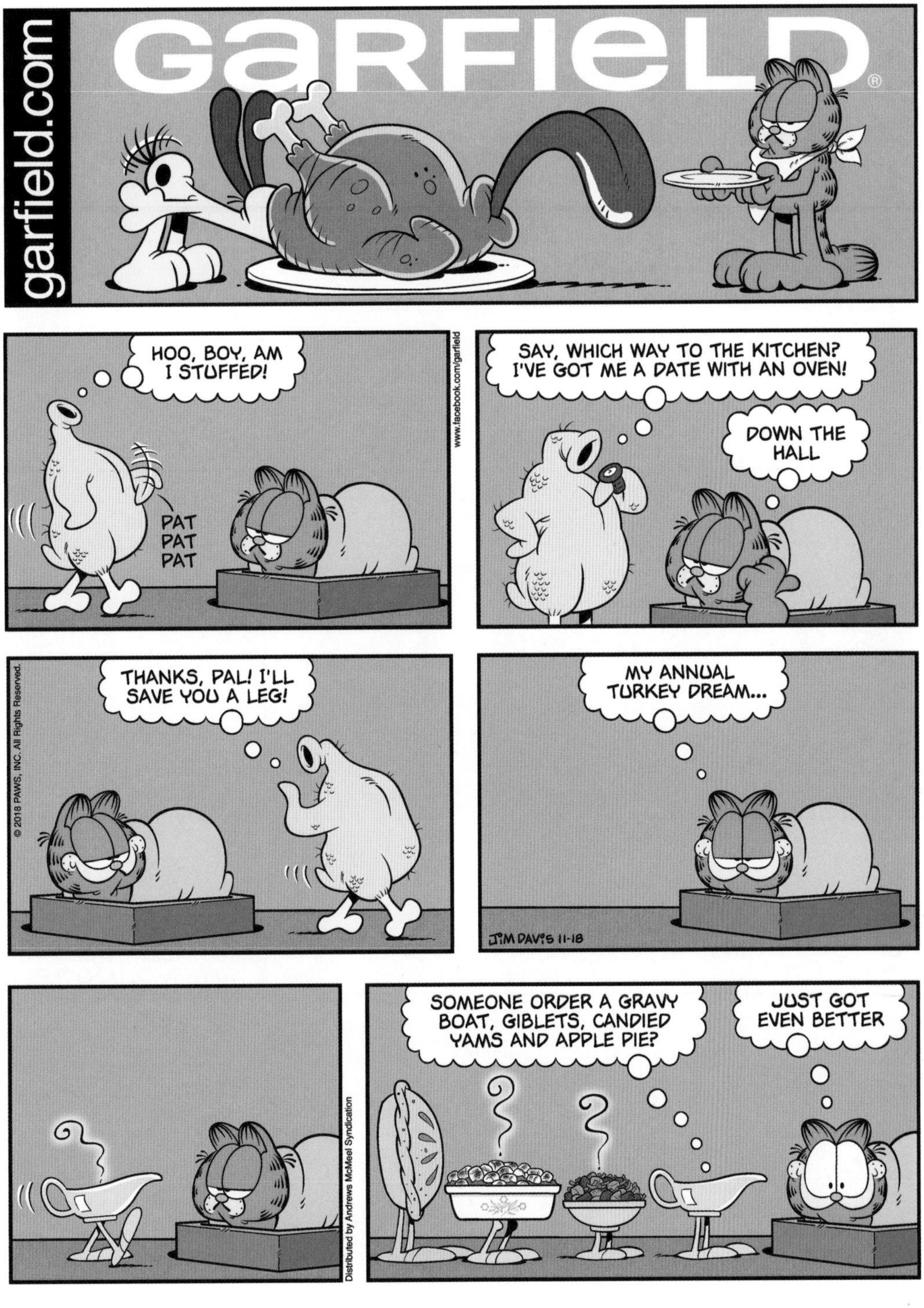
GARFIELD
garfield.com
HOO, BOY, AM I STUFFED!
PAT PAT PAT
SAY, WHICH WAY TO THE KITCHEN? I'VE GOT ME A DATE WITH AN OVEN!
DOWN THE HALL
THANKS, PAL! I'LL SAVE YOU A LEG!
MY ANNUAL TURKEY DREAM...
JIM DAVIS 11-18
SOMEONE ORDER A GRAVY BOAT, GIBLETS, CANDIED YAMS AND APPLE PIE?
JUST GOT EVEN BETTER
www.facebook.com/garfield
© 2018 PAWS, INC. All Rights Reserved.
Distributed by Andrews McMeel Syndication

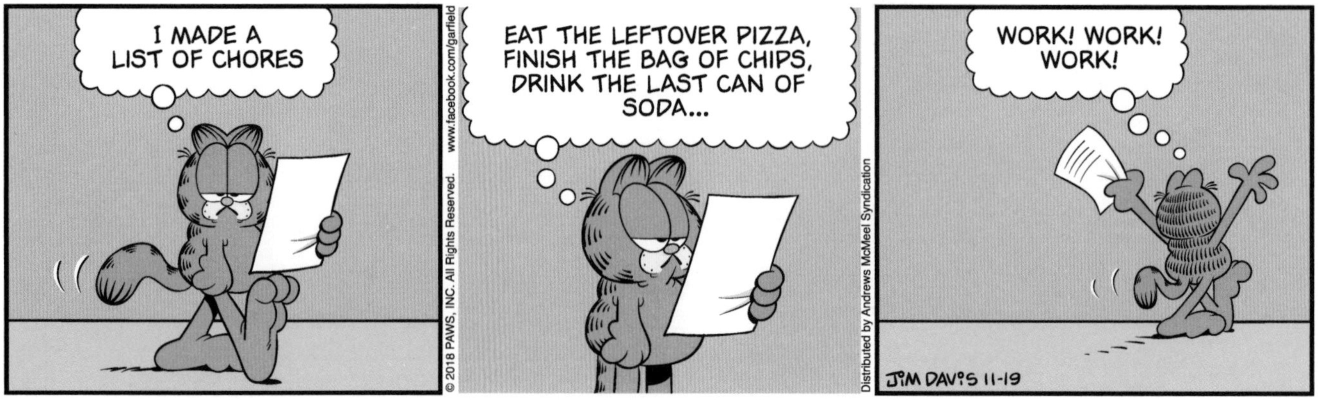
I MADE A LIST OF CHORES
EAT THE LEFTOVER PIZZA, FINISH THE BAG OF CHIPS, DRINK THE LAST CAN OF SODA...
WORK! WORK! WORK!
© 2018 PAWS, INC. All Rights Reserved. www.facebook.com/garfield
Distributed by Andrews McMeel Syndication
JIM DAVIS 11-19

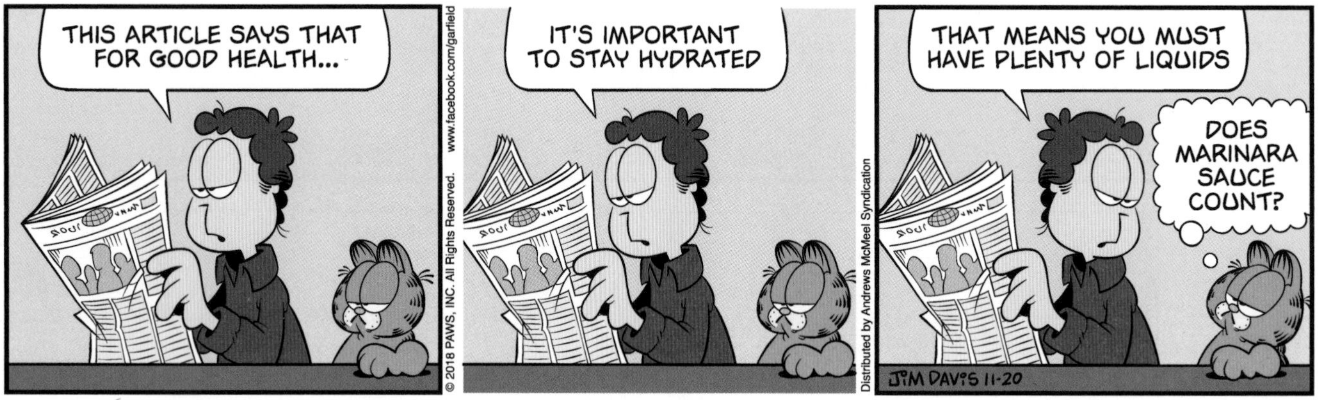
THIS ARTICLE SAYS THAT FOR GOOD HEALTH...
IT'S IMPORTANT TO STAY HYDRATED
THAT MEANS YOU MUST HAVE PLENTY OF LIQUIDS
DOES MARINARA SAUCE COUNT?
© 2018 PAWS, INC. All Rights Reserved. www.facebook.com/garfield
Distributed by Andrews McMeel Syndication
JIM DAVIS 11-20

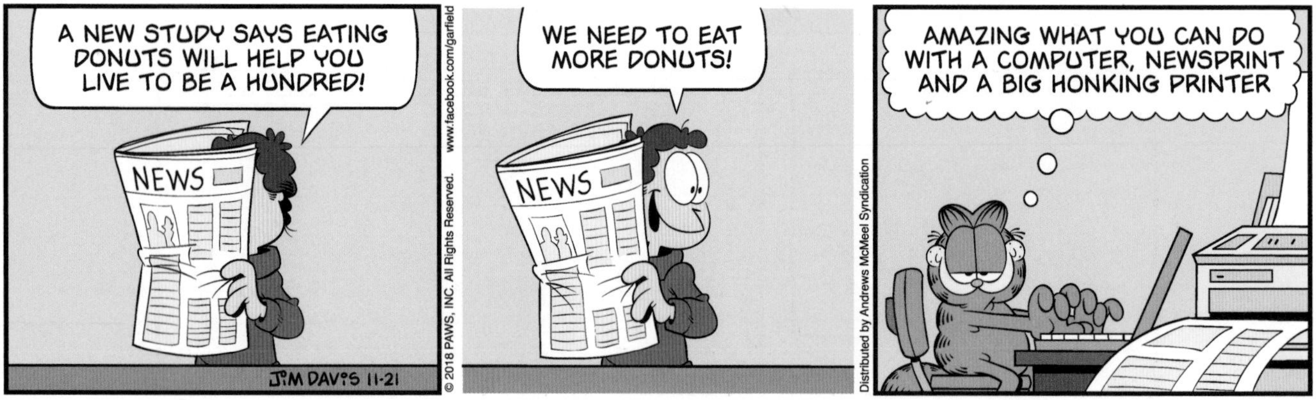
A NEW STUDY SAYS EATING DONUTS WILL HELP YOU LIVE TO BE A HUNDRED!
NEWS
JIM DAVIS 11-21
WE NEED TO EAT MORE DONUTS!
NEWS
AMAZING WHAT YOU CAN DO WITH A COMPUTER, NEWSPRINT AND A BIG HONKING PRINTER
© 2018 PAWS, INC. All Rights Reserved. www.facebook.com/garfield
Distributed by Andrews McMeel Syndication

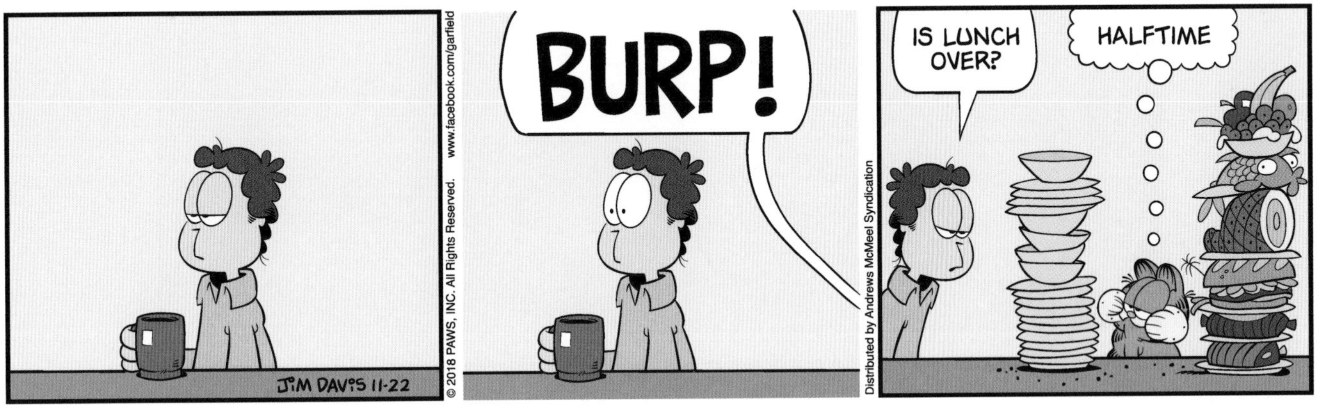
JIM DAVIS 11-22
© 2018 PAWS, INC. All Rights Reserved. www.facebook.com/garfield
BURP!
Distributed by Andrews McMeel Syndication
IS LUNCH OVER?
HALFTIME

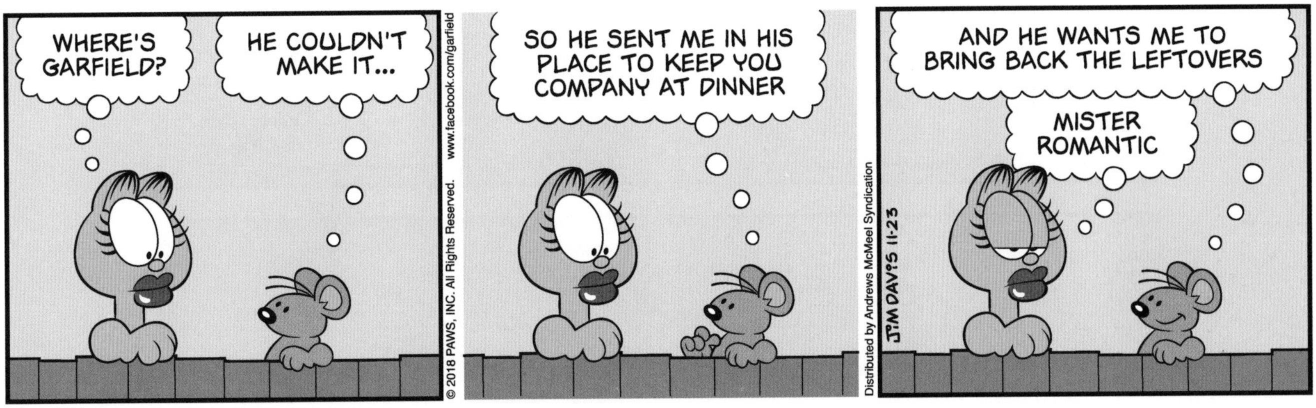
WHERE'S GARFIELD?
HE COULDN'T MAKE IT...
© 2018 PAWS, INC. All Rights Reserved. www.facebook.com/garfield
SO HE SENT ME IN HIS PLACE TO KEEP YOU COMPANY AT DINNER
Distributed by Andrews McMeel Syndication
JIM DAVIS 11-23
AND HE WANTS ME TO BRING BACK THE LEFTOVERS
MISTER ROMANTIC

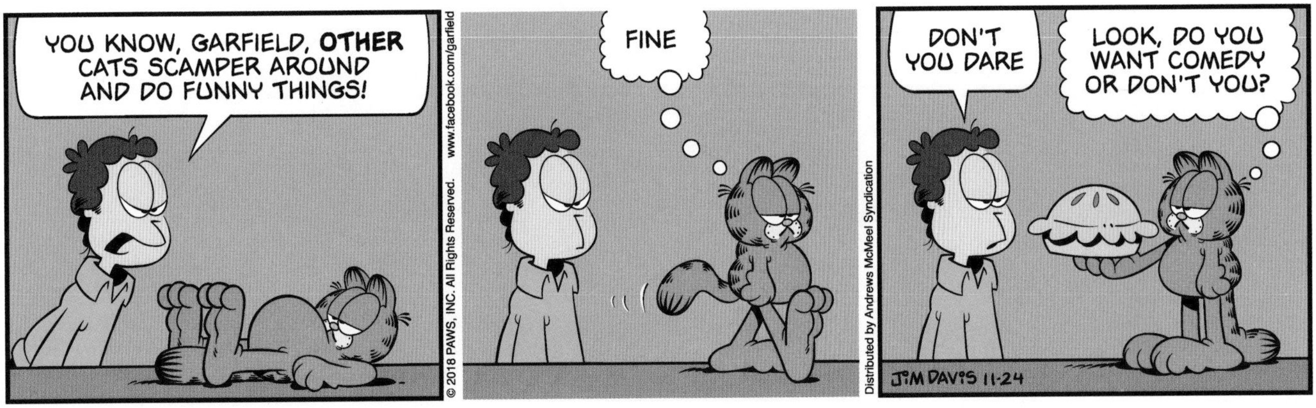
YOU KNOW, GARFIELD, OTHER CATS SCAMPER AROUND AND DO FUNNY THINGS!
© 2018 PAWS, INC. All Rights Reserved. www.facebook.com/garfield
FINE
Distributed by Andrews McMeel Syndication
DON'T YOU DARE
LOOK, DO YOU WANT COMEDY OR DON'T YOU?
JIM DAVIS 11-24

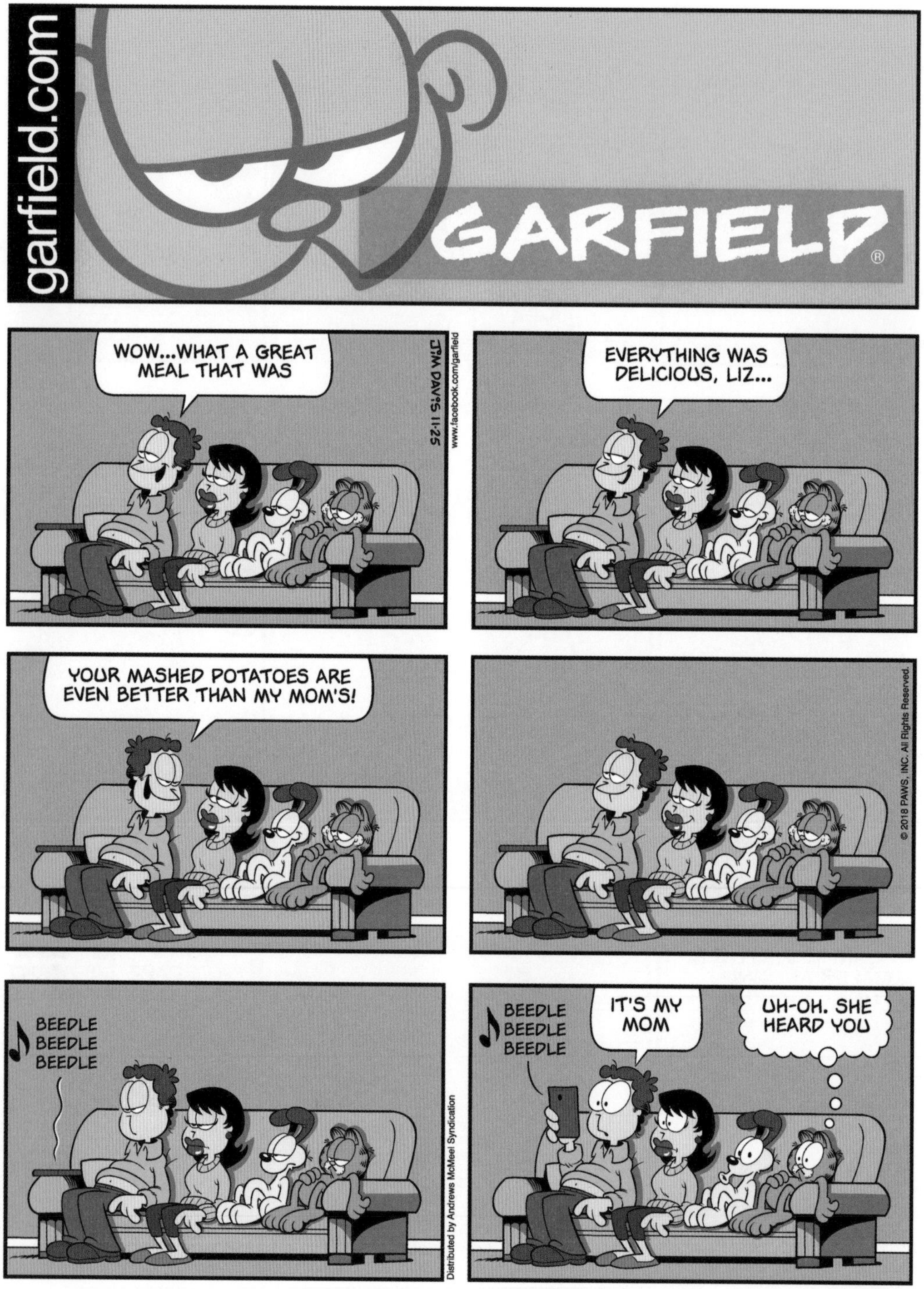
garfield.com
GARFIELD®
WOW...WHAT A GREAT MEAL THAT WAS
JIM DAVIS 11-25
www.facebook.com/garfield
EVERYTHING WAS DELICIOUS, LIZ...
YOUR MASHED POTATOES ARE EVEN BETTER THAN MY MOM'S!
© 2018 PAWS, INC. All Rights Reserved.
BEEDLE BEEDLE BEEDLE
Distributed by Andrews McMeel Syndication
BEEDLE BEEDLE BEEDLE
IT'S MY MOM
UH-OH. SHE HEARD YOU

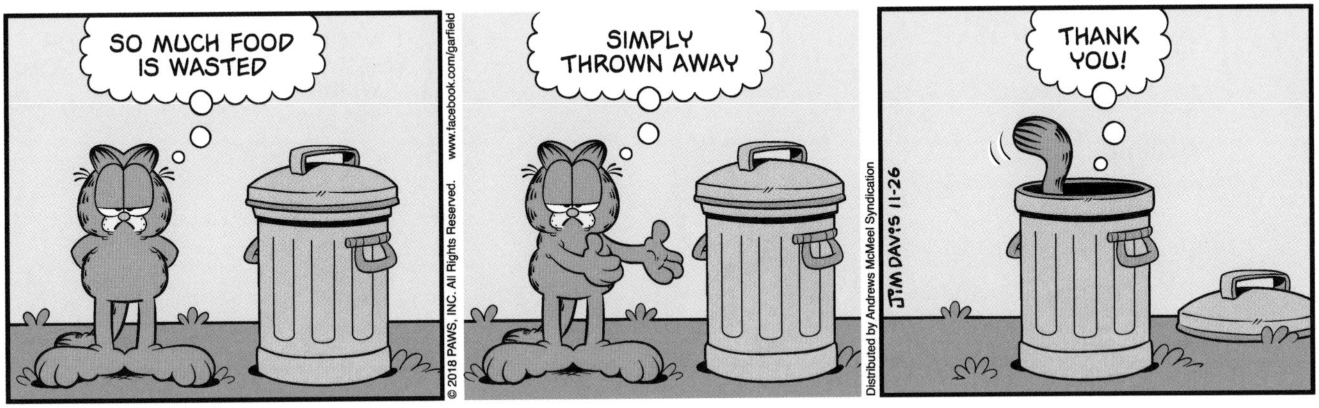
SO MUCH FOOD IS WASTED
SIMPLY THROWN AWAY
THANK YOU!
JIM DAVIS 11-26

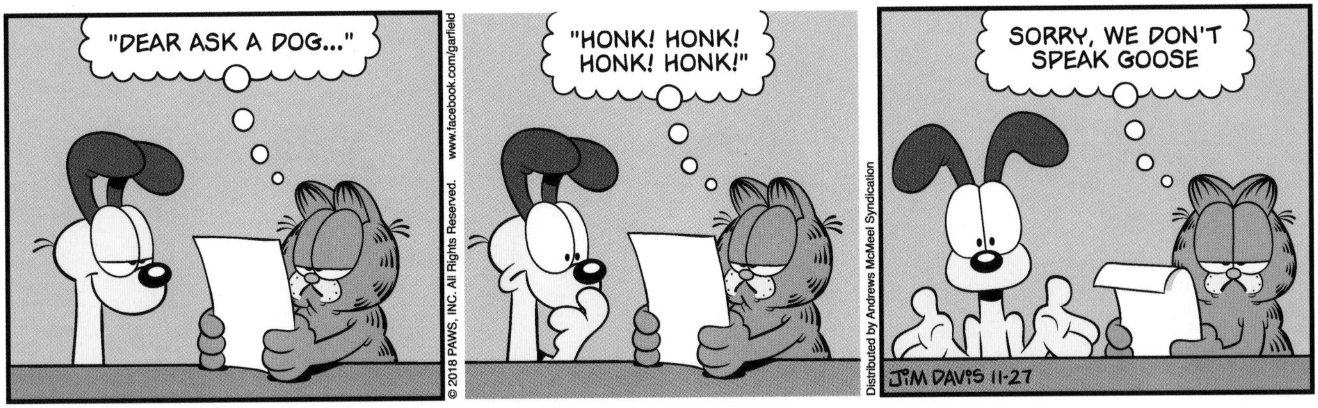
"DEAR ASK A DOG..."
"HONK! HONK! HONK! HONK!"
SORRY, WE DON'T SPEAK GOOSE
JIM DAVIS 11-27

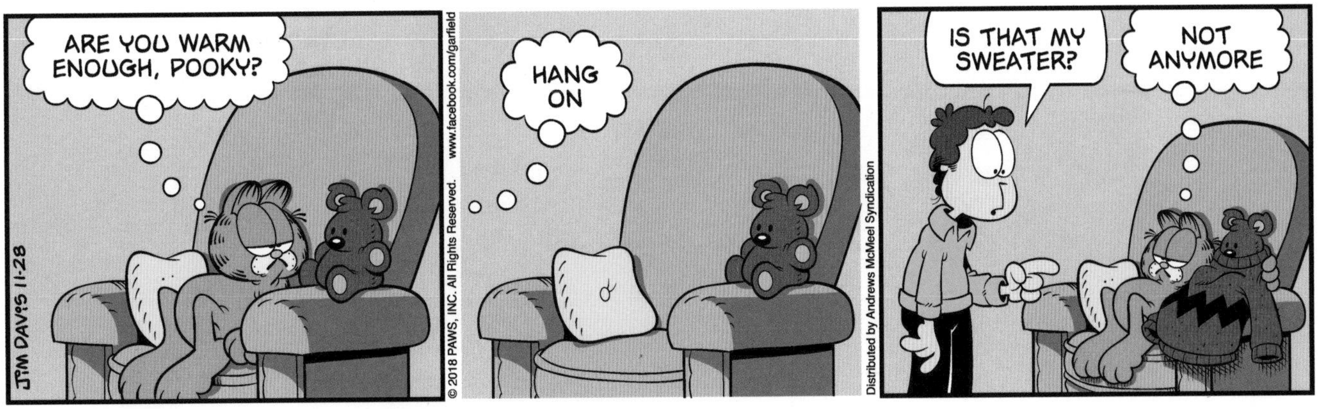
ARE YOU WARM ENOUGH, POOKY?
JIM DAVIS 11-28
HANG ON
IS THAT MY SWEATER?
NOT ANYMORE

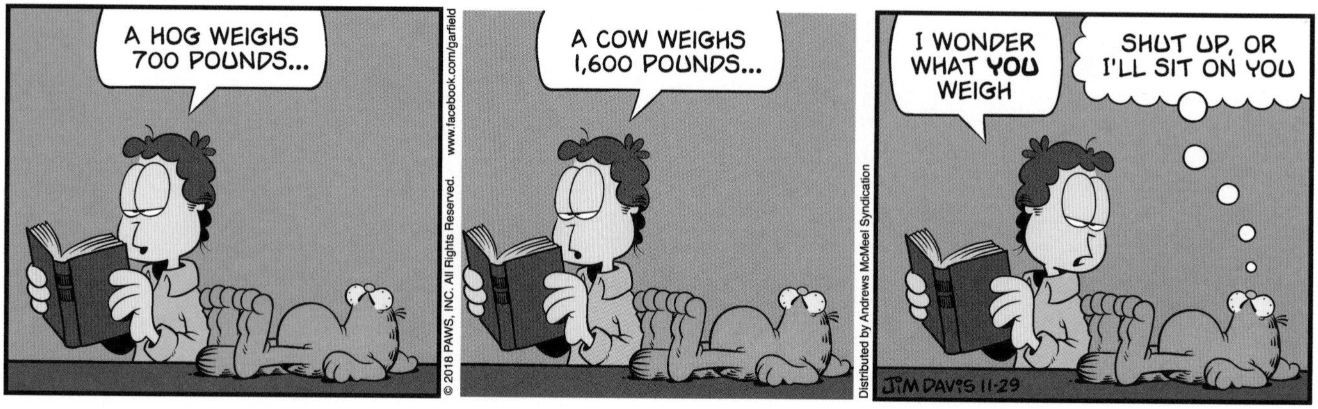
A HOG WEIGHS 700 POUNDS...
A COW WEIGHS 1,600 POUNDS...
I WONDER WHAT **YOU** WEIGH
SHUT UP, OR I'LL SIT ON YOU
JIM DAVIS 11-29

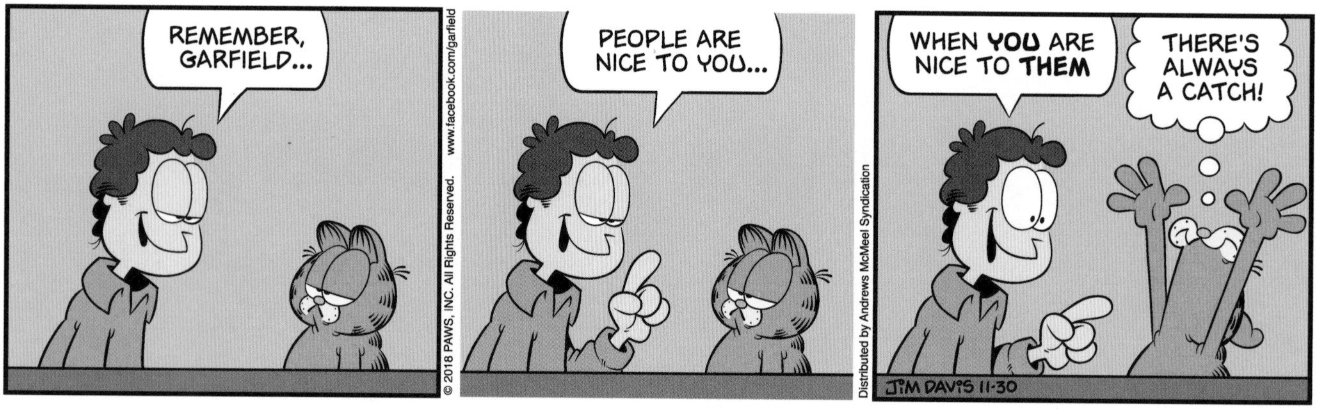
REMEMBER, GARFIELD...
PEOPLE ARE NICE TO YOU...
WHEN **YOU** ARE NICE TO **THEM**
THERE'S ALWAYS A CATCH!
JIM DAVIS 11-30

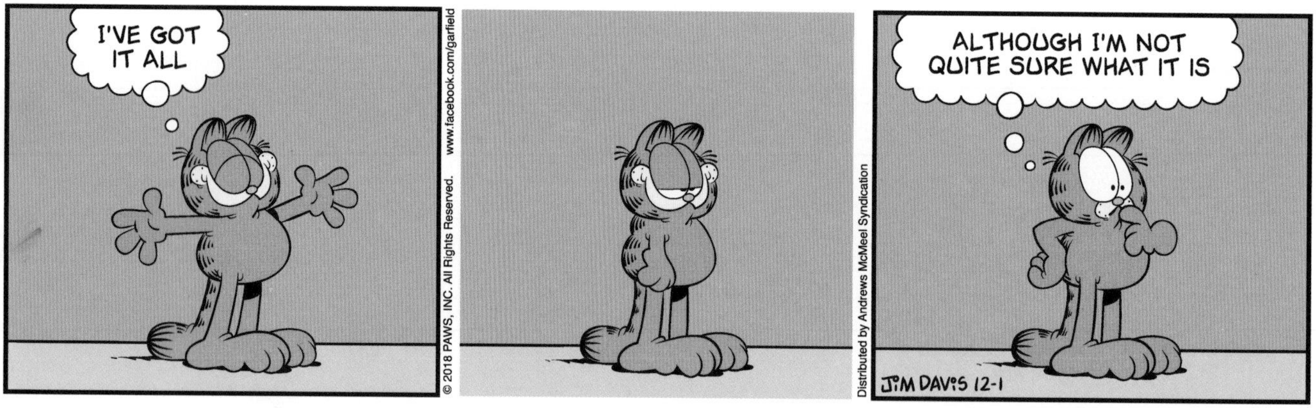
I'VE GOT IT ALL
ALTHOUGH I'M NOT QUITE SURE WHAT IT IS
JIM DAVIS 12-1

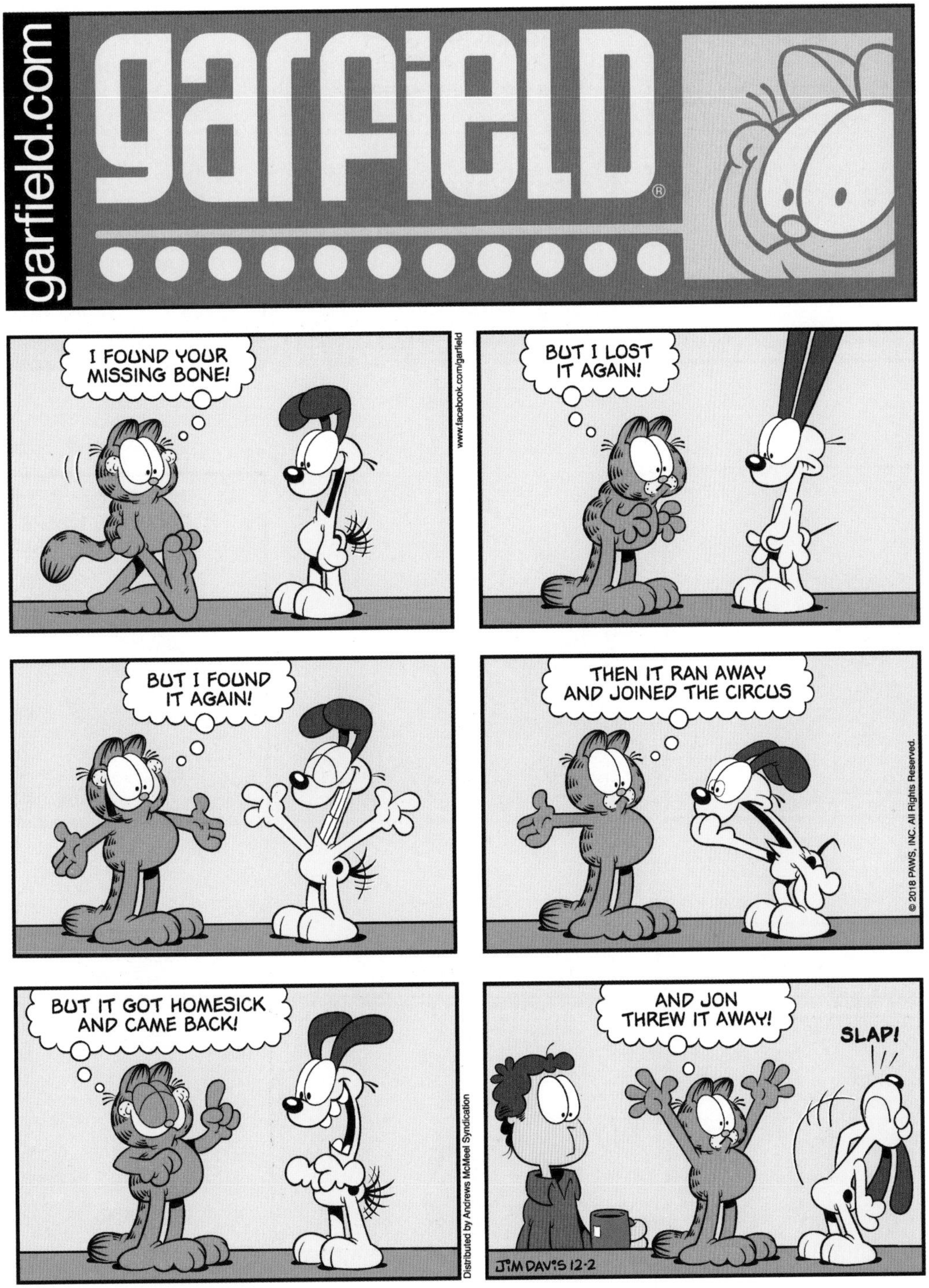
garfield.com
garfield
I FOUND YOUR MISSING BONE!
www.facebook.com/garfield
BUT I LOST IT AGAIN!
BUT I FOUND IT AGAIN!
THEN IT RAN AWAY AND JOINED THE CIRCUS
© 2018 PAWS, INC. All Rights Reserved.
BUT IT GOT HOMESICK AND CAME BACK!
Distributed by Andrews McMeel Syndication
AND JON THREW IT AWAY!
SLAP!
JIM DAVIS 12-2

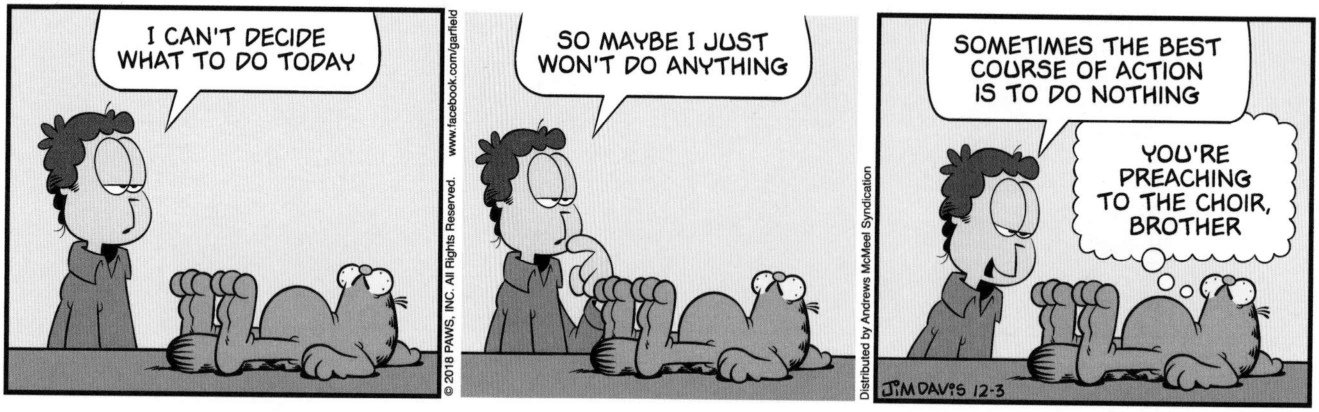
I CAN'T DECIDE WHAT TO DO TODAY
SO MAYBE I JUST WON'T DO ANYTHING
SOMETIMES THE BEST COURSE OF ACTION IS TO DO NOTHING
YOU'RE PREACHING TO THE CHOIR, BROTHER
© 2018 PAWS, INC. All Rights Reserved. www.facebook.com/garfield
Distributed by Andrews McMeel Syndication
JIM DAVIS 12-3

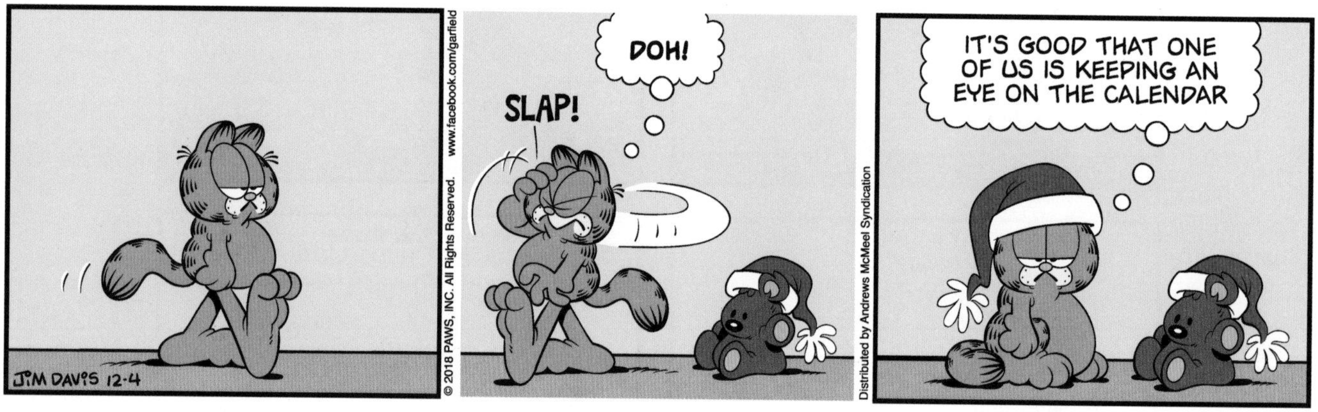
SLAP!
DOH!
IT'S GOOD THAT ONE OF US IS KEEPING AN EYE ON THE CALENDAR
JIM DAVIS 12-4
© 2018 PAWS, INC. All Rights Reserved. www.facebook.com/garfield
Distributed by Andrews McMeel Syndication

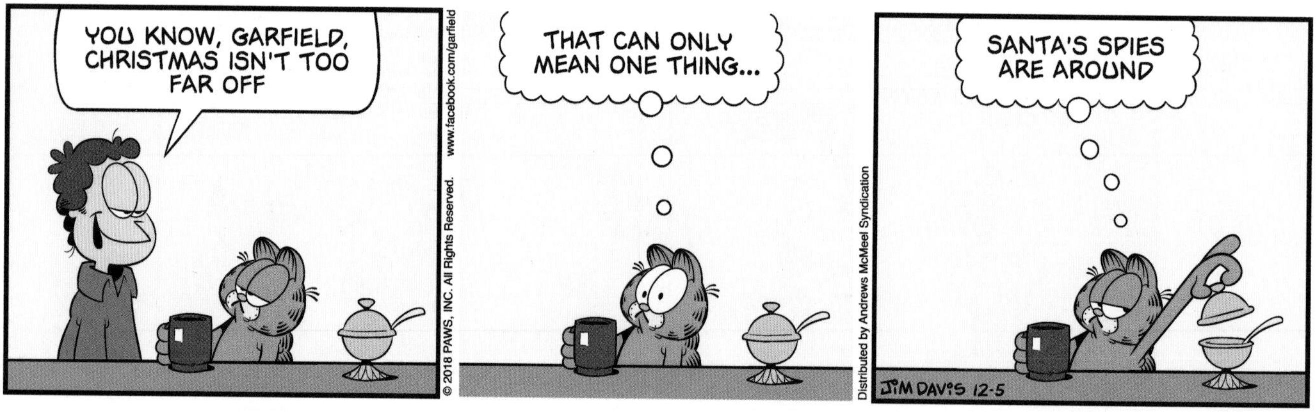
YOU KNOW, GARFIELD, CHRISTMAS ISN'T TOO FAR OFF
THAT CAN ONLY MEAN ONE THING...
SANTA'S SPIES ARE AROUND
© 2018 PAWS, INC. All Rights Reserved. www.facebook.com/garfield
Distributed by Andrews McMeel Syndication
JIM DAVIS 12-5

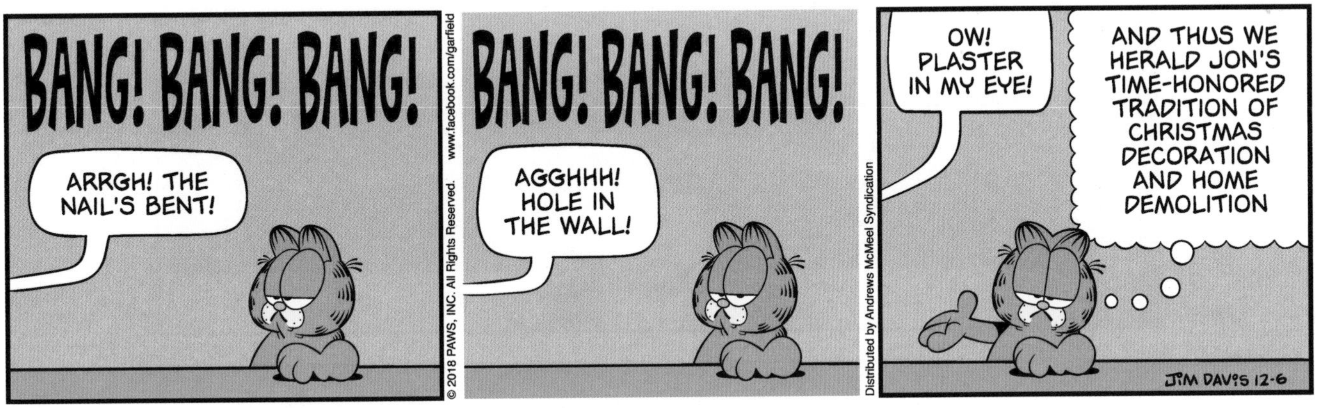
BANG! BANG! BANG!
ARRGH! THE NAIL'S BENT!
BANG! BANG! BANG!
AGGHHH! HOLE IN THE WALL!
OW! PLASTER IN MY EYE!
AND THUS WE HERALD JON'S TIME-HONORED TRADITION OF CHRISTMAS DECORATION AND HOME DEMOLITION
JIM DAVIS 12-6
© 2018 PAWS, INC. All Rights Reserved. www.facebook.com/garfield
Distributed by Andrews McMeel Syndication

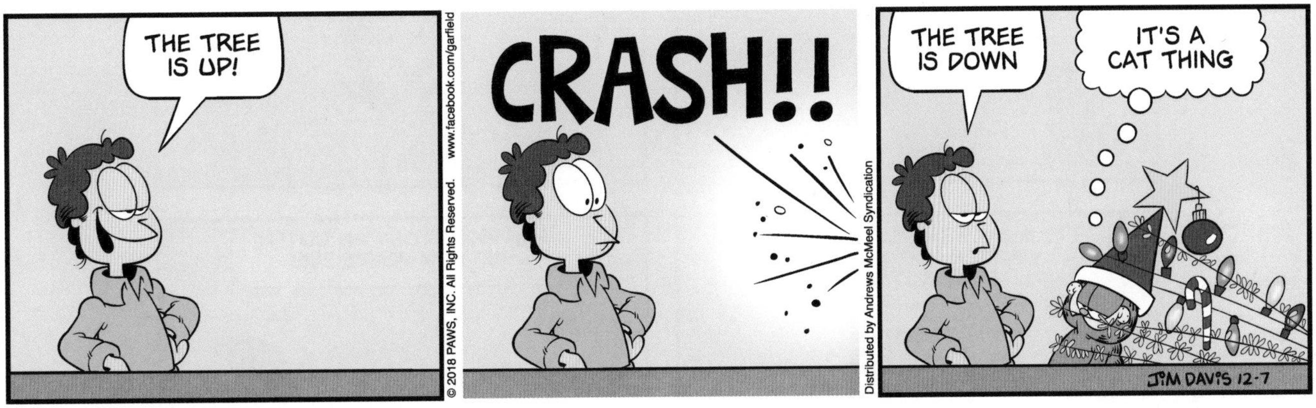
THE TREE IS UP!
CRASH!!
THE TREE IS DOWN
IT'S A CAT THING
JIM DAVIS 12-7
© 2018 PAWS, INC. All Rights Reserved. www.facebook.com/garfield
Distributed by Andrews McMeel Syndication

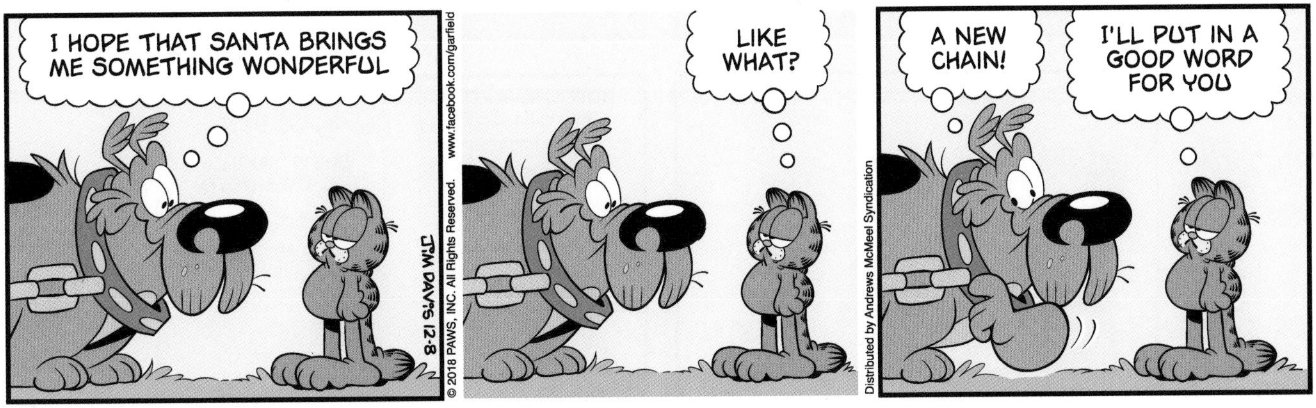
I HOPE THAT SANTA BRINGS ME SOMETHING WONDERFUL
JIM DAVIS 12-8
LIKE WHAT?
A NEW CHAIN!
I'LL PUT IN A GOOD WORD FOR YOU
© 2018 PAWS, INC. All Rights Reserved. www.facebook.com/garfield
Distributed by Andrews McMeel Syndication

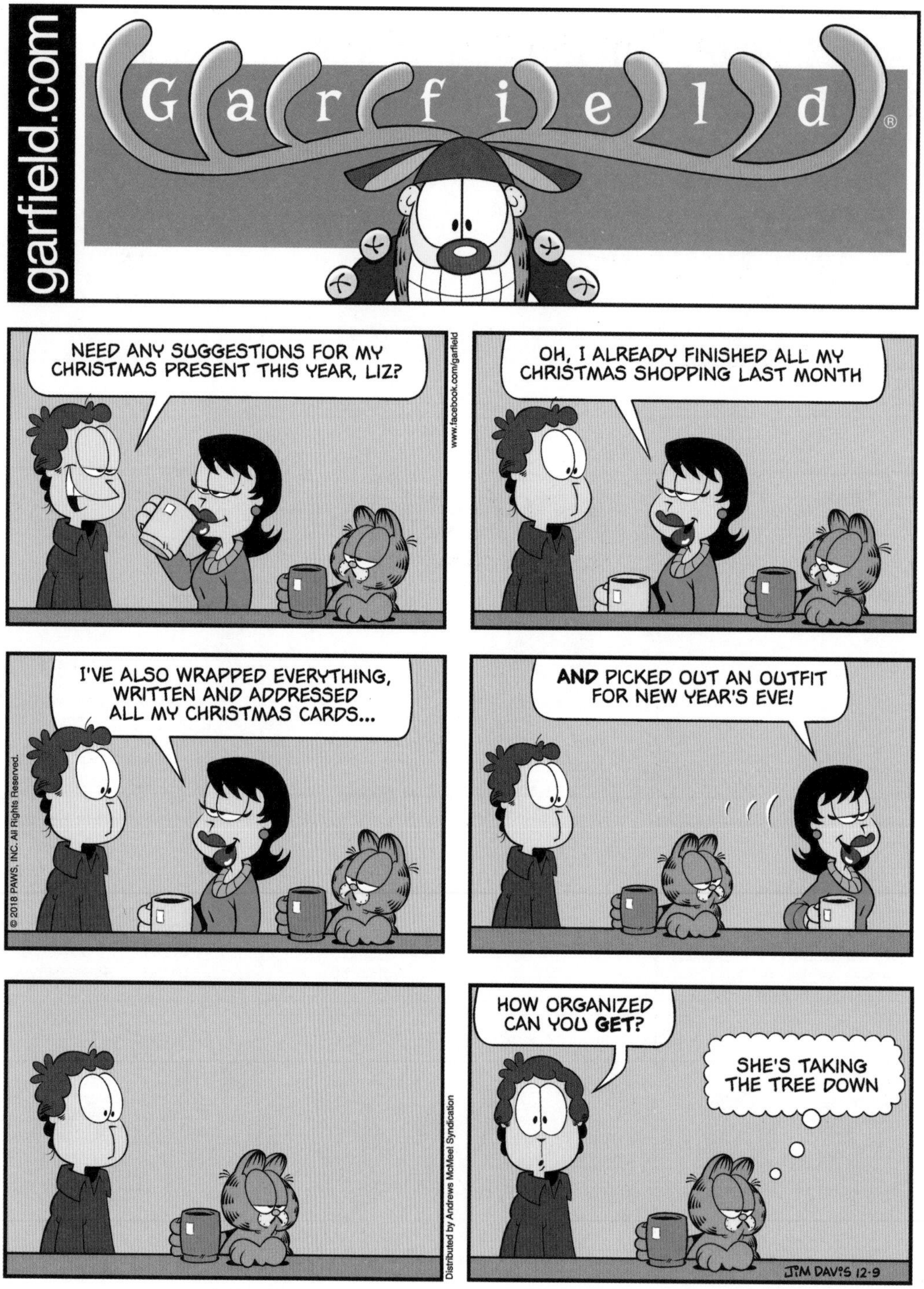
garfield.com
Garfield®
NEED ANY SUGGESTIONS FOR MY CHRISTMAS PRESENT THIS YEAR, LIZ?
www.facebook.com/garfield
OH, I ALREADY FINISHED ALL MY CHRISTMAS SHOPPING LAST MONTH
I'VE ALSO WRAPPED EVERYTHING, WRITTEN AND ADDRESSED ALL MY CHRISTMAS CARDS...
© 2018 PAWS, INC. All Rights Reserved.
AND PICKED OUT AN OUTFIT FOR NEW YEAR'S EVE!
Distributed by Andrews McMeel Syndication
HOW ORGANIZED CAN YOU GET?
SHE'S TAKING THE TREE DOWN
JIM DAVIS 12-9

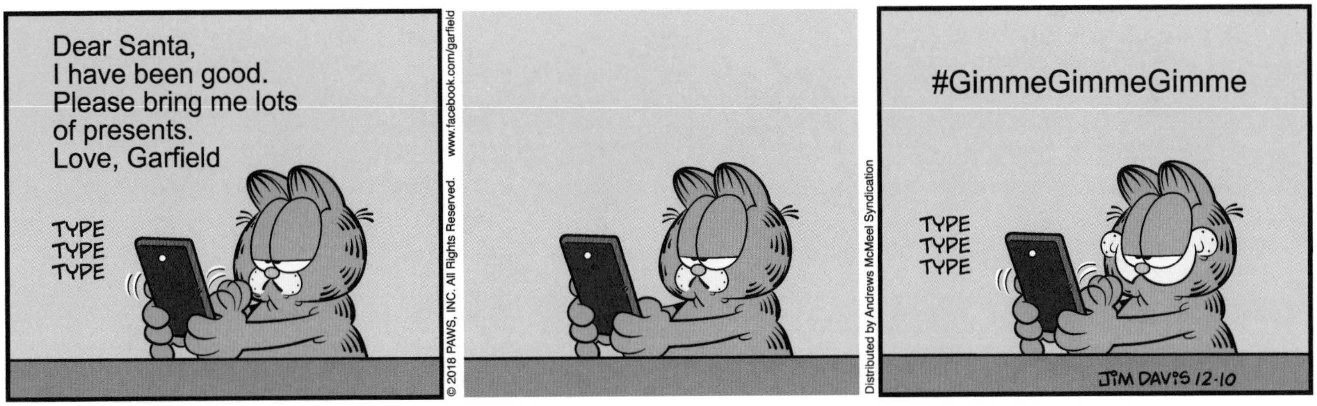
Dear Santa,
I have been good.
Please bring me lots
of presents.
Love, Garfield
TYPE
TYPE
TYPE
#GimmeGimmeGimme
TYPE
TYPE
TYPE
JIM DAVIS 12-10
© 2018 PAWS, INC. All Rights Reserved. www.facebook.com/garfield
Distributed by Andrews McMeel Syndication

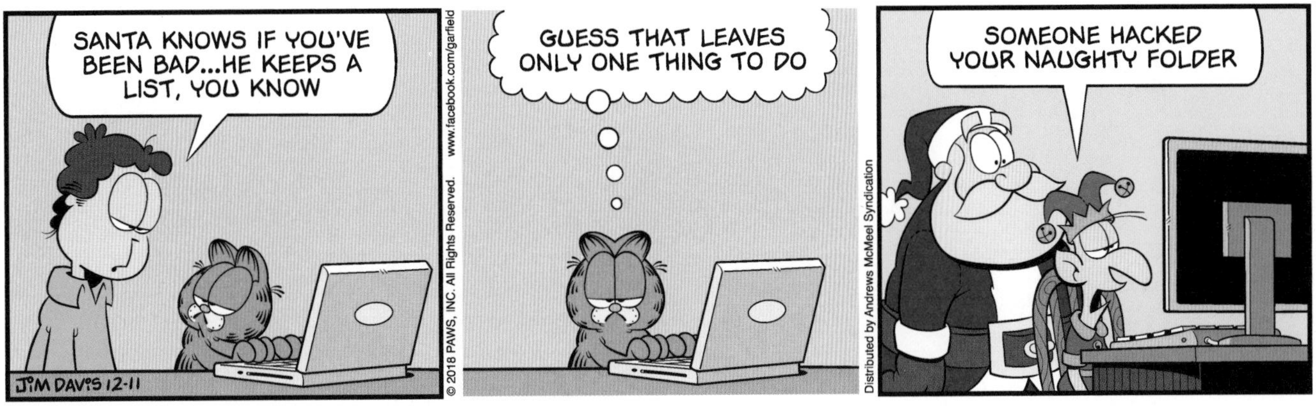
SANTA KNOWS IF YOU'VE BEEN BAD...HE KEEPS A LIST, YOU KNOW
JIM DAVIS 12-11
GUESS THAT LEAVES ONLY ONE THING TO DO
SOMEONE HACKED YOUR NAUGHTY FOLDER
© 2018 PAWS, INC. All Rights Reserved. www.facebook.com/garfield
Distributed by Andrews McMeel Syndication

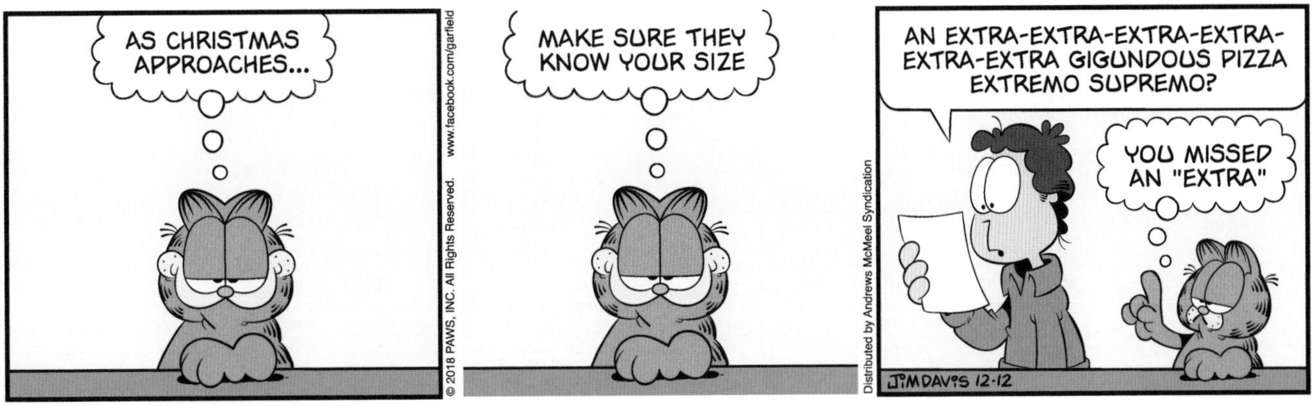
AS CHRISTMAS APPROACHES...
MAKE SURE THEY KNOW YOUR SIZE
AN EXTRA-EXTRA-EXTRA-EXTRA-EXTRA-EXTRA GIGUNDOUS PIZZA EXTREMO SUPREMO?
YOU MISSED AN "EXTRA"
JIM DAVIS 12-12
© 2018 PAWS, INC. All Rights Reserved. www.facebook.com/garfield
Distributed by Andrews McMeel Syndication

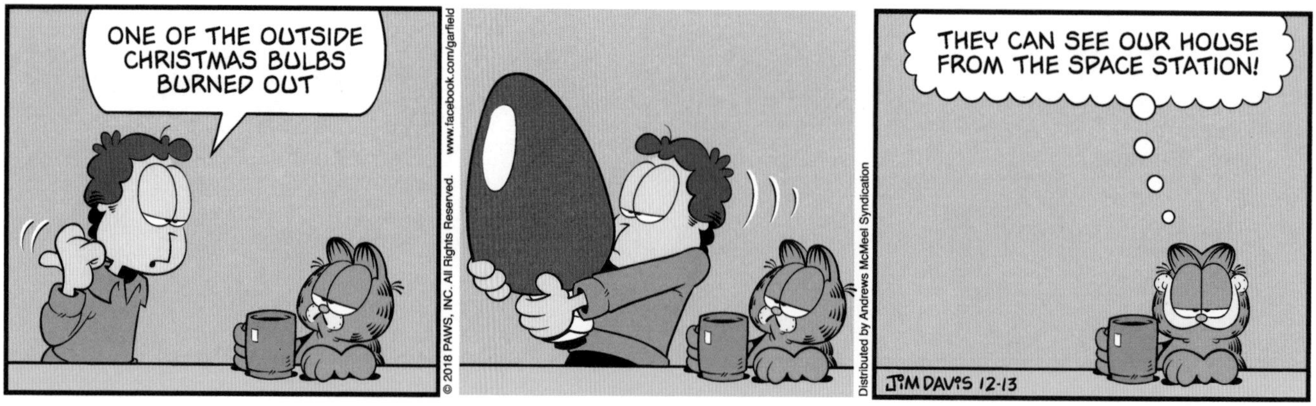
ONE OF THE OUTSIDE CHRISTMAS BULBS BURNED OUT
© 2018 PAWS, INC. All Rights Reserved. www.facebook.com/garfield
Distributed by Andrews McMeel Syndication
THEY CAN SEE OUR HOUSE FROM THE SPACE STATION!
JIM DAVIS 12-13

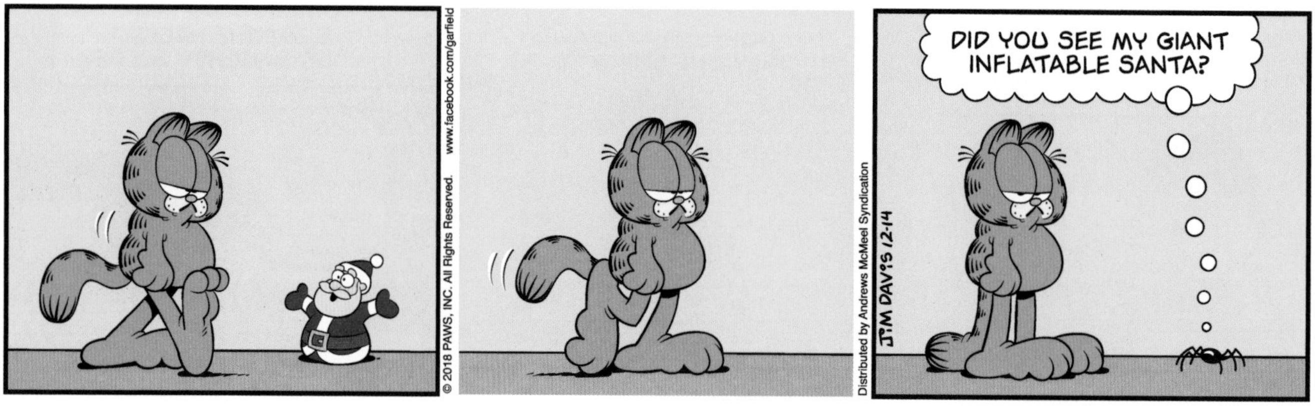
© 2018 PAWS, INC. All Rights Reserved. www.facebook.com/garfield
Distributed by Andrews McMeel Syndication
JIM DAVIS 12-14
DID YOU SEE MY GIANT INFLATABLE SANTA?

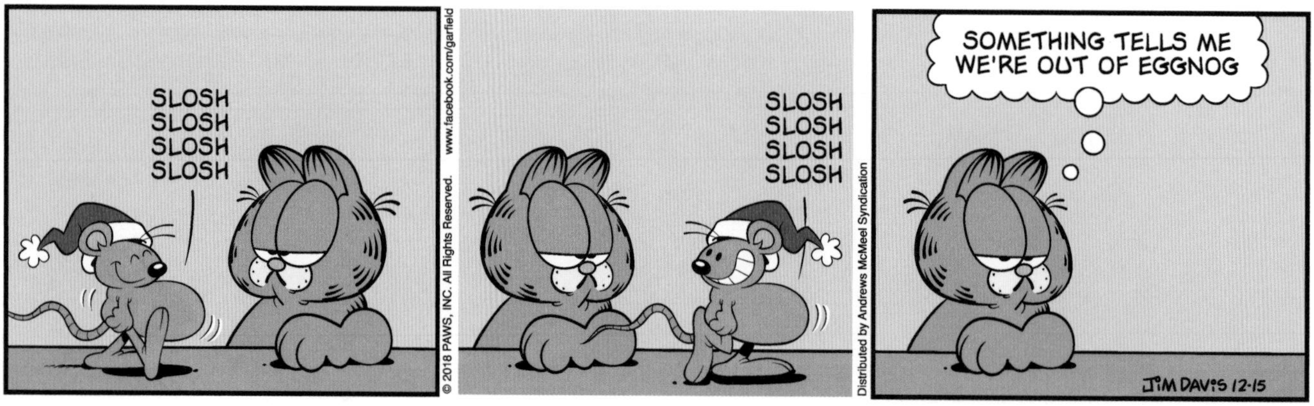
SLOSH SLOSH SLOSH SLOSH
© 2018 PAWS, INC. All Rights Reserved. www.facebook.com/garfield
SLOSH SLOSH SLOSH SLOSH
Distributed by Andrews McMeel Syndication
SOMETHING TELLS ME WE'RE OUT OF EGGNOG
JIM DAVIS 12-15

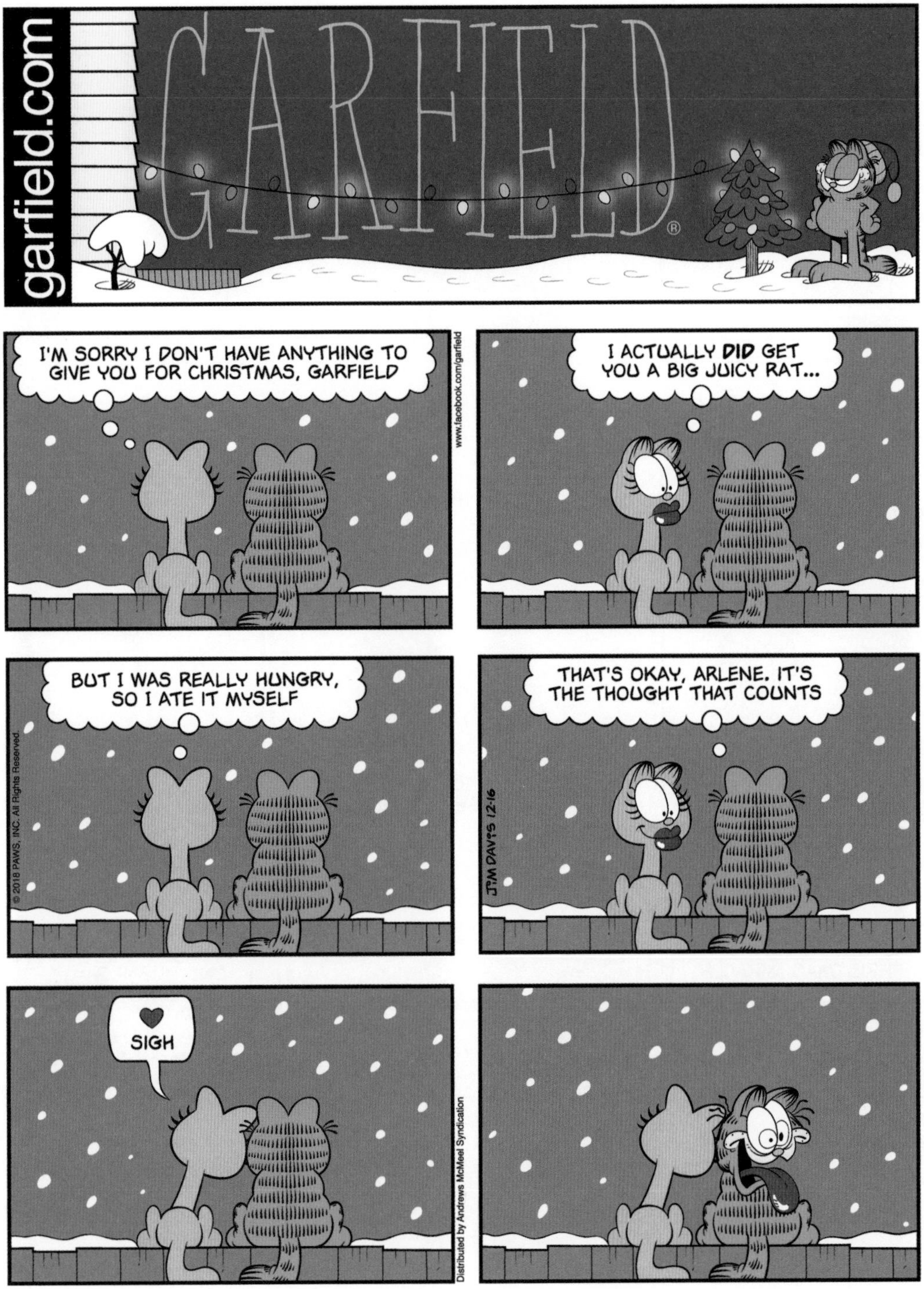
garfield.com
GARFIELD
I'M SORRY I DON'T HAVE ANYTHING TO GIVE YOU FOR CHRISTMAS, GARFIELD
www.facebook.com/garfield
I ACTUALLY DID GET YOU A BIG JUICY RAT...
BUT I WAS REALLY HUNGRY, SO I ATE IT MYSELF
© 2018 PAWS, INC. All Rights Reserved
THAT'S OKAY, ARLENE. IT'S THE THOUGHT THAT COUNTS
JIM DAVIS 12-16
SIGH
Distributed by Andrews McMeel Syndication

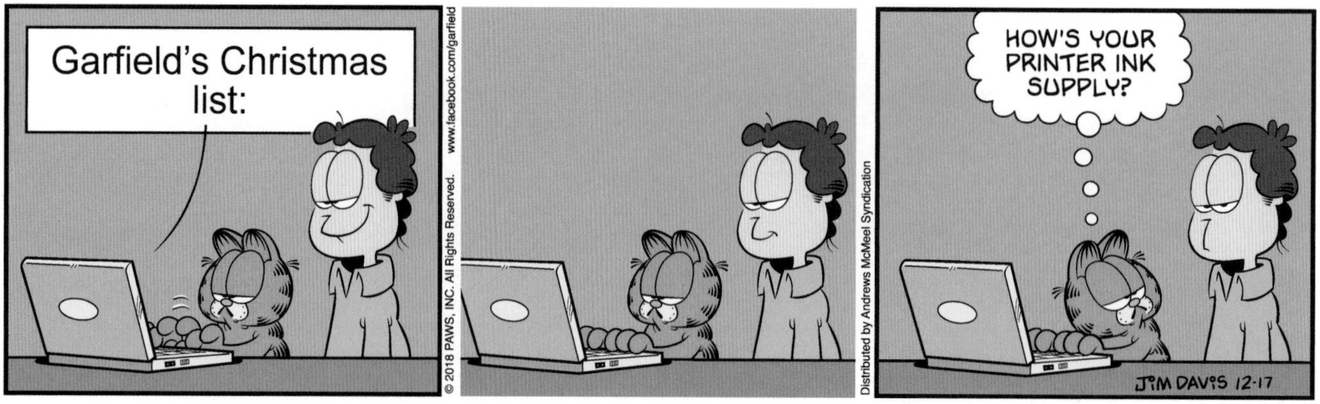
Garfield's Christmas list:
© 2018 PAWS, INC. All Rights Reserved. www.facebook.com/garfield
Distributed by Andrews McMeel Syndication
HOW'S YOUR PRINTER INK SUPPLY?
JIM DAVIS 12-17

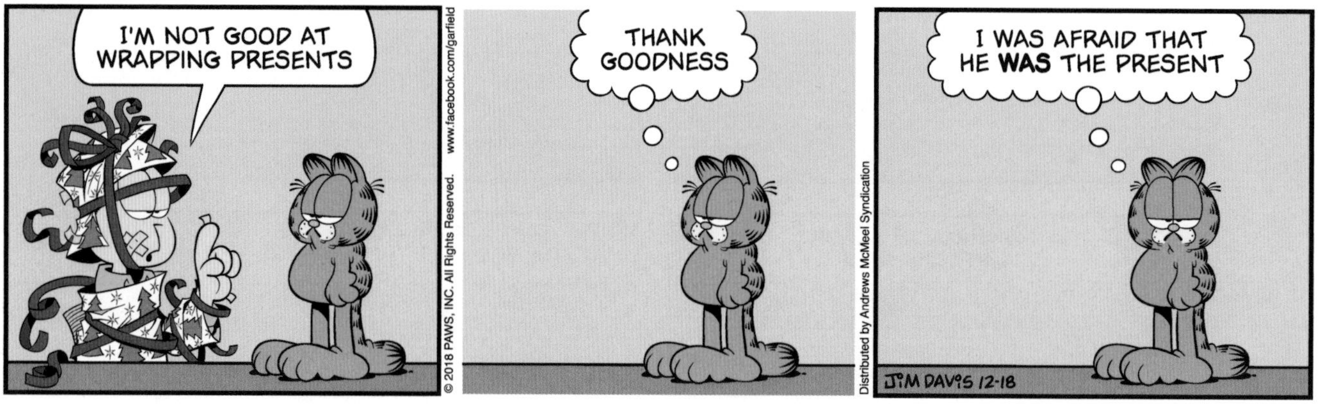
I'M NOT GOOD AT WRAPPING PRESENTS
© 2018 PAWS, INC. All Rights Reserved. www.facebook.com/garfield
THANK GOODNESS
Distributed by Andrews McMeel Syndication
I WAS AFRAID THAT HE **WAS** THE PRESENT
JIM DAVIS 12-18

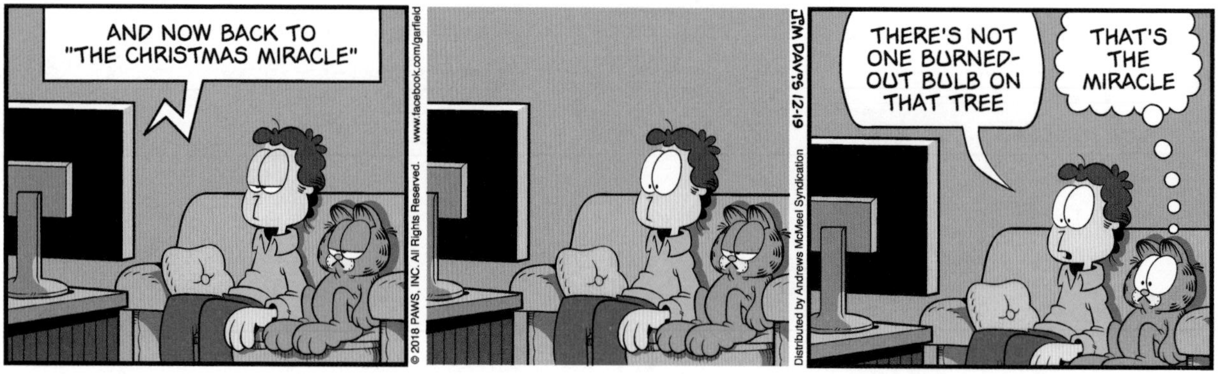
AND NOW BACK TO "THE CHRISTMAS MIRACLE"
© 2018 PAWS, INC. All Rights Reserved. www.facebook.com/garfield
JIM DAVIS 12-19
Distributed by Andrews McMeel Syndication
THERE'S NOT ONE BURNED-OUT BULB ON THAT TREE
THAT'S THE MIRACLE

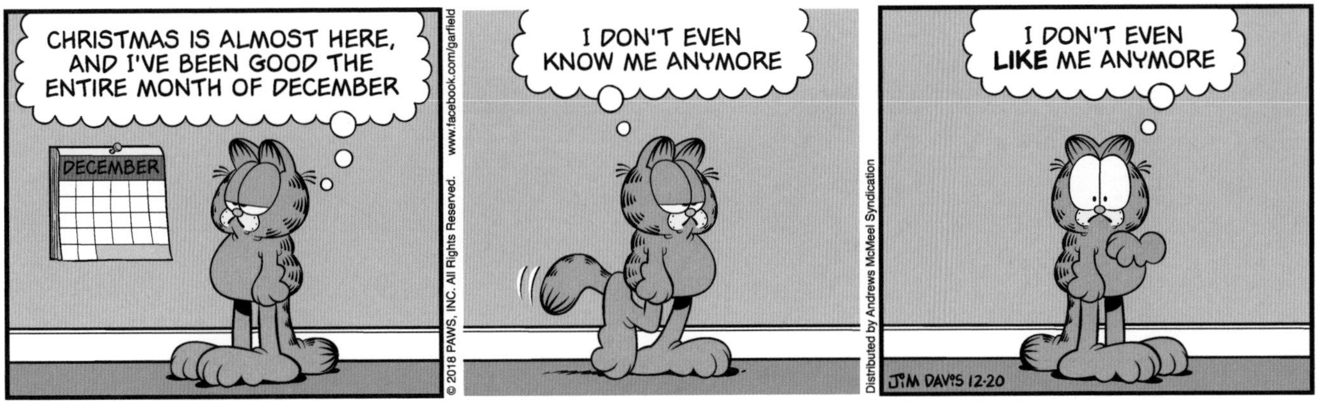
CHRISTMAS IS ALMOST HERE, AND I'VE BEEN GOOD THE ENTIRE MONTH OF DECEMBER
DECEMBER
I DON'T EVEN KNOW ME ANYMORE
I DON'T EVEN **LIKE** ME ANYMORE
JIM DAVIS 12-20
© 2018 PAWS, INC. All Rights Reserved. www.facebook.com/garfield
Distributed by Andrews McMeel Syndication

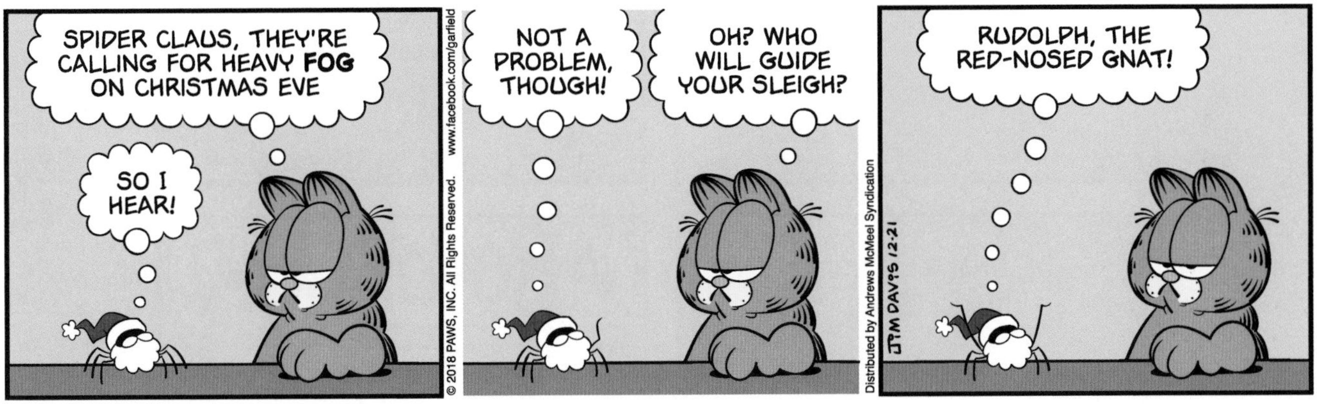
SPIDER CLAUS, THEY'RE CALLING FOR HEAVY **FOG** ON CHRISTMAS EVE
SO I HEAR!
NOT A PROBLEM, THOUGH!
OH? WHO WILL GUIDE YOUR SLEIGH?
RUDOLPH, THE RED-NOSED GNAT!
JIM DAVIS 12-21
© 2018 PAWS, INC. All Rights Reserved. www.facebook.com/garfield
Distributed by Andrews McMeel Syndication

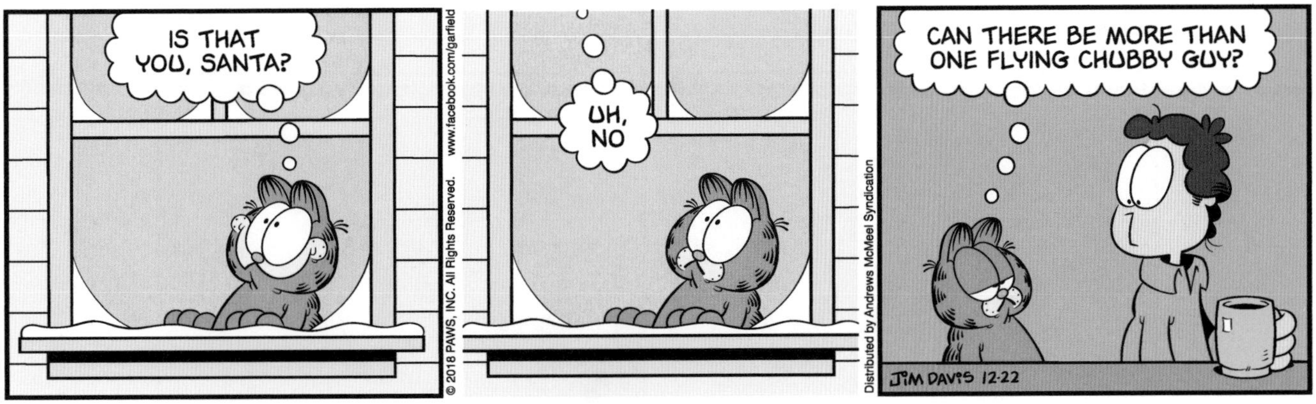
IS THAT YOU, SANTA?
UH, NO
CAN THERE BE MORE THAN ONE FLYING CHUBBY GUY?
JIM DAVIS 12-22
© 2018 PAWS, INC. All Rights Reserved. www.facebook.com/garfield
Distributed by Andrews McMeel Syndication

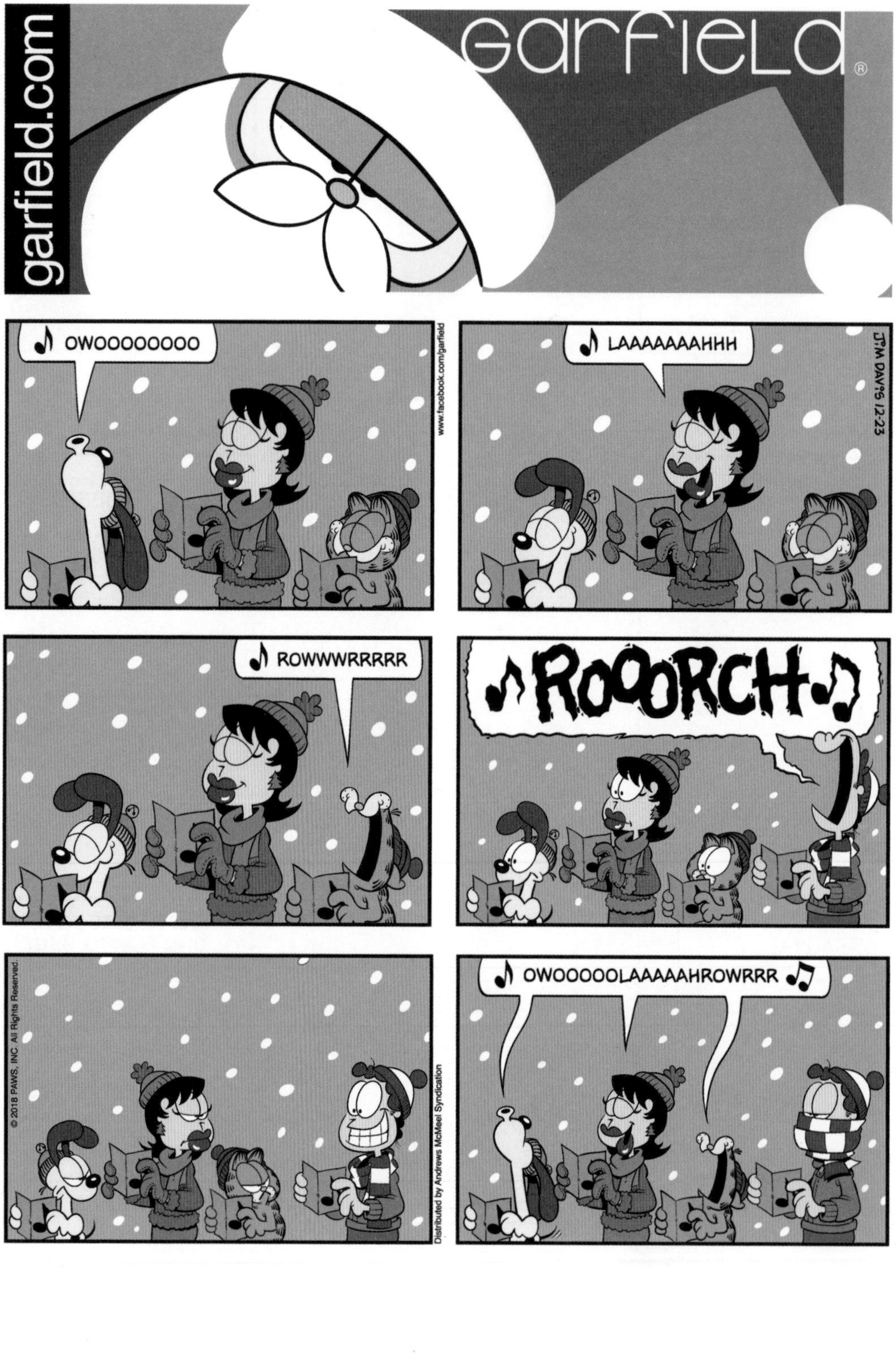
garfield.com
GARFIELD
♪ OWOOOOOOOO
www.facebook.com/garfield
♪ LAAAAAAAHHH
JPM DAVIS 12-23
♪ ROWWWRRRRR
♪ ROOORCH ♫
© 2018 PAWS, INC. All Rights Reserved.
Distributed by Andrews McMeel Syndication
♪ OWOOOOOLAAAAAHROWRRR ♫

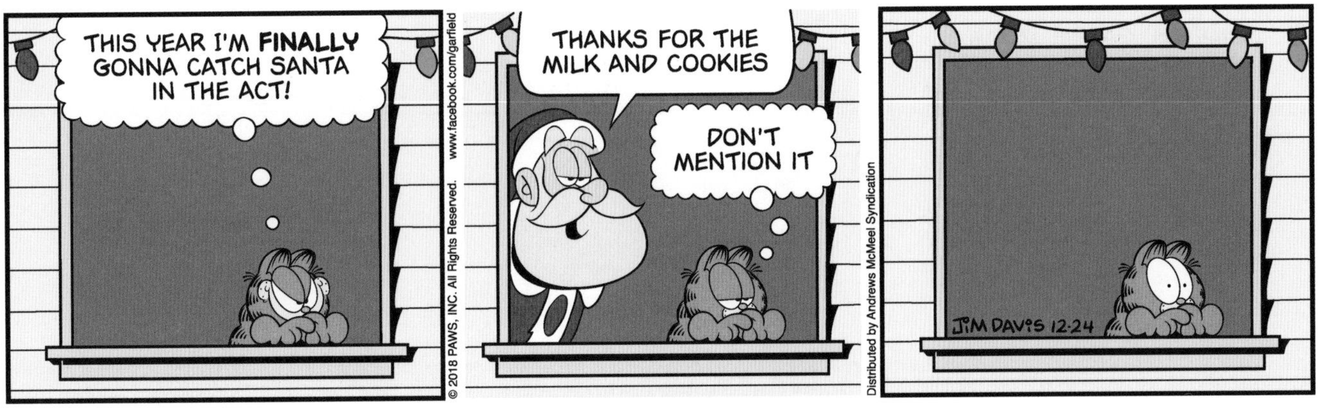
THIS YEAR I'M **FINALLY** GONNA CATCH SANTA IN THE ACT!
© 2018 PAWS, INC. All Rights Reserved. www.facebook.com/garfield
THANKS FOR THE MILK AND COOKIES
DON'T MENTION IT
Distributed by Andrews McMeel Syndication
JIM DAVIS 12-24

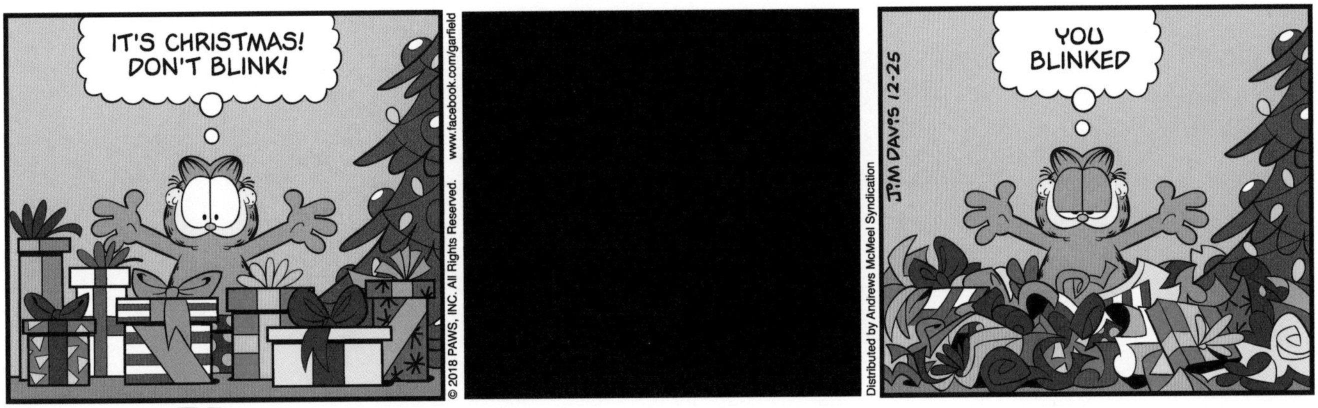
IT'S CHRISTMAS! DON'T BLINK!
© 2018 PAWS, INC. All Rights Reserved. www.facebook.com/garfield
Distributed by Andrews McMeel Syndication
JIM DAVIS 12-25
YOU BLINKED

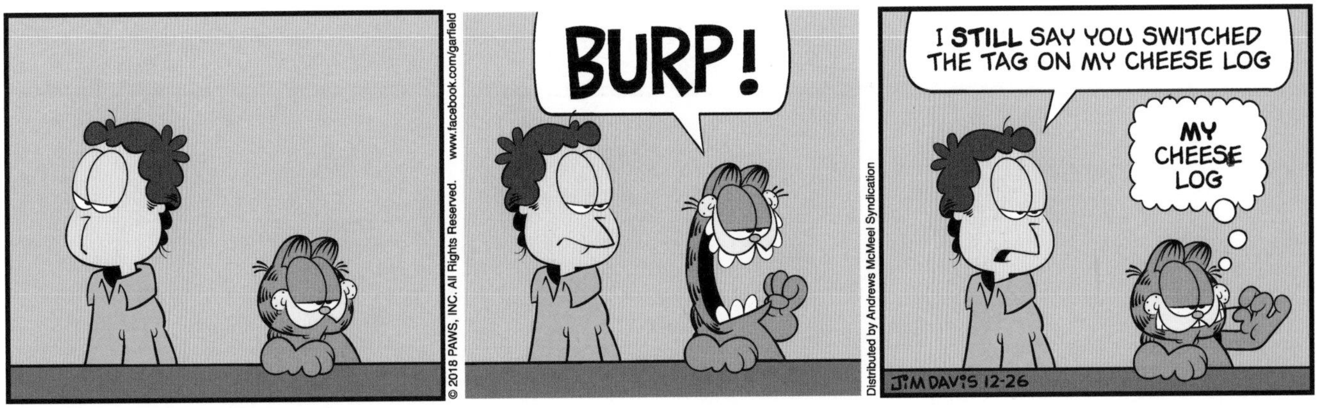
© 2018 PAWS, INC. All Rights Reserved. www.facebook.com/garfield
BURP!
Distributed by Andrews McMeel Syndication
I **STILL** SAY YOU SWITCHED THE TAG ON MY CHEESE LOG
MY CHEESE LOG
JIM DAVIS 12-26

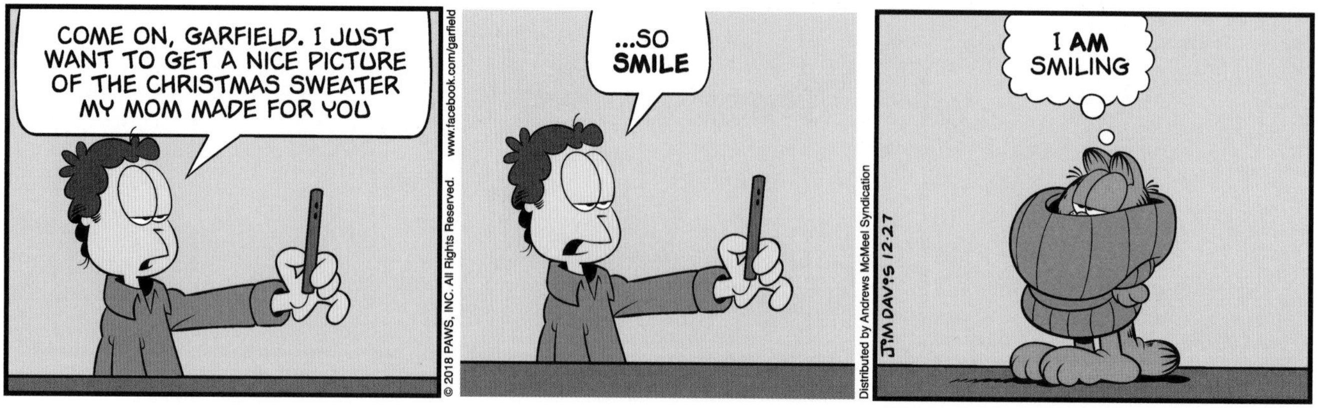
COME ON, GARFIELD. I JUST WANT TO GET A NICE PICTURE OF THE CHRISTMAS SWEATER MY MOM MADE FOR YOU
© 2018 PAWS, INC. All Rights Reserved. www.facebook.com/garfield
...SO SMILE
Distributed by Andrews McMeel Syndication
JIM DAVIS 12-27
I AM SMILING

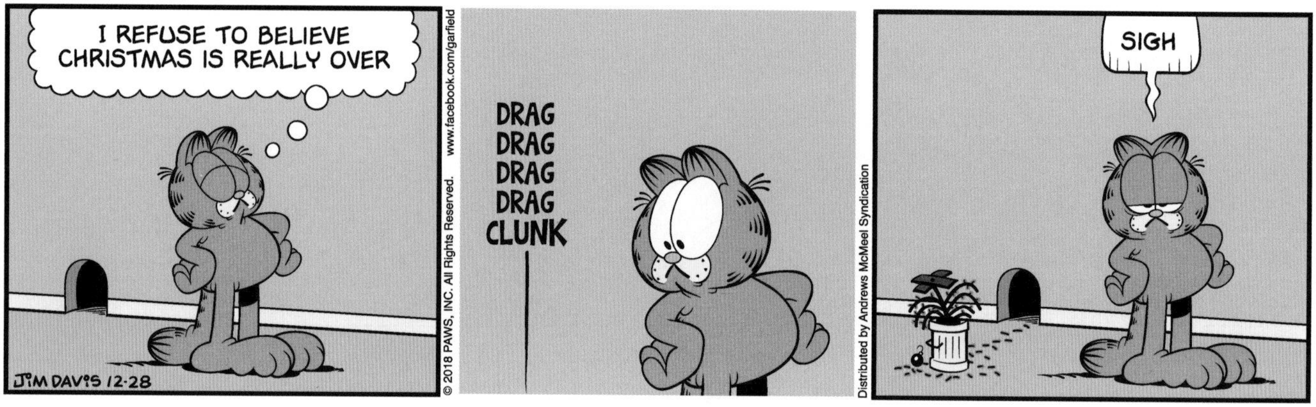
I REFUSE TO BELIEVE CHRISTMAS IS REALLY OVER
JIM DAVIS 12-28
© 2018 PAWS, INC. All Rights Reserved. www.facebook.com/garfield
DRAG
DRAG
DRAG
DRAG
CLUNK
Distributed by Andrews McMeel Syndication
SIGH

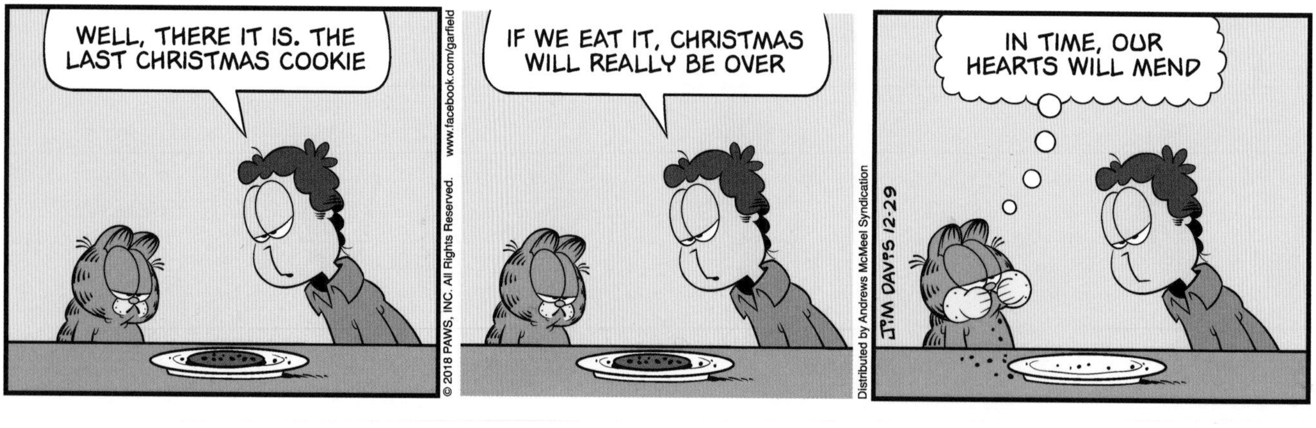
WELL, THERE IT IS. THE LAST CHRISTMAS COOKIE
© 2018 PAWS, INC. All Rights Reserved. www.facebook.com/garfield
IF WE EAT IT, CHRISTMAS WILL REALLY BE OVER
Distributed by Andrews McMeel Syndication
JIM DAVIS 12-29
IN TIME, OUR HEARTS WILL MEND

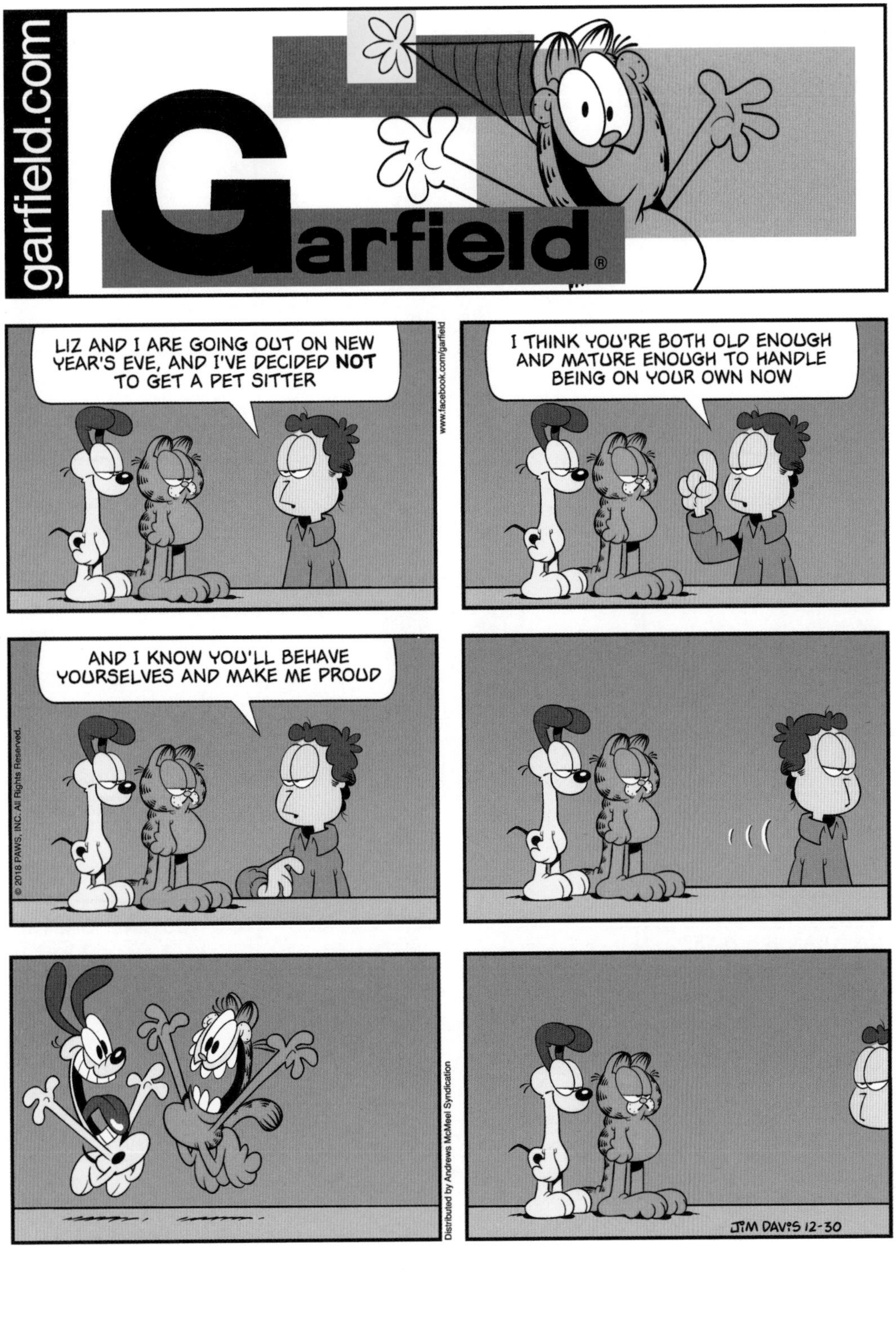
garfield.com
Garfield®
LIZ AND I ARE GOING OUT ON NEW YEAR'S EVE, AND I'VE DECIDED **NOT** TO GET A PET SITTER
www.facebook.com/garfield
I THINK YOU'RE BOTH OLD ENOUGH AND MATURE ENOUGH TO HANDLE BEING ON YOUR OWN NOW
© 2018 PAWS, INC. All Rights Reserved.
AND I KNOW YOU'LL BEHAVE YOURSELVES AND MAKE ME PROUD
Distributed by Andrews McMeel Syndication
JIM DAVIS 12-30

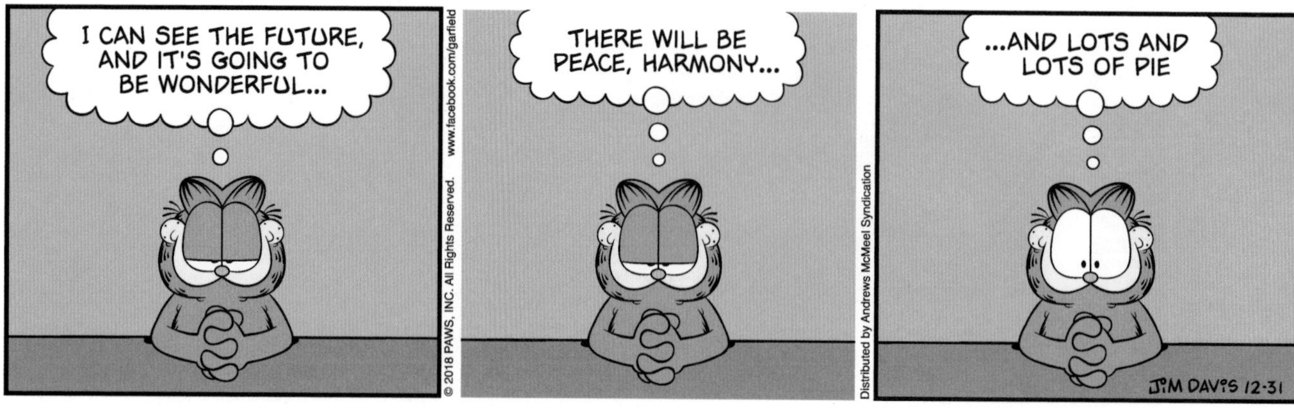
I CAN SEE THE FUTURE, AND IT'S GOING TO BE WONDERFUL...
THERE WILL BE PEACE, HARMONY...
...AND LOTS AND LOTS OF PIE
JIM DAVIS 12-31

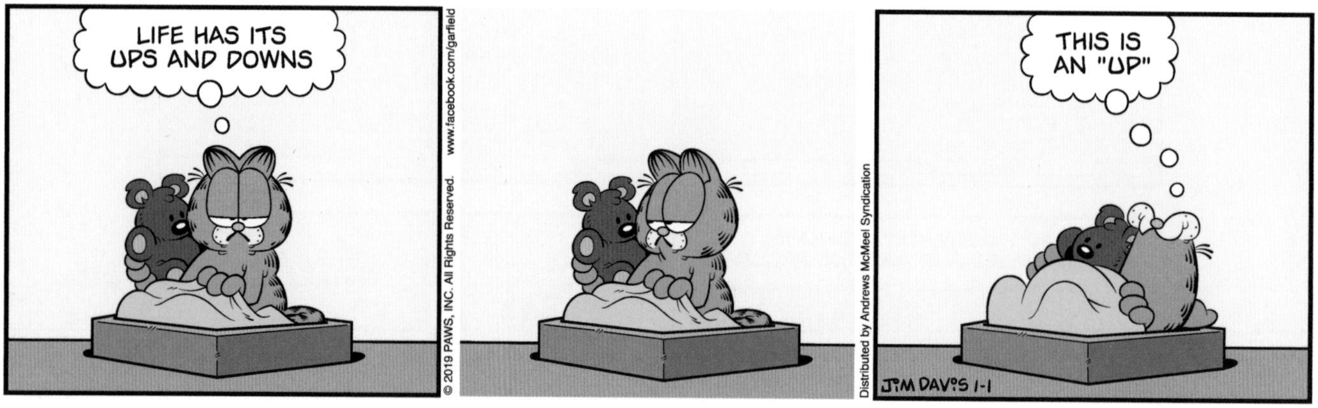
LIFE HAS ITS UPS AND DOWNS
THIS IS AN "UP"
JIM DAVIS 1-1

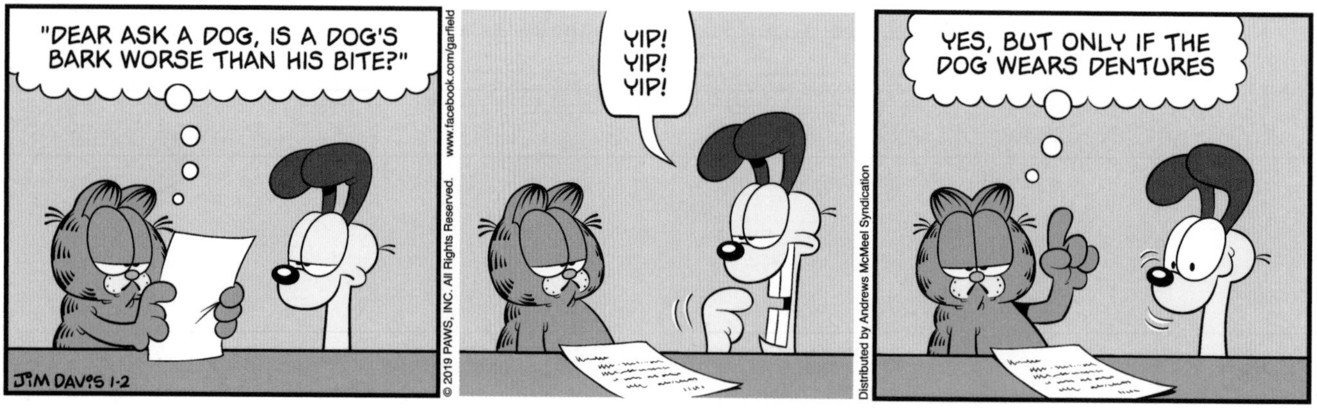
"DEAR ASK A DOG, IS A DOG'S BARK WORSE THAN HIS BITE?"
YIP! YIP! YIP!
YES, BUT ONLY IF THE DOG WEARS DENTURES
JIM DAVIS 1-2

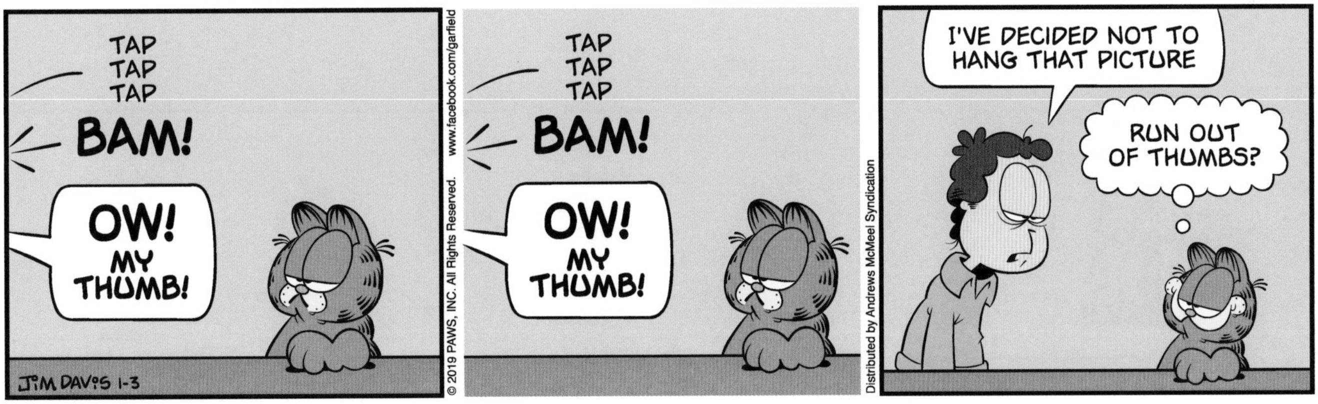
TAP
TAP
TAP
BAM!
OW! MY THUMB!
JIM DAVIS 1-3
© 2019 PAWS, INC. All Rights Reserved. www.facebook.com/garfield
TAP
TAP
TAP
BAM!
OW! MY THUMB!
Distributed by Andrews McMeel Syndication
I'VE DECIDED NOT TO HANG THAT PICTURE
RUN OUT OF THUMBS?

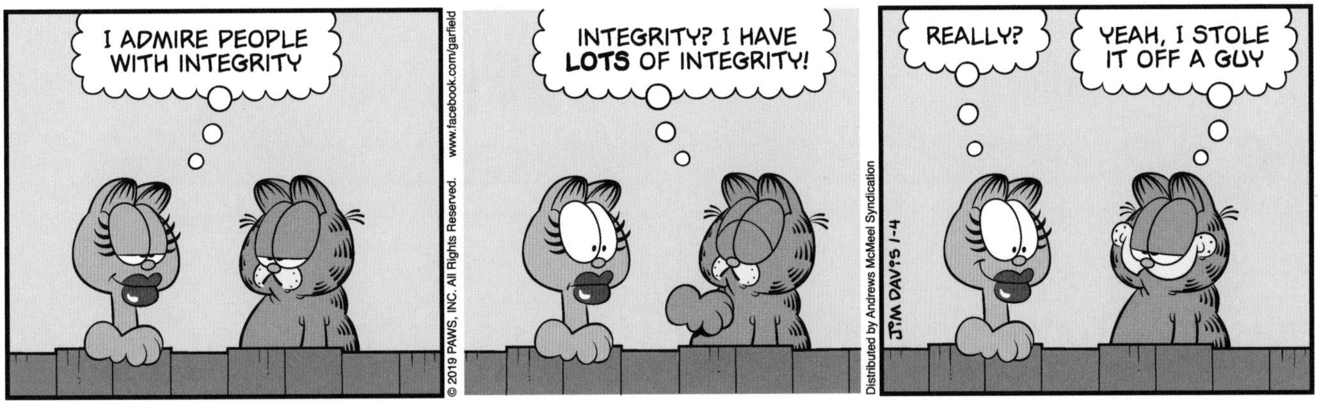
I ADMIRE PEOPLE WITH INTEGRITY
© 2019 PAWS, INC. All Rights Reserved. www.facebook.com/garfield
INTEGRITY? I HAVE **LOTS** OF INTEGRITY!
Distributed by Andrews McMeel Syndication
JIM DAVIS 1-4
REALLY?
YEAH, I STOLE IT OFF A GUY

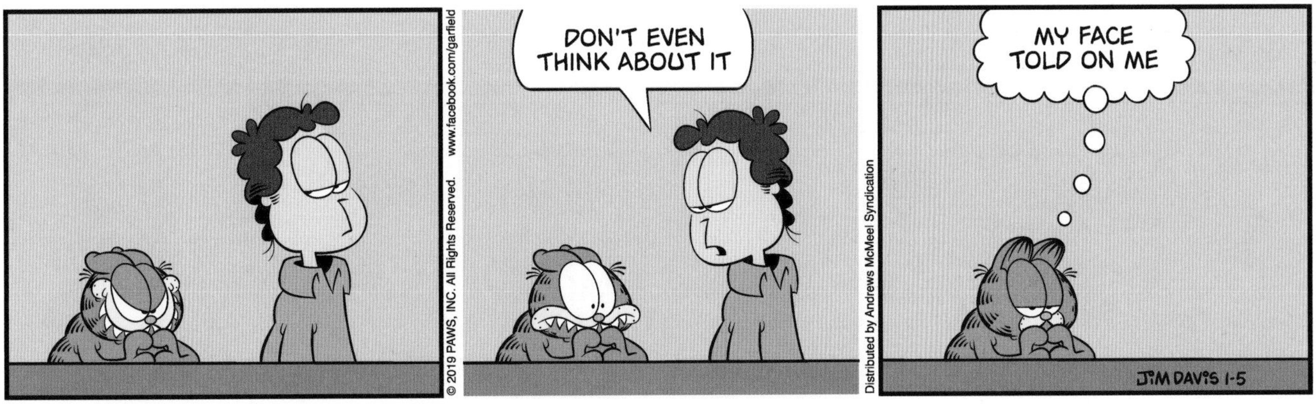
© 2019 PAWS, INC. All Rights Reserved. www.facebook.com/garfield
DON'T EVEN THINK ABOUT IT
Distributed by Andrews McMeel Syndication
MY FACE TOLD ON ME
JIM DAVIS 1-5

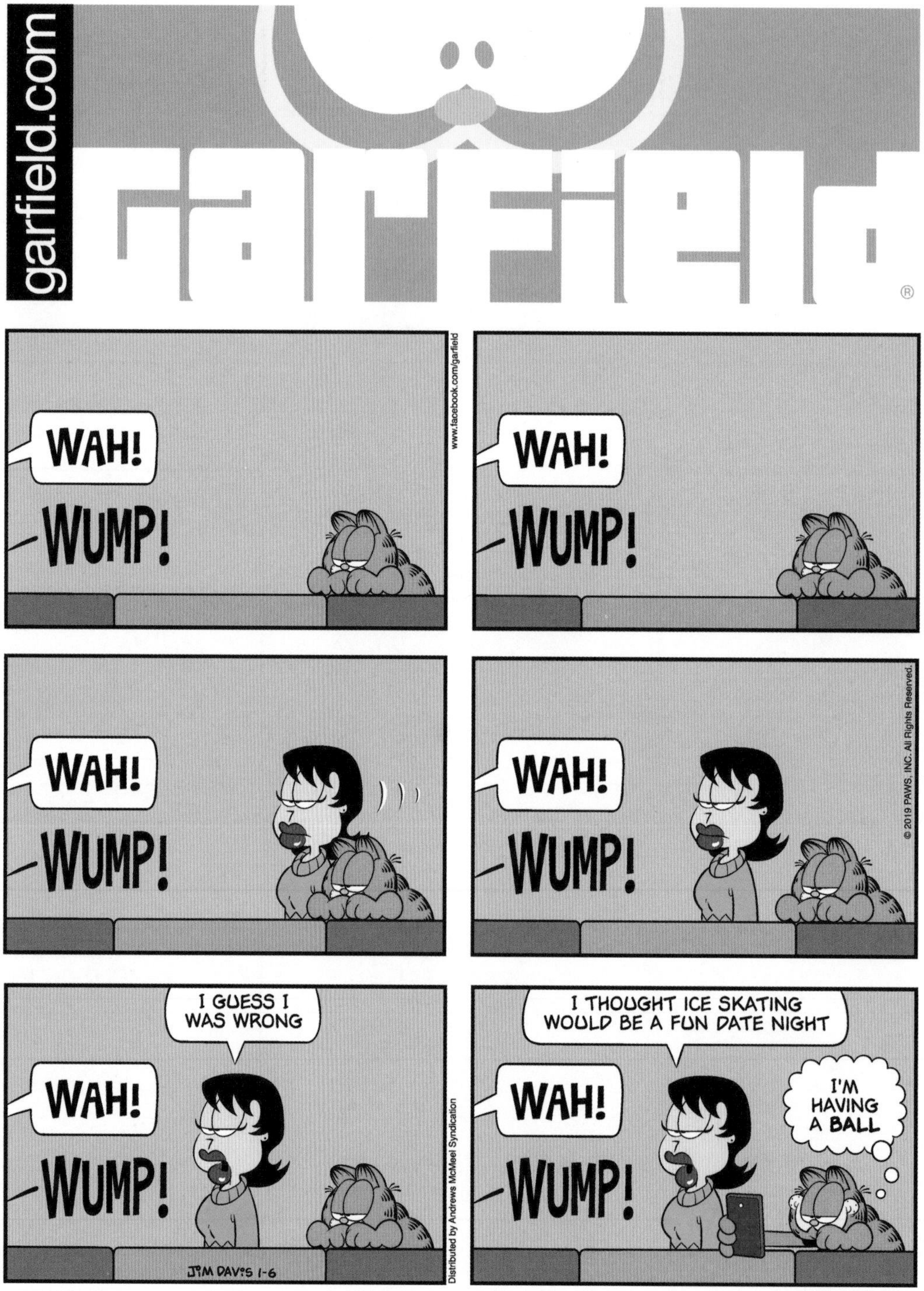
garfield.com
GARFIELD®
www.facebook.com/garfield
WAH!
WUMP!
WAH!
WUMP!
WAH!
WUMP!
WAH!
WUMP!
© 2019 PAWS, INC. All Rights Reserved.
I GUESS I WAS WRONG
WAH!
WUMP!
JIM DAVIS 1-6
Distributed by Andrews McMeel Syndication
I THOUGHT ICE SKATING WOULD BE A FUN DATE NIGHT
WAH!
WUMP!
I'M HAVING A BALL

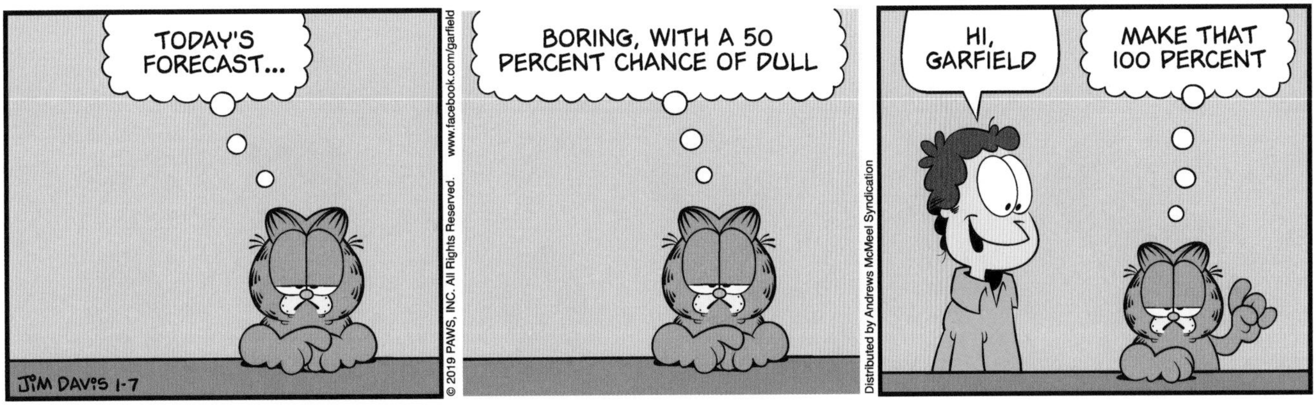
TODAY'S FORECAST...
JIM DAVIS 1-7
© 2019 PAWS, INC. All Rights Reserved. www.facebook.com/garfield
BORING, WITH A 50 PERCENT CHANCE OF DULL
Distributed by Andrews McMeel Syndication
HI, GARFIELD
MAKE THAT 100 PERCENT

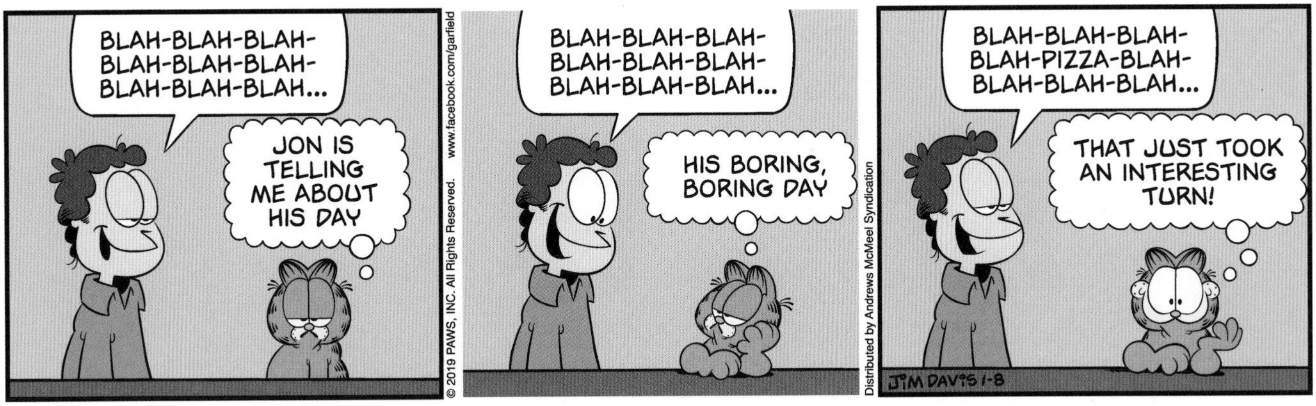
BLAH-BLAH-BLAH-BLAH-BLAH-BLAH-BLAH-BLAH-BLAH...
JON IS TELLING ME ABOUT HIS DAY
© 2019 PAWS, INC. All Rights Reserved. www.facebook.com/garfield
BLAH-BLAH-BLAH-BLAH-BLAH-BLAH-BLAH-BLAH-BLAH...
HIS BORING, BORING DAY
Distributed by Andrews McMeel Syndication
BLAH-BLAH-BLAH-BLAH-PIZZA-BLAH-BLAH-BLAH-BLAH...
THAT JUST TOOK AN INTERESTING TURN!
JIM DAVIS 1-8

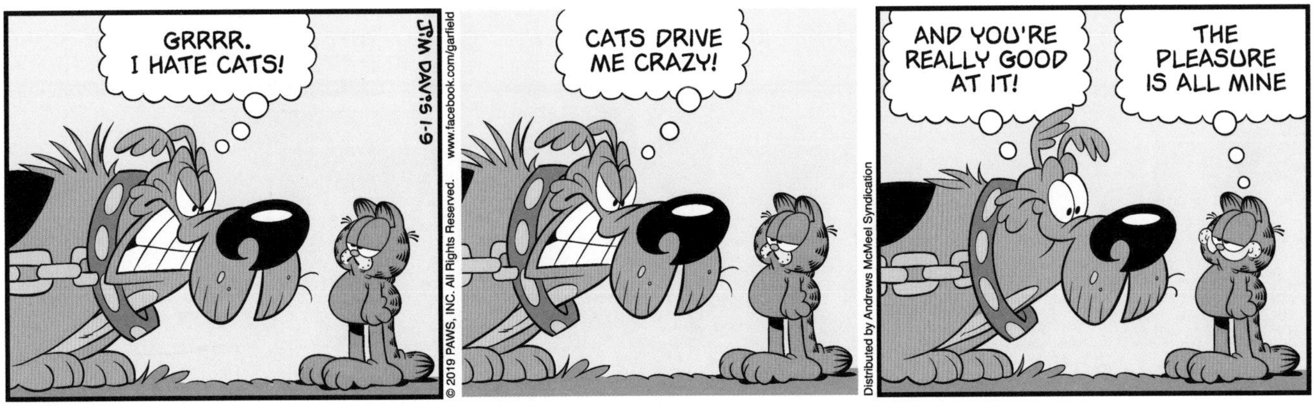
GRRRR. I HATE CATS!
JIM DAVIS 1-9
© 2019 PAWS, INC. All Rights Reserved. www.facebook.com/garfield
CATS DRIVE ME CRAZY!
Distributed by Andrews McMeel Syndication
AND YOU'RE REALLY GOOD AT IT!
THE PLEASURE IS ALL MINE

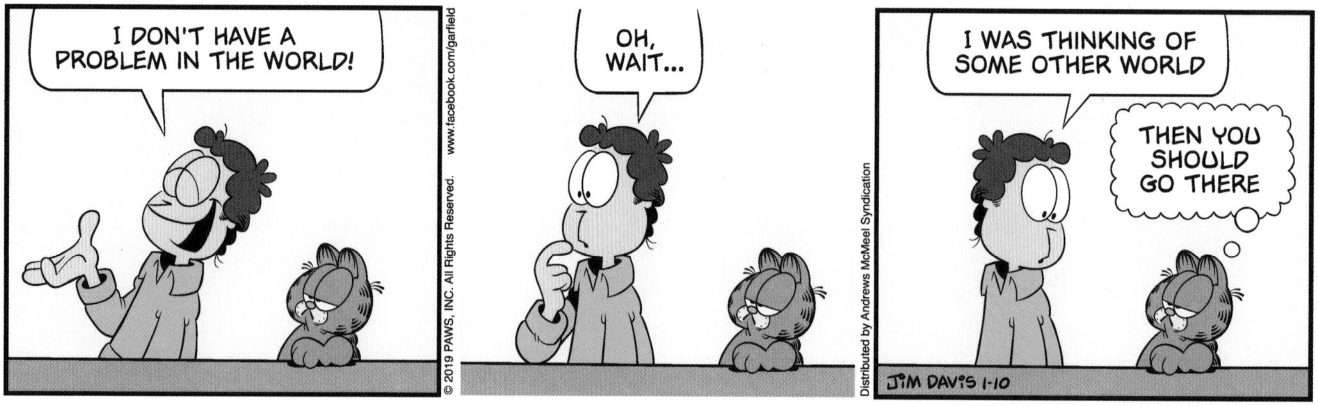
I DON'T HAVE A PROBLEM IN THE WORLD!
© 2019 PAWS, INC. All Rights Reserved. www.facebook.com/garfield
OH, WAIT...
Distributed by Andrews McMeel Syndication
I WAS THINKING OF SOME OTHER WORLD
THEN YOU SHOULD GO THERE
JIM DAVIS 1-10

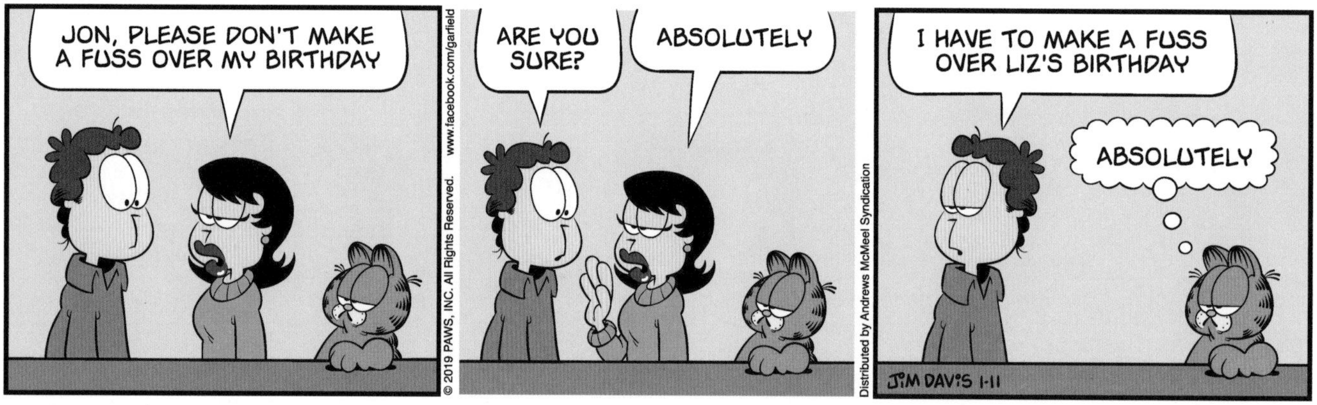
JON, PLEASE DON'T MAKE A FUSS OVER MY BIRTHDAY
© 2019 PAWS, INC. All Rights Reserved. www.facebook.com/garfield
ARE YOU SURE?
ABSOLUTELY
Distributed by Andrews McMeel Syndication
I HAVE TO MAKE A FUSS OVER LIZ'S BIRTHDAY
ABSOLUTELY
JIM DAVIS 1-11

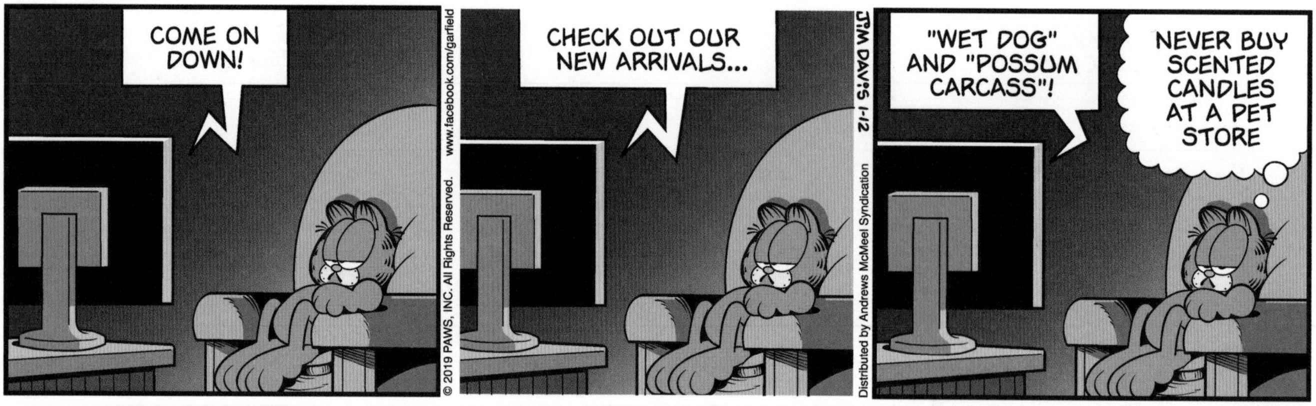
COME ON DOWN!
© 2019 PAWS, INC. All Rights Reserved. www.facebook.com/garfield
CHECK OUT OUR NEW ARRIVALS...
JIM DAVIS 1-12
Distributed by Andrews McMeel Syndication
"WET DOG" AND "POSSUM CARCASS"!
NEVER BUY SCENTED CANDLES AT A PET STORE

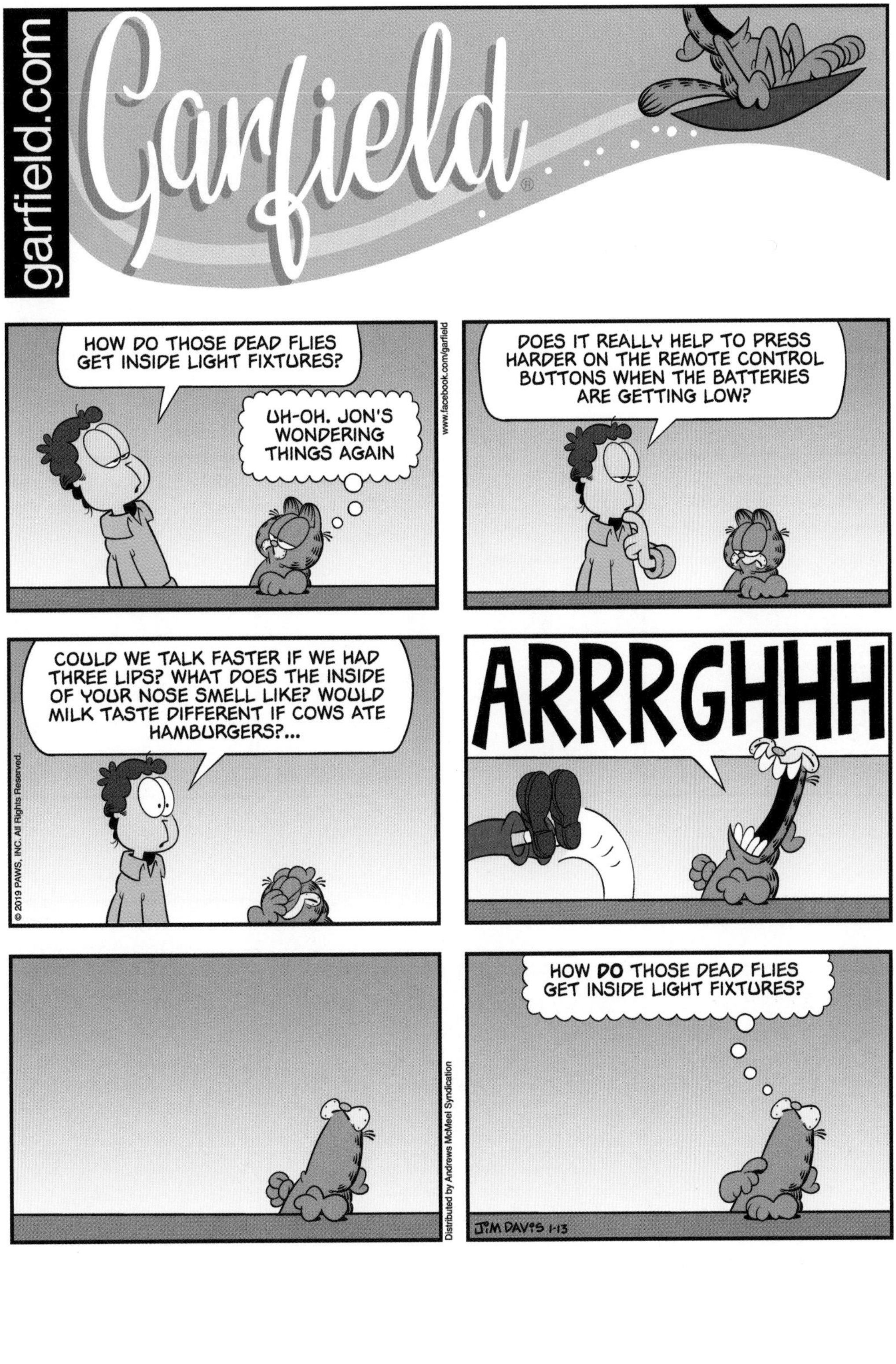
garfield.com
Garfield
HOW DO THOSE DEAD FLIES GET INSIDE LIGHT FIXTURES?
UH-OH. JON'S WONDERING THINGS AGAIN
www.facebook.com/garfield
DOES IT REALLY HELP TO PRESS HARDER ON THE REMOTE CONTROL BUTTONS WHEN THE BATTERIES ARE GETTING LOW?
COULD WE TALK FASTER IF WE HAD THREE LIPS? WHAT DOES THE INSIDE OF YOUR NOSE SMELL LIKE? WOULD MILK TASTE DIFFERENT IF COWS ATE HAMBURGERS?...
© 2019 PAWS, INC. All Rights Reserved.
ARRRGHHH
Distributed by Andrews McMeel Syndication
HOW **DO** THOSE DEAD FLIES GET INSIDE LIGHT FIXTURES?
JIM DAVIS 1-13

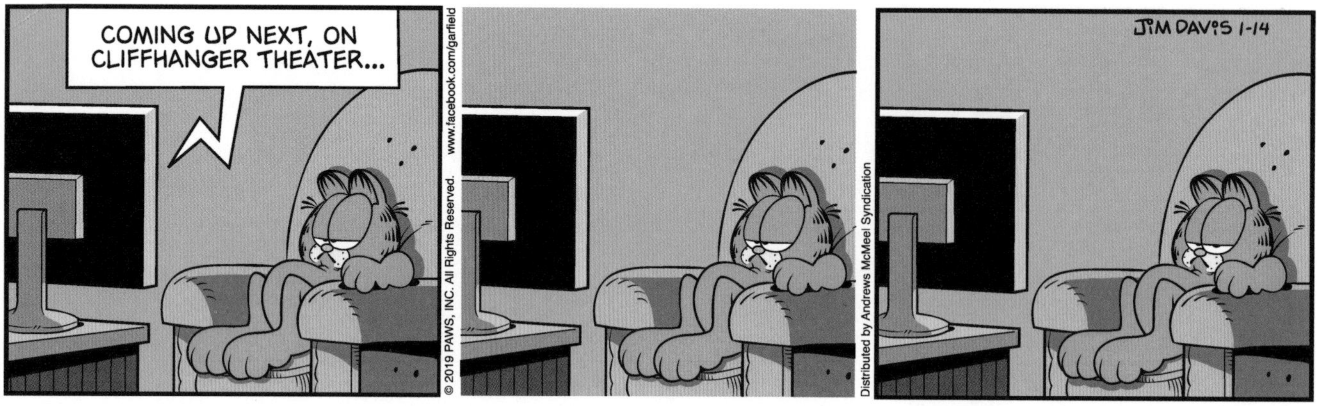
COMING UP NEXT, ON CLIFFHANGER THEATER...
JIM DAVIS 1-14
© 2019 PAWS, INC. All Rights Reserved. www.facebook.com/garfield
Distributed by Andrews McMeel Syndication

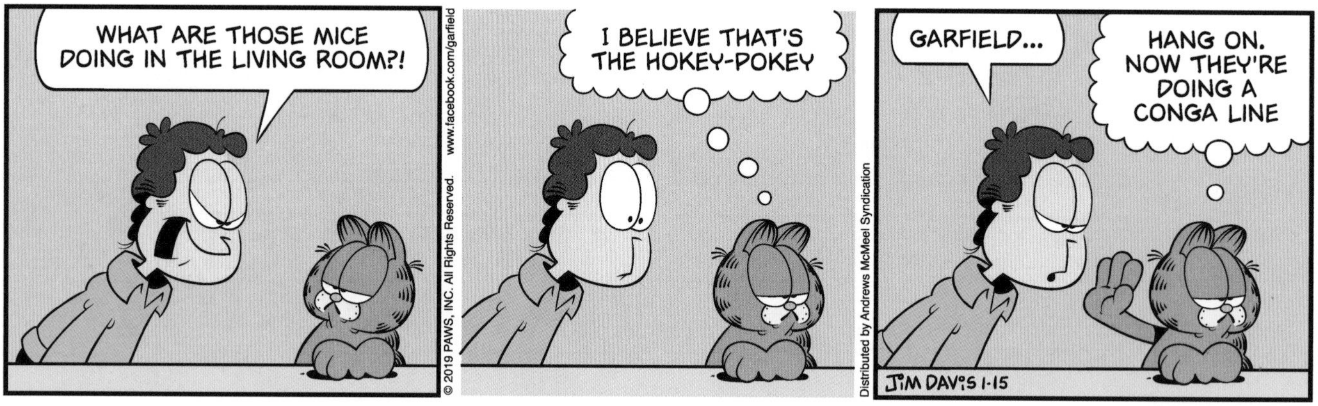
WHAT ARE THOSE MICE DOING IN THE LIVING ROOM?!
I BELIEVE THAT'S THE HOKEY-POKEY
GARFIELD...
HANG ON. NOW THEY'RE DOING A CONGA LINE
JIM DAVIS 1-15
© 2019 PAWS, INC. All Rights Reserved. www.facebook.com/garfield
Distributed by Andrews McMeel Syndication

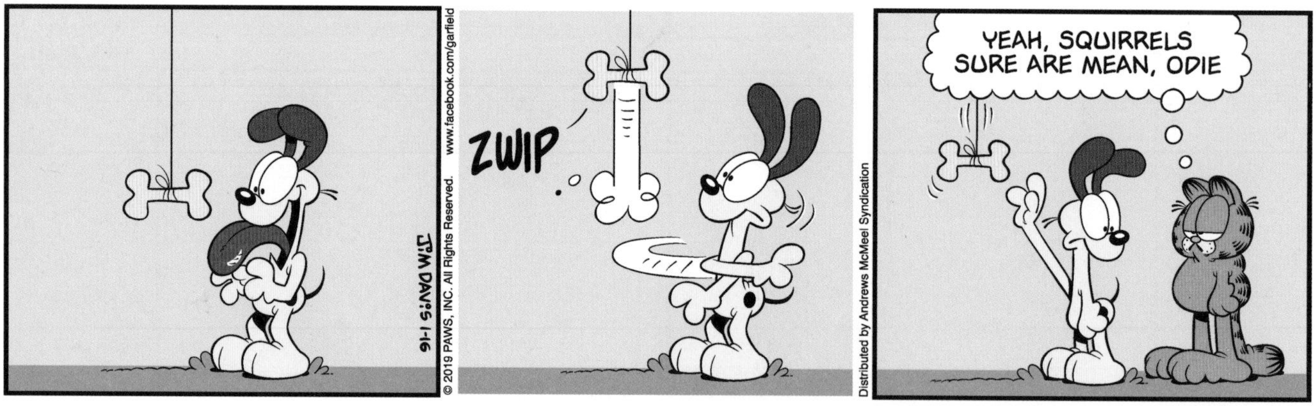
JIM DAVIS 1-16
ZWIP
YEAH, SQUIRRELS SURE ARE MEAN, ODIE
© 2019 PAWS, INC. All Rights Reserved. www.facebook.com/garfield
Distributed by Andrews McMeel Syndication

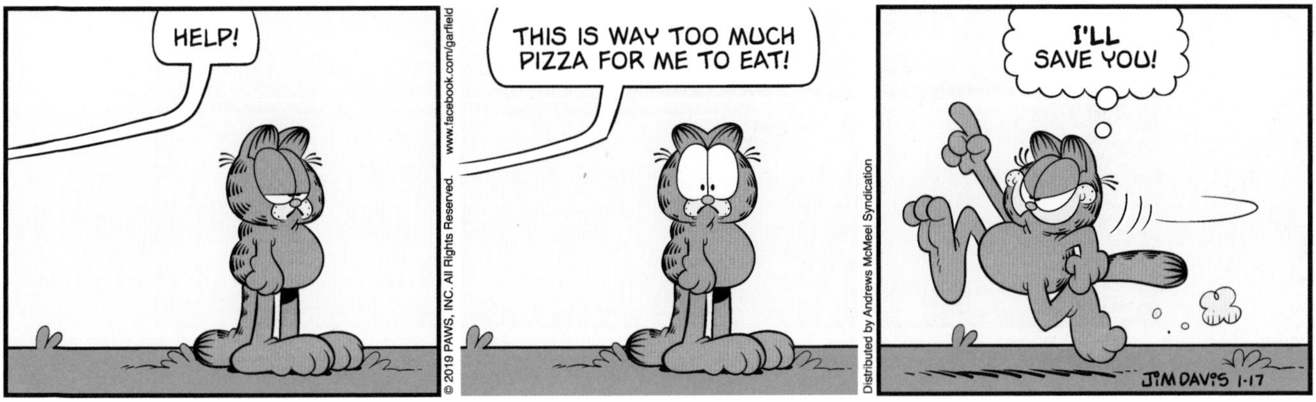
HELP!
THIS IS WAY TOO MUCH PIZZA FOR ME TO EAT!
I'LL SAVE YOU!
JIM DAVIS 1-17
© 2019 PAWS, INC. All Rights Reserved. www.facebook.com/garfield
Distributed by Andrews McMeel Syndication

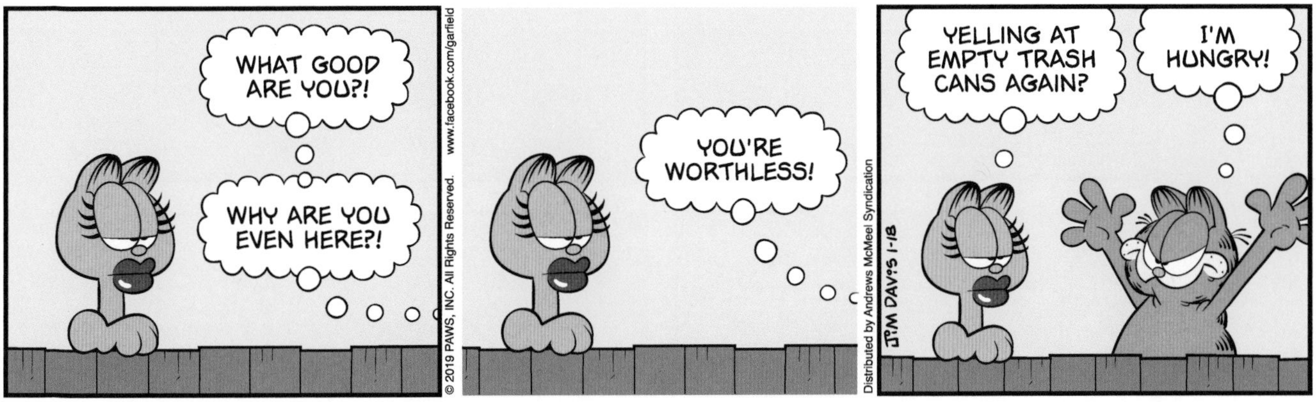
WHAT GOOD ARE YOU?!
WHY ARE YOU EVEN HERE?!
YOU'RE WORTHLESS!
YELLING AT EMPTY TRASH CANS AGAIN?
I'M HUNGRY!
JIM DAVIS 1-18
© 2019 PAWS, INC. All Rights Reserved. www.facebook.com/garfield
Distributed by Andrews McMeel Syndication

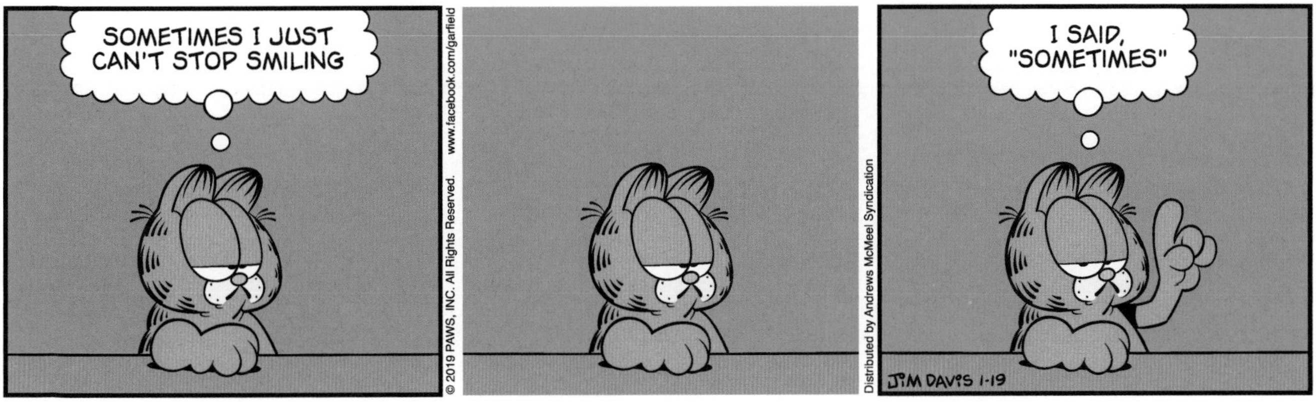
SOMETIMES I JUST CAN'T STOP SMILING
I SAID, "SOMETIMES"
JIM DAVIS 1-19
© 2019 PAWS, INC. All Rights Reserved. www.facebook.com/garfield
Distributed by Andrews McMeel Syndication

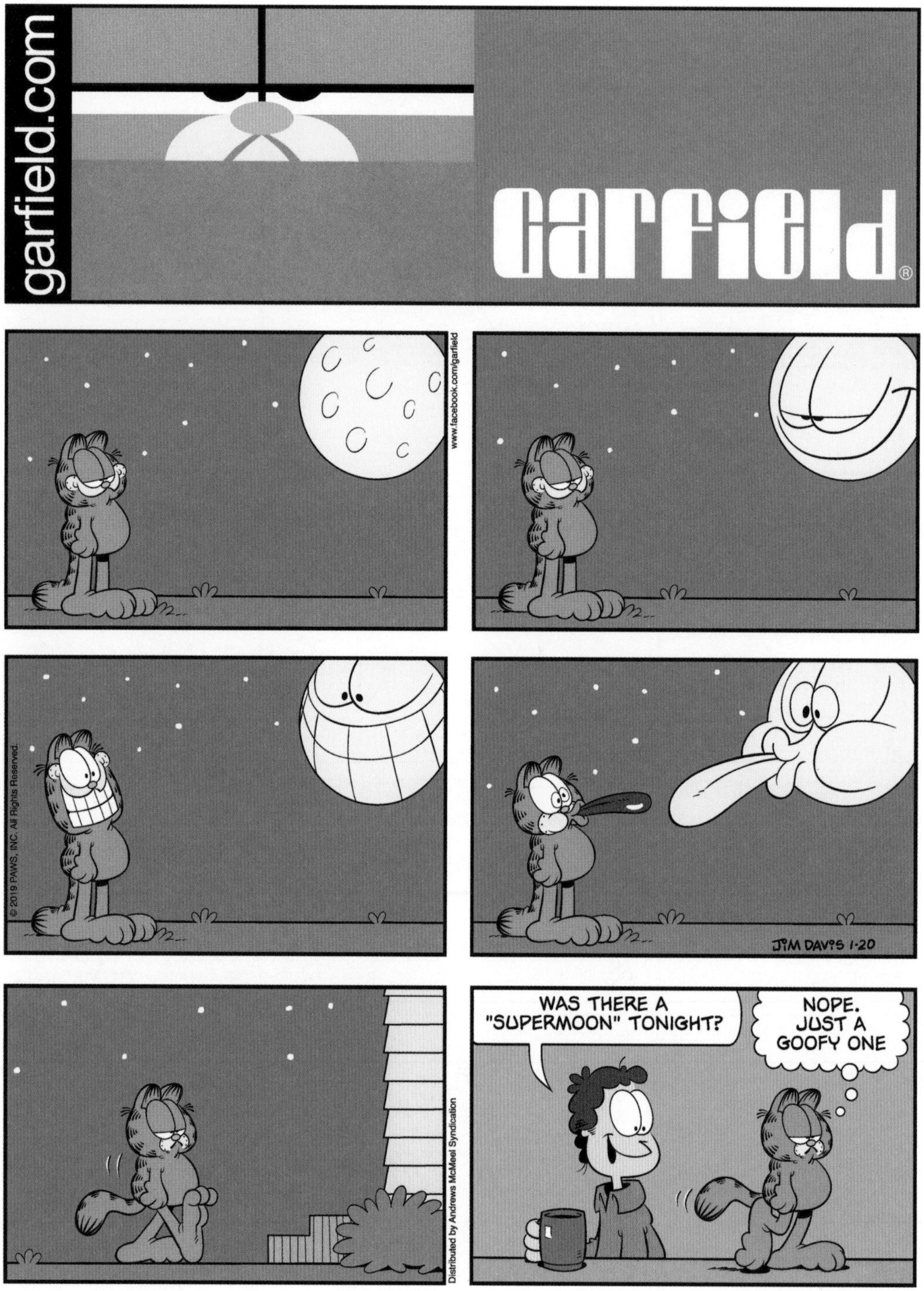

garfield.com
GARFIELD
www.facebook.com/garfield
© 2019 PAWS, INC. All Rights Reserved.
JIM DAVIS 1-20
Distributed by Andrews McMeel Syndication
WAS THERE A "SUPERMOON" TONIGHT?
NOPE. JUST A GOOFY ONE

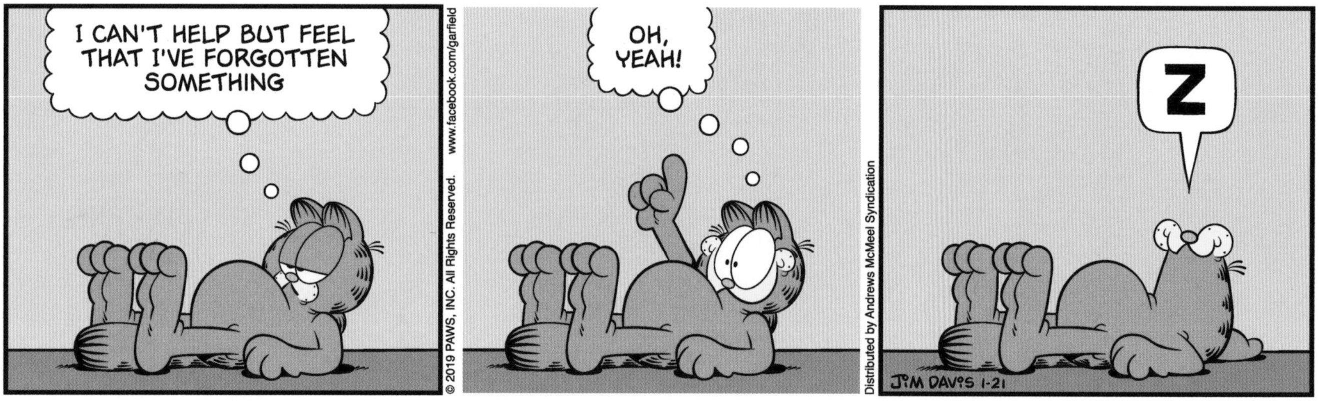
I CAN'T HELP BUT FEEL THAT I'VE FORGOTTEN SOMETHING
OH, YEAH!
Z
JIM DAVIS 1-21
© 2019 PAWS, INC. All Rights Reserved. www.facebook.com/garfield
Distributed by Andrews McMeel Syndication

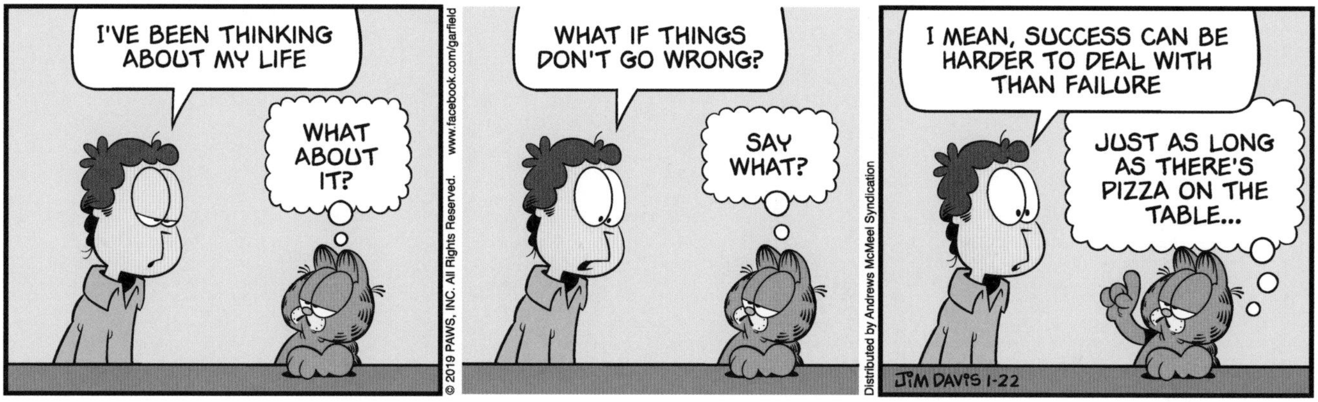
I'VE BEEN THINKING ABOUT MY LIFE
WHAT ABOUT IT?
WHAT IF THINGS DON'T GO WRONG?
SAY WHAT?
I MEAN, SUCCESS CAN BE HARDER TO DEAL WITH THAN FAILURE
JUST AS LONG AS THERE'S PIZZA ON THE TABLE...
JIM DAVIS 1-22
© 2019 PAWS, INC. All Rights Reserved. www.facebook.com/garfield
Distributed by Andrews McMeel Syndication

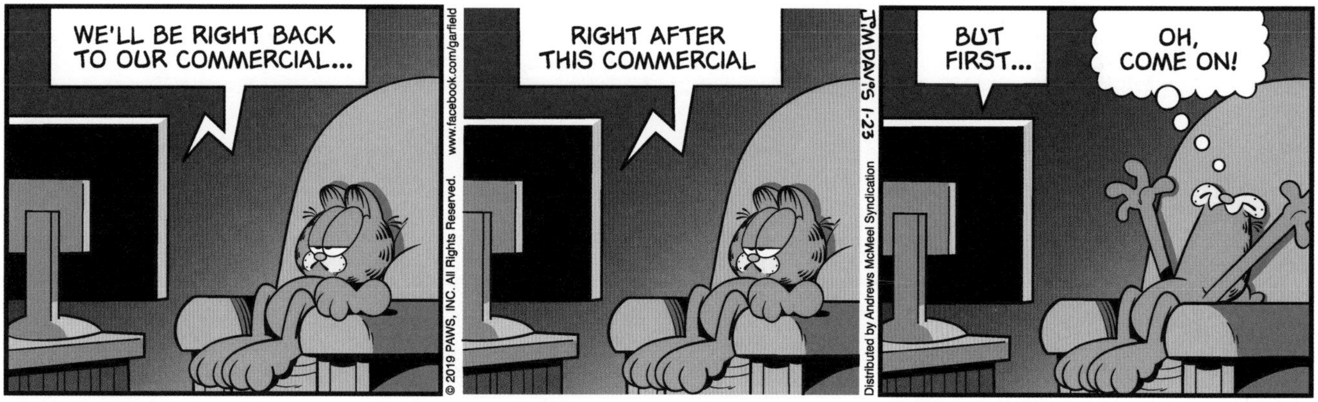
WE'LL BE RIGHT BACK TO OUR COMMERCIAL...
RIGHT AFTER THIS COMMERCIAL
BUT FIRST...
OH, COME ON!
JIM DAVIS 1-23
© 2019 PAWS, INC. All Rights Reserved. www.facebook.com/garfield
Distributed by Andrews McMeel Syndication

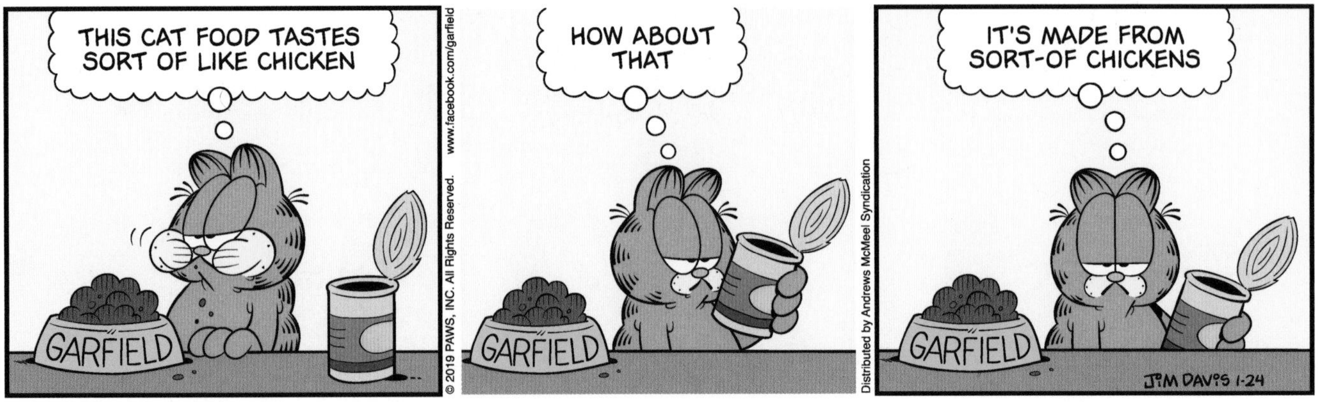
THIS CAT FOOD TASTES SORT OF LIKE CHICKEN
GARFIELD
© 2019 PAWS, INC. All Rights Reserved. www.facebook.com/garfield
HOW ABOUT THAT
GARFIELD
Distributed by Andrews McMeel Syndication
IT'S MADE FROM SORT-OF CHICKENS
GARFIELD
JIM DAVIS 1-24

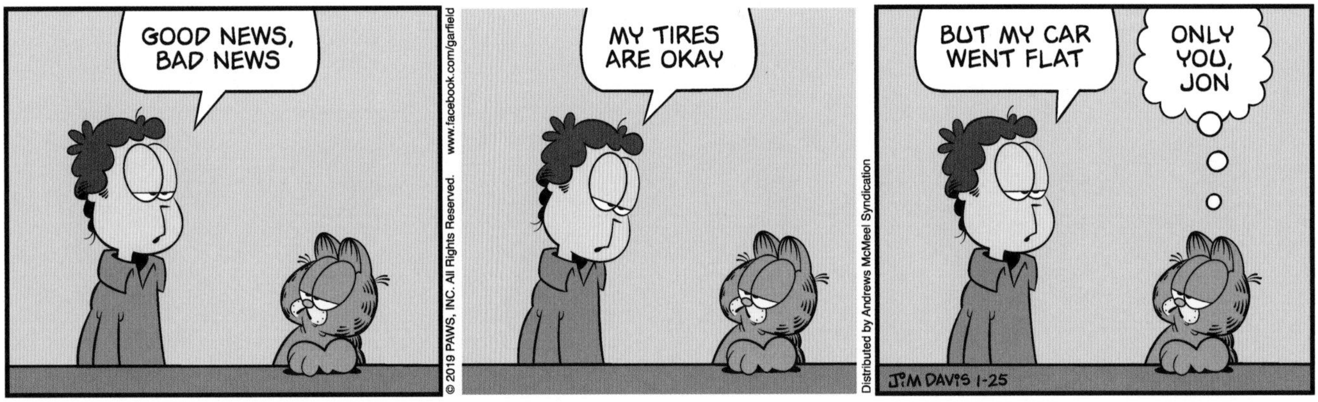
GOOD NEWS, BAD NEWS
© 2019 PAWS, INC. All Rights Reserved. www.facebook.com/garfield
MY TIRES ARE OKAY
Distributed by Andrews McMeel Syndication
BUT MY CAR WENT FLAT
ONLY YOU, JON
JIM DAVIS 1-25

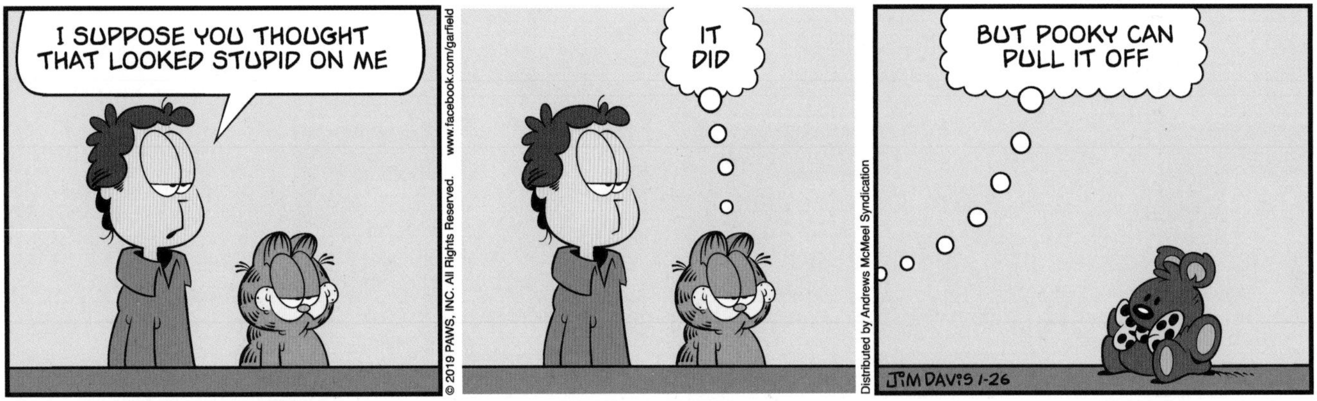
I SUPPOSE YOU THOUGHT THAT LOOKED STUPID ON ME
© 2019 PAWS, INC. All Rights Reserved. www.facebook.com/garfield
IT DID
Distributed by Andrews McMeel Syndication
BUT POOKY CAN PULL IT OFF
JIM DAVIS 1-26

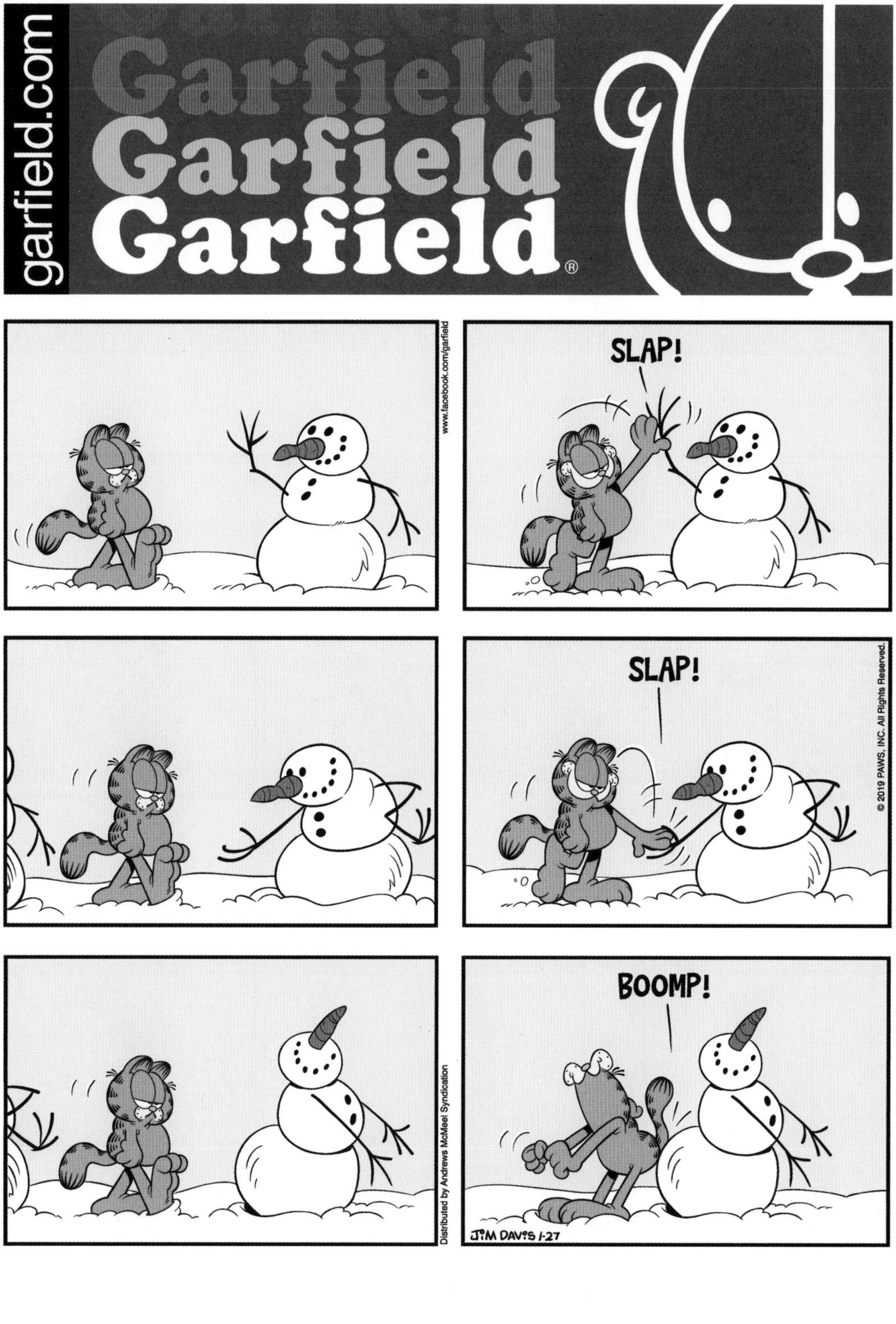
garfield.com
Garfield
Garfield
Garfield®
www.facebook.com/garfield
SLAP!
SLAP!
© 2019 PAWS, INC. All Rights Reserved.
Distributed by Andrews McMeel Syndication
BOOMP!
JIM DAVIS 1-27

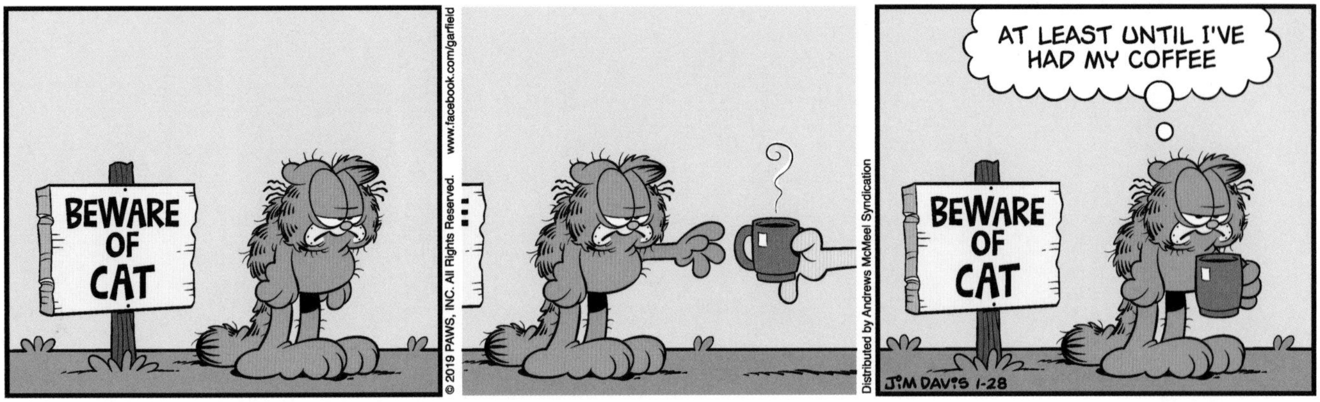
BEWARE OF CAT
© 2019 PAWS, INC. All Rights Reserved. www.facebook.com/garfield
Distributed by Andrews McMeel Syndication
AT LEAST UNTIL I'VE HAD MY COFFEE
BEWARE OF CAT
JIM DAVIS 1-28

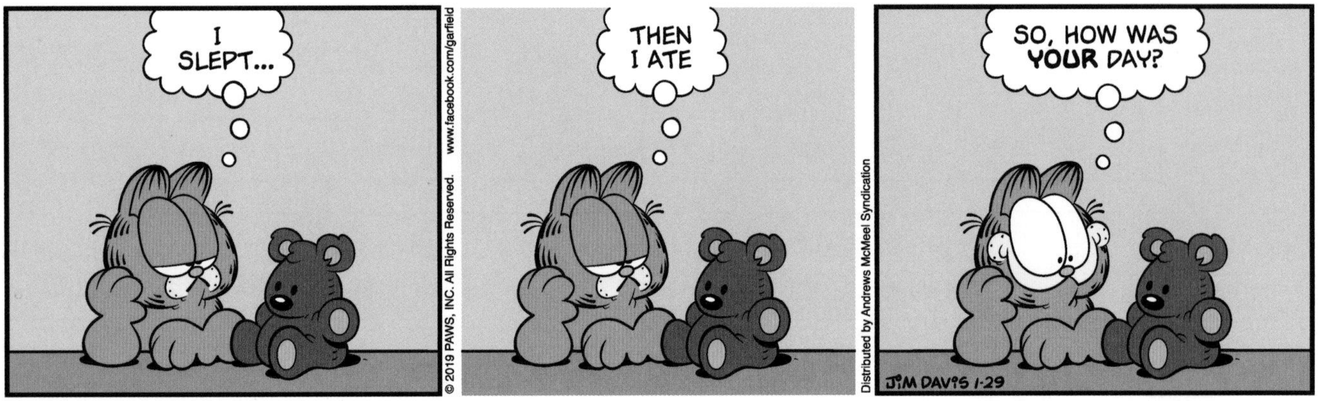
I SLEPT...
© 2019 PAWS, INC. All Rights Reserved. www.facebook.com/garfield
THEN I ATE
Distributed by Andrews McMeel Syndication
SO, HOW WAS YOUR DAY?
JIM DAVIS 1-29

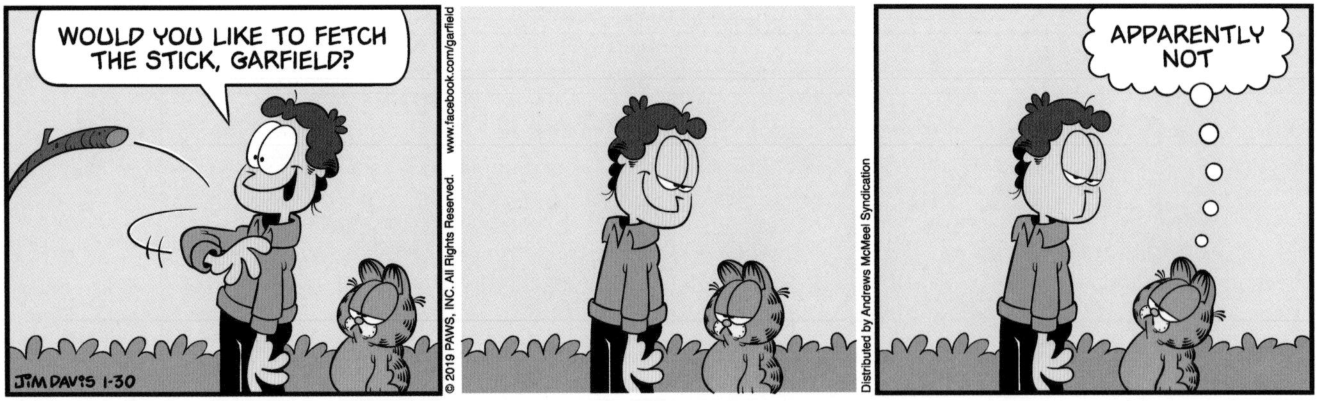
WOULD YOU LIKE TO FETCH THE STICK, GARFIELD?
JIM DAVIS 1-30
© 2019 PAWS, INC. All Rights Reserved. www.facebook.com/garfield
Distributed by Andrews McMeel Syndication
APPARENTLY NOT

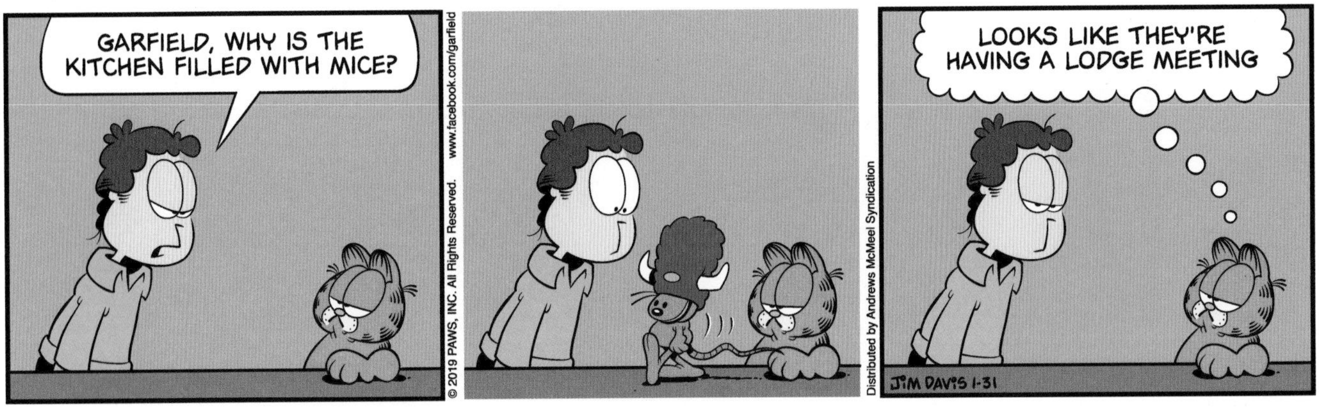
GARFIELD, WHY IS THE KITCHEN FILLED WITH MICE?
LOOKS LIKE THEY'RE HAVING A LODGE MEETING
JIM DAVIS 1-31
© 2019 PAWS, INC. All Rights Reserved. www.facebook.com/garfield
Distributed by Andrews McMeel Syndication

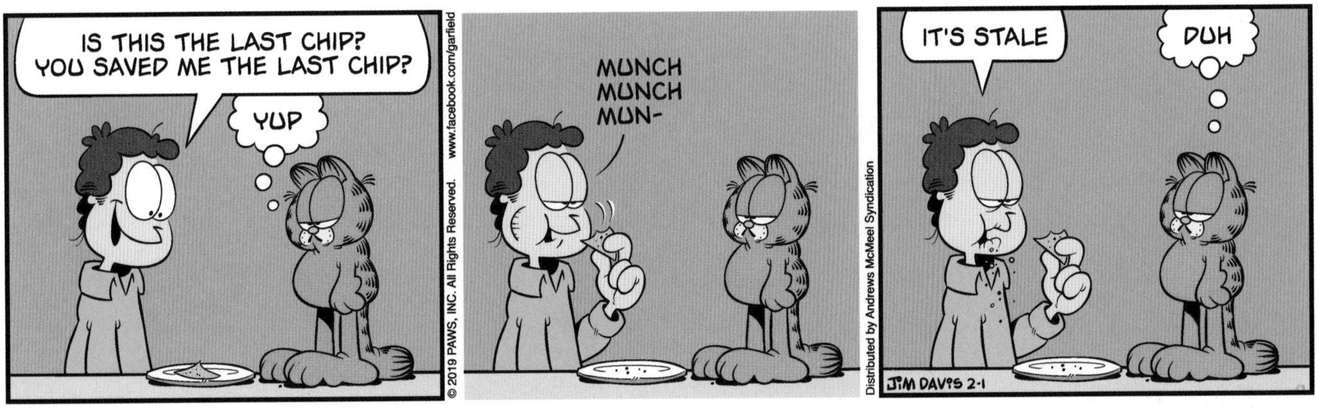
IS THIS THE LAST CHIP? YOU SAVED ME THE LAST CHIP?
YUP
MUNCH MUNCH MUN-
IT'S STALE
DUH
JIM DAVIS 2-1
© 2019 PAWS, INC. All Rights Reserved. www.facebook.com/garfield
Distributed by Andrews McMeel Syndication

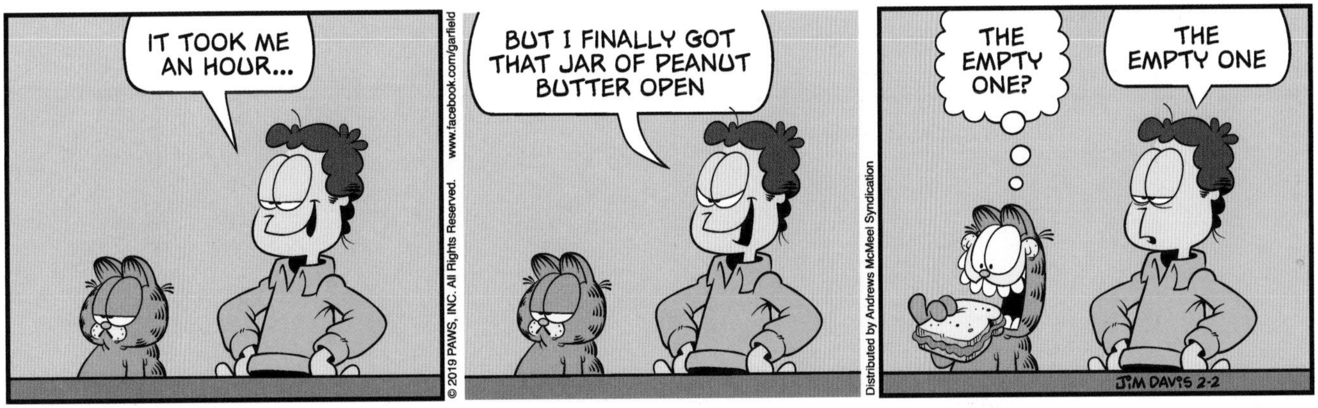
IT TOOK ME AN HOUR...
BUT I FINALLY GOT THAT JAR OF PEANUT BUTTER OPEN
THE EMPTY ONE?
THE EMPTY ONE
JIM DAVIS 2-2
© 2019 PAWS, INC. All Rights Reserved. www.facebook.com/garfield
Distributed by Andrews McMeel Syndication

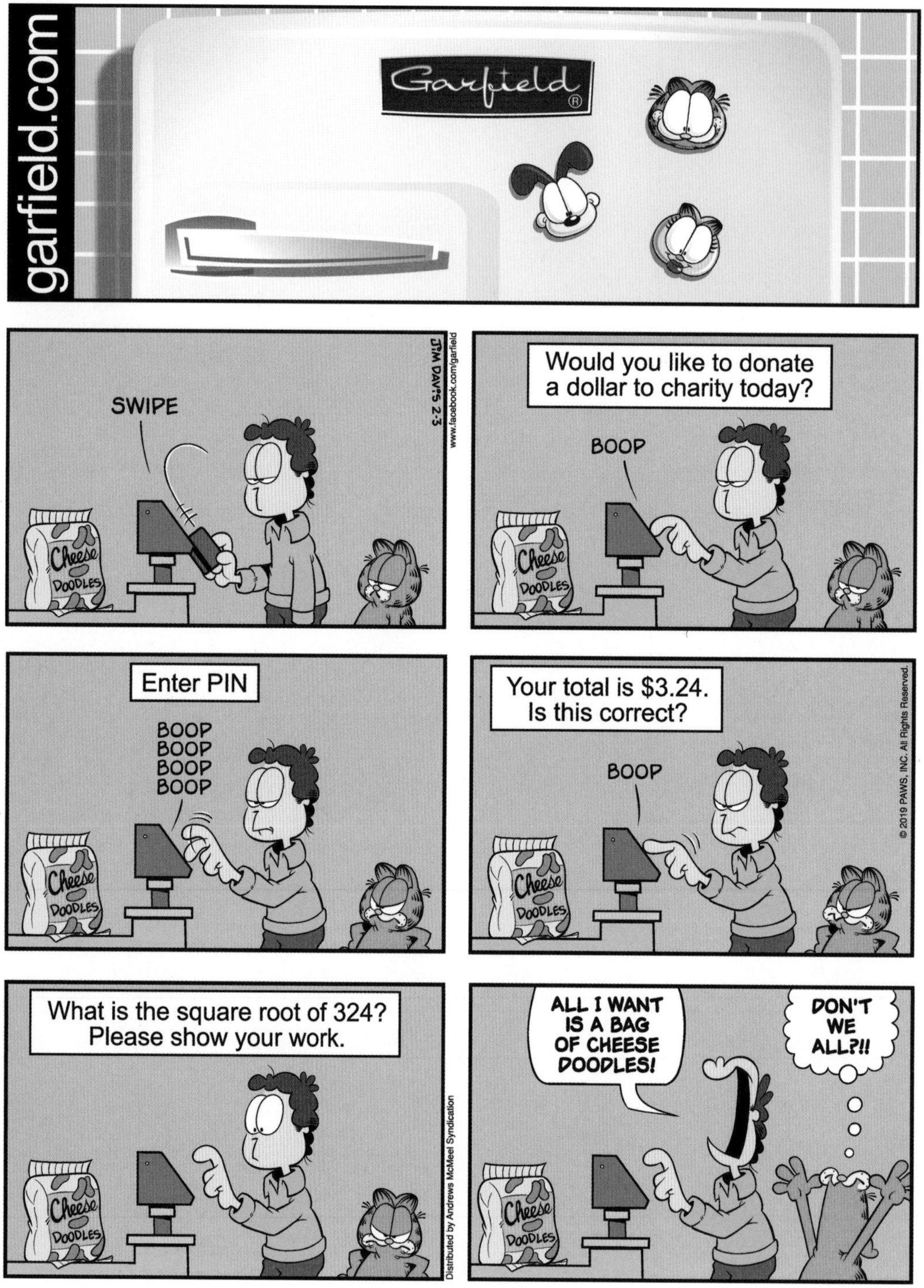
garfield.com
Garfield
JIM DAVIS 2-3
www.facebook.com/garfield
SWIPE
Would you like to donate a dollar to charity today?
BOOP
Enter PIN
BOOP BOOP BOOP BOOP
Your total is $3.24. Is this correct?
BOOP
© 2019 PAWS, INC. All Rights Reserved.
What is the square root of 324? Please show your work.
Distributed by Andrews McMeel Syndication
ALL I WANT IS A BAG OF CHEESE DOODLES!
DON'T WE ALL?!!

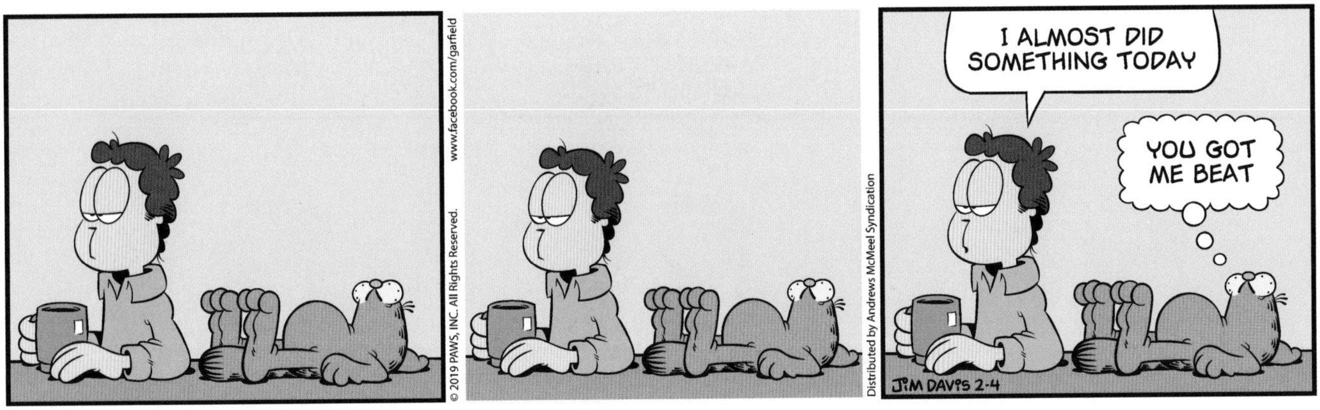
© 2019 PAWS, INC. All Rights Reserved. www.facebook.com/garfield
Distributed by Andrews McMeel Syndication
I ALMOST DID SOMETHING TODAY
YOU GOT ME BEAT
JIM DAVIS 2-4

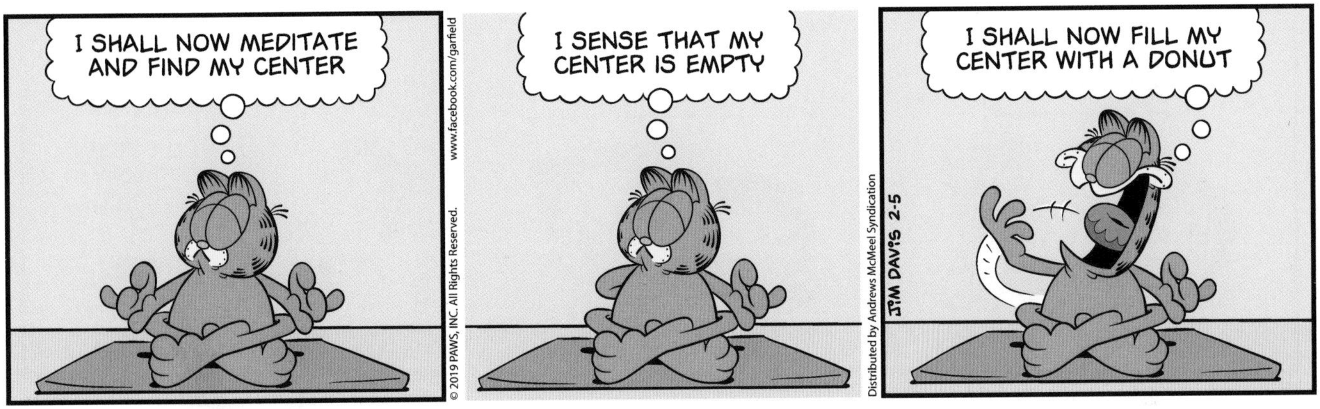
I SHALL NOW MEDITATE AND FIND MY CENTER
© 2019 PAWS, INC. All Rights Reserved. www.facebook.com/garfield
I SENSE THAT MY CENTER IS EMPTY
Distributed by Andrews McMeel Syndication
JIM DAVIS 2-5
I SHALL NOW FILL MY CENTER WITH A DONUT

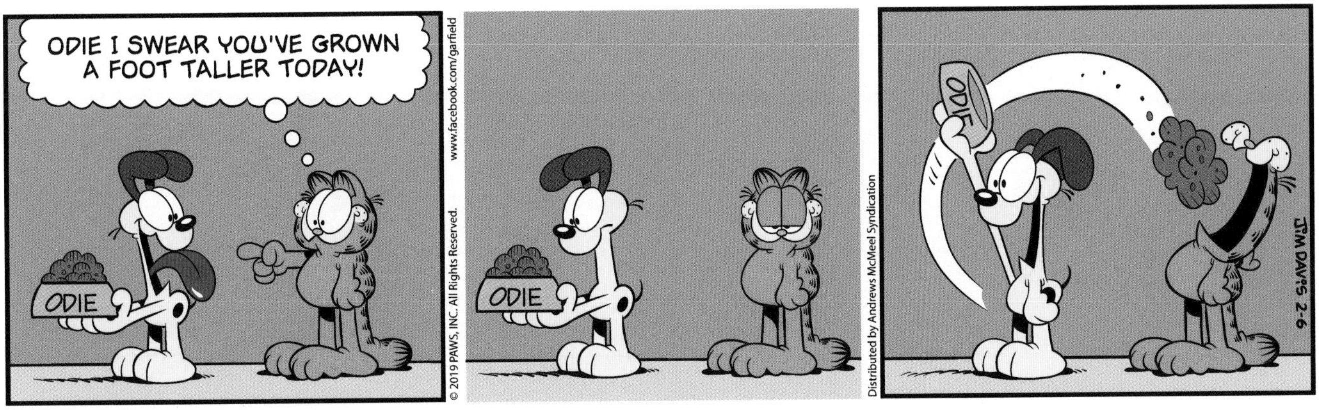
ODIE I SWEAR YOU'VE GROWN A FOOT TALLER TODAY!
ODIE
© 2019 PAWS, INC. All Rights Reserved. www.facebook.com/garfield
ODIE
Distributed by Andrews McMeel Syndication
ODIE
JIM DAVIS 2-6

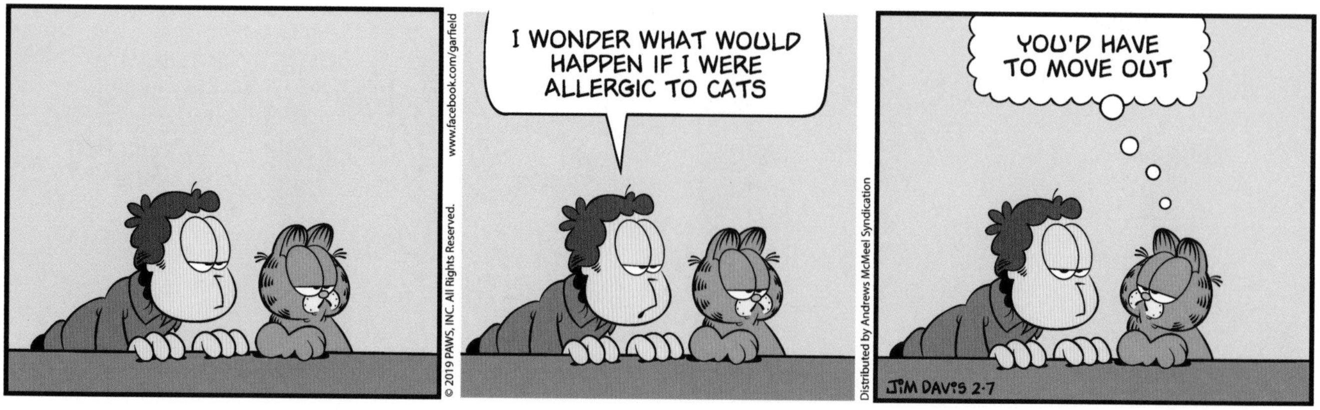
© 2019 PAWS, INC. All Rights Reserved. www.facebook.com/garfield
I WONDER WHAT WOULD HAPPEN IF I WERE ALLERGIC TO CATS
YOU'D HAVE TO MOVE OUT
Distributed by Andrews McMeel Syndication
JIM DAVIS 2-7

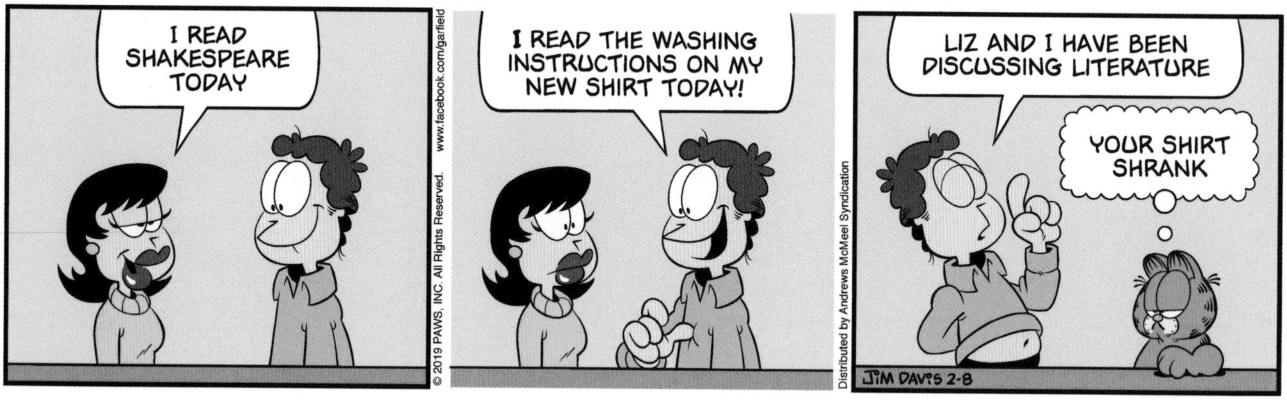
I READ SHAKESPEARE TODAY
© 2019 PAWS, INC. All Rights Reserved. www.facebook.com/garfield
I READ THE WASHING INSTRUCTIONS ON MY NEW SHIRT TODAY!
Distributed by Andrews McMeel Syndication
LIZ AND I HAVE BEEN DISCUSSING LITERATURE
YOUR SHIRT SHRANK
JIM DAVIS 2-8

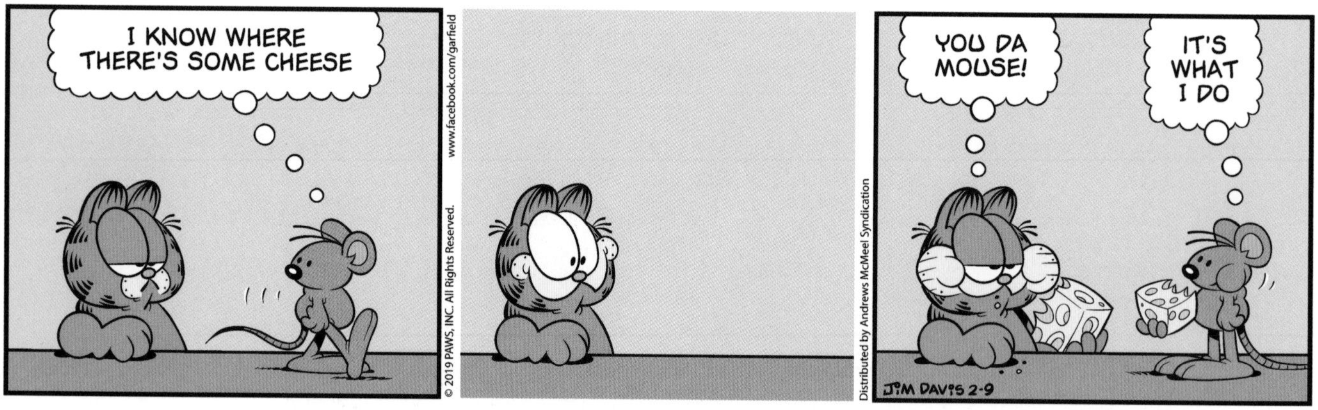
I KNOW WHERE THERE'S SOME CHEESE
© 2019 PAWS, INC. All Rights Reserved. www.facebook.com/garfield
Distributed by Andrews McMeel Syndication
YOU DA MOUSE!
IT'S WHAT I DO
JIM DAVIS 2-9

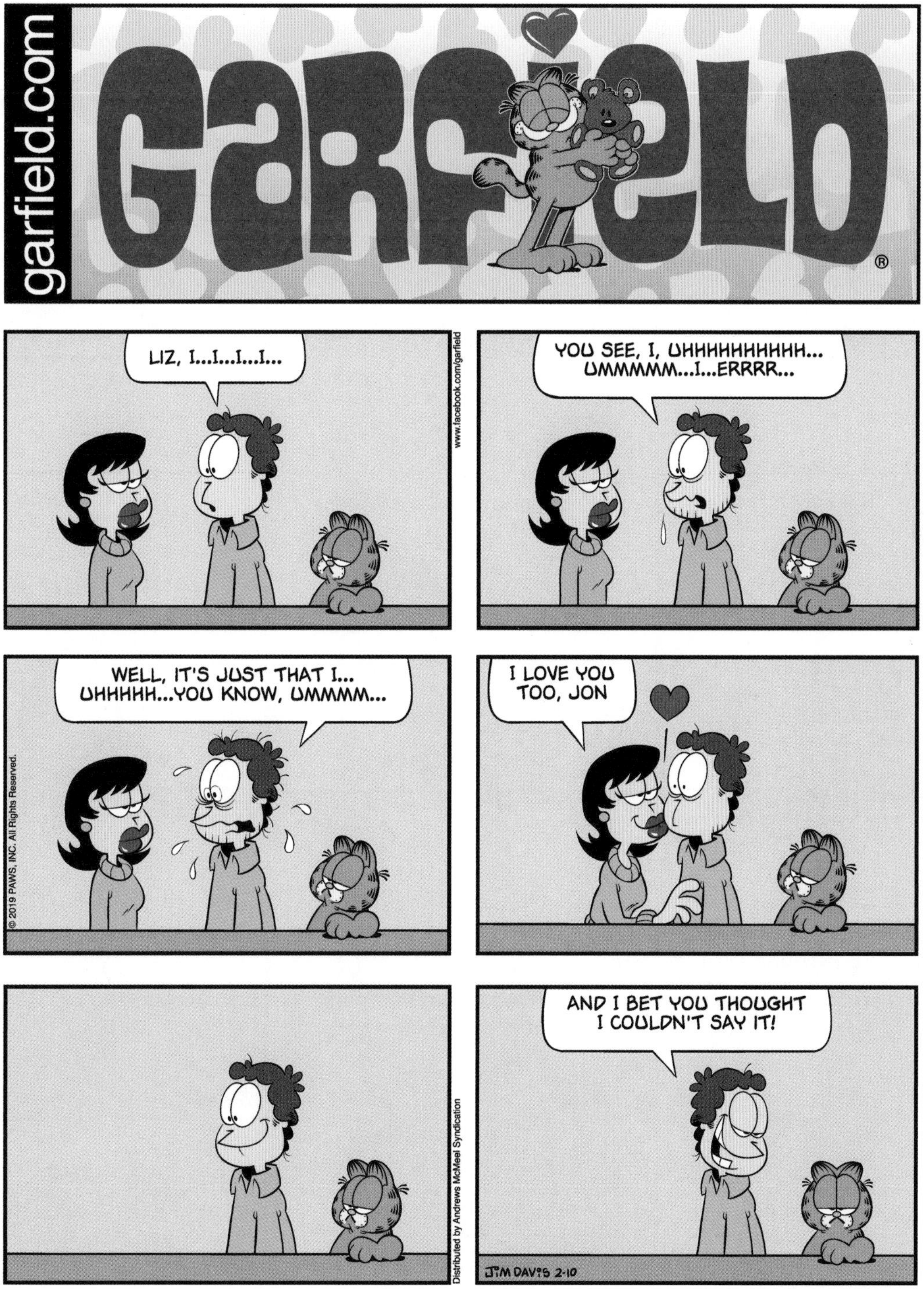
garfield.com
GARFIELD
LIZ, I...I...I...I...
www.facebook.com/garfield
YOU SEE, I, UHHHHHHHHHH... UMMMMM...I...ERRRR...
WELL, IT'S JUST THAT I... UHHHHH...YOU KNOW, UMMMM...
© 2019 PAWS, INC. All Rights Reserved.
I LOVE YOU TOO, JON
Distributed by Andrews McMeel Syndication
AND I BET YOU THOUGHT I COULDN'T SAY IT!
JIM DAVIS 2-10

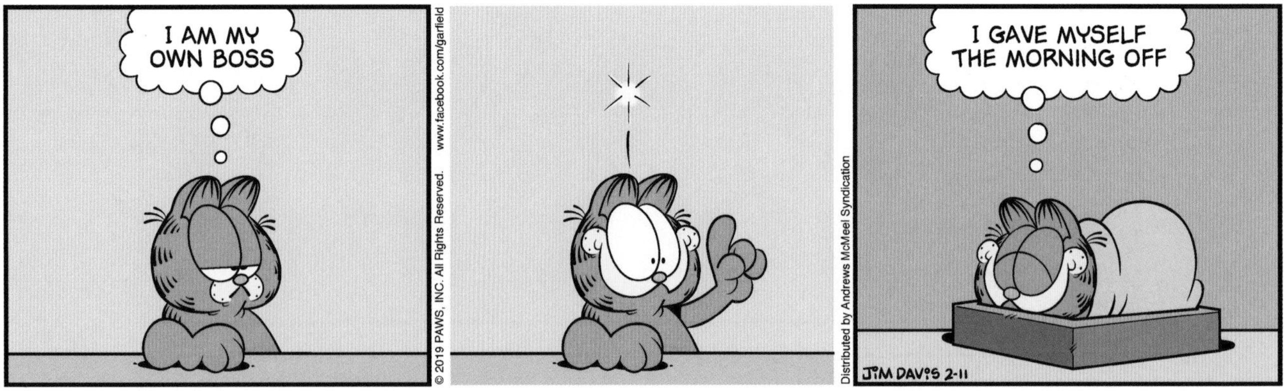
I AM MY OWN BOSS
I GAVE MYSELF THE MORNING OFF
© 2019 PAWS, INC. All Rights Reserved. www.facebook.com/garfield
Distributed by Andrews McMeel Syndication
JIM DAVIS 2-11

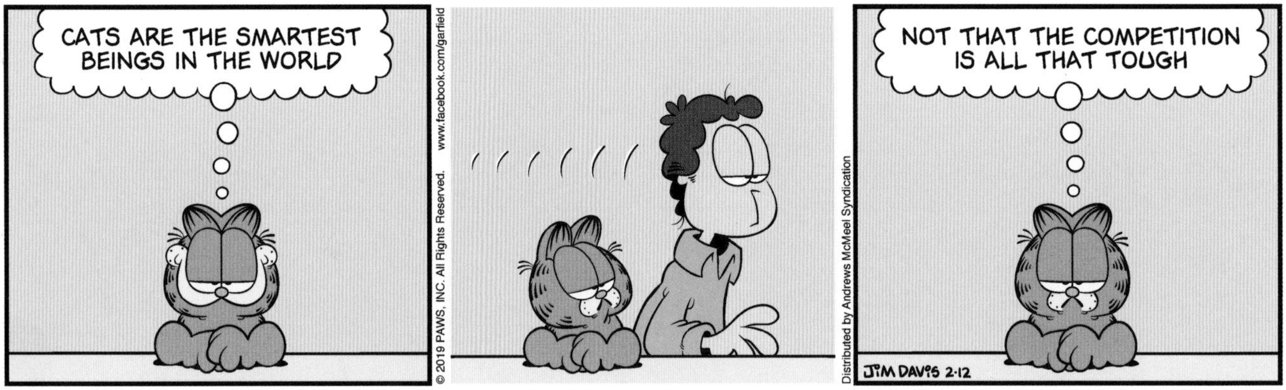
CATS ARE THE SMARTEST BEINGS IN THE WORLD
NOT THAT THE COMPETITION IS ALL THAT TOUGH
© 2019 PAWS, INC. All Rights Reserved. www.facebook.com/garfield
Distributed by Andrews McMeel Syndication
JIM DAVIS 2-12

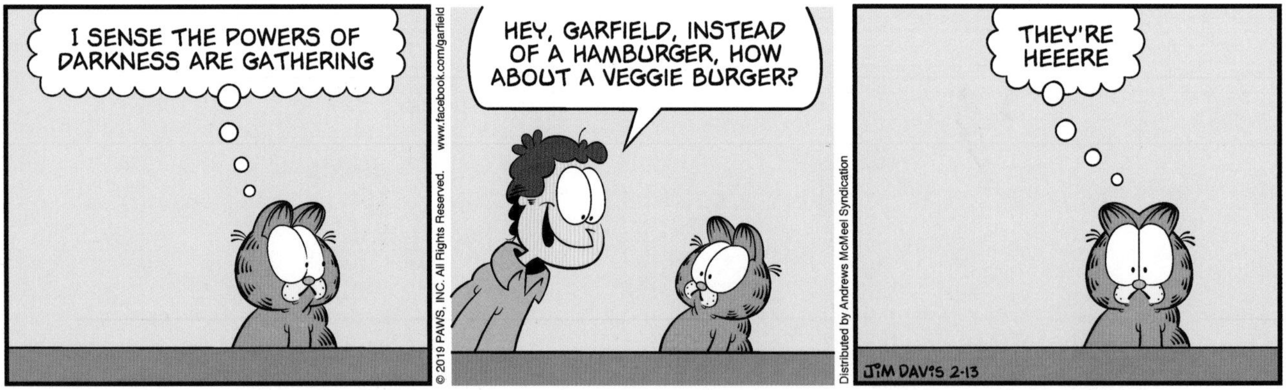
I SENSE THE POWERS OF DARKNESS ARE GATHERING
HEY, GARFIELD, INSTEAD OF A HAMBURGER, HOW ABOUT A VEGGIE BURGER?
THEY'RE HEEERE
© 2019 PAWS, INC. All Rights Reserved. www.facebook.com/garfield
Distributed by Andrews McMeel Syndication
JIM DAVIS 2-13

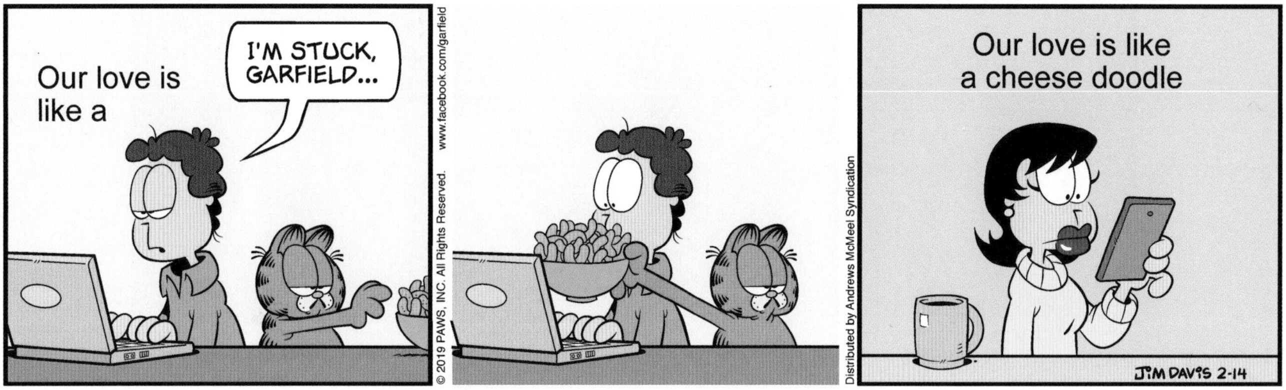
Our love is like a
I'M STUCK, GARFIELD...
© 2019 PAWS, INC. All Rights Reserved. www.facebook.com/garfield
Distributed by Andrews McMeel Syndication
Our love is like a cheese doodle
JIM DAVIS 2-14

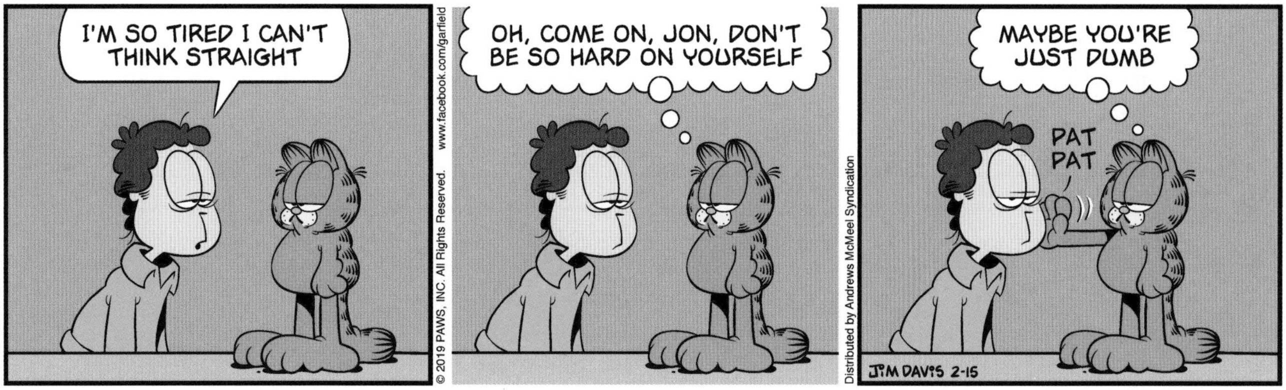
I'M SO TIRED I CAN'T THINK STRAIGHT
© 2019 PAWS, INC. All Rights Reserved. www.facebook.com/garfield
OH, COME ON, JON, DON'T BE SO HARD ON YOURSELF
Distributed by Andrews McMeel Syndication
MAYBE YOU'RE JUST DUMB
PAT PAT
JIM DAVIS 2-15

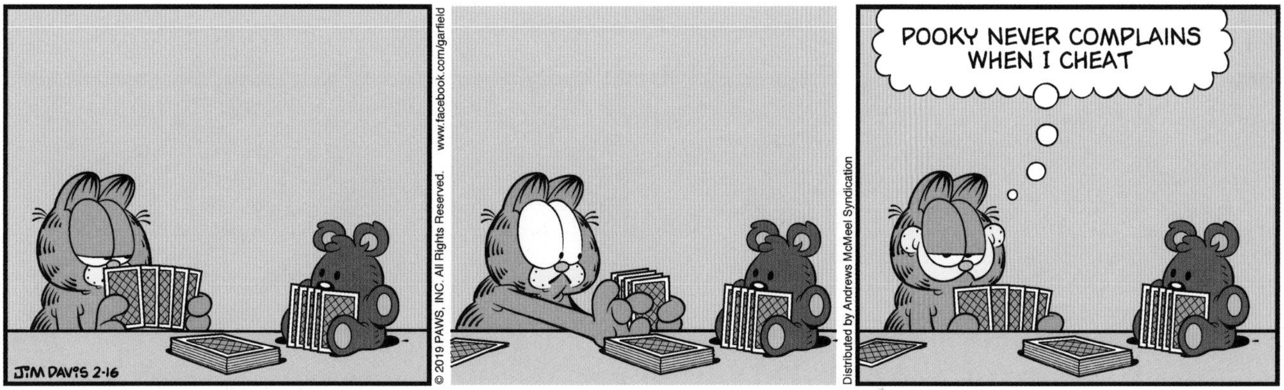
JIM DAVIS 2-16
© 2019 PAWS, INC. All Rights Reserved. www.facebook.com/garfield
Distributed by Andrews McMeel Syndication
POOKY NEVER COMPLAINS WHEN I CHEAT

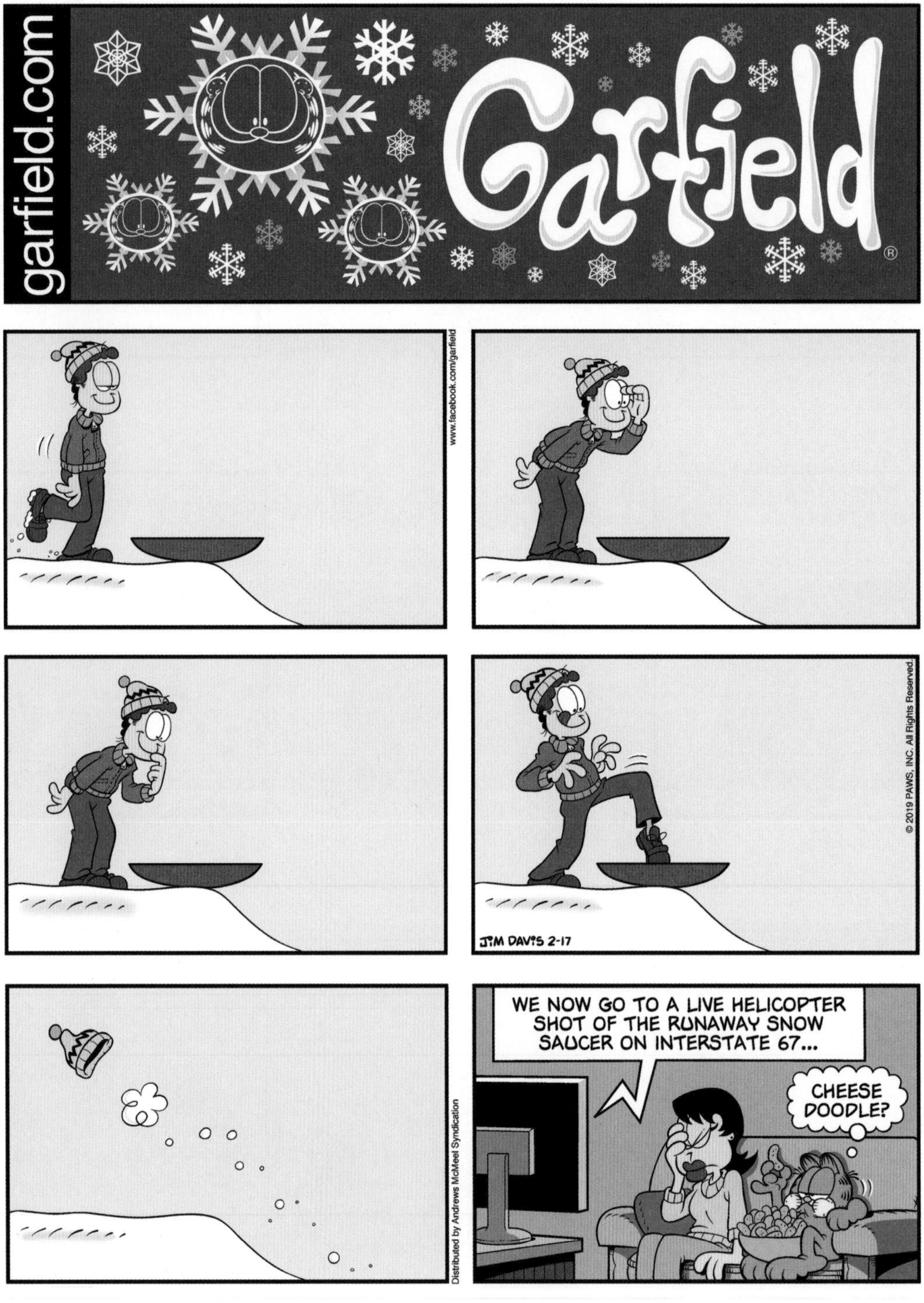
garfield.com
Garfield®
www.facebook.com/garfield
© 2019 PAWS, INC. All Rights Reserved.
JIM DAVIS 2-17
Distributed by Andrews McMeel Syndication
WE NOW GO TO A LIVE HELICOPTER SHOT OF THE RUNAWAY SNOW SAUCER ON INTERSTATE 67...
CHEESE DOODLE?

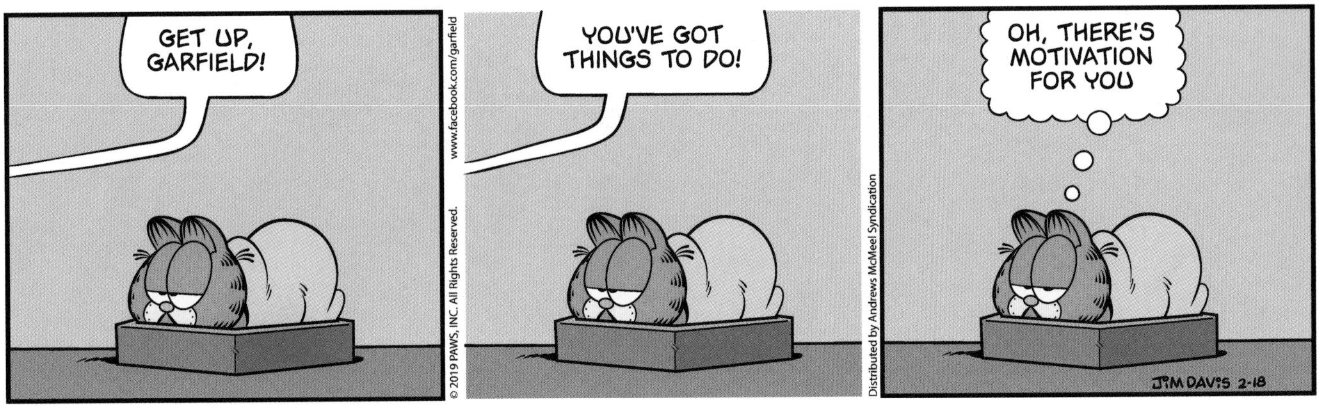
GET UP, GARFIELD!
YOU'VE GOT THINGS TO DO!
OH, THERE'S MOTIVATION FOR YOU
JIM DAVIS 2-18
© 2019 PAWS, INC. All Rights Reserved.
www.facebook.com/garfield
Distributed by Andrews McMeel Syndication

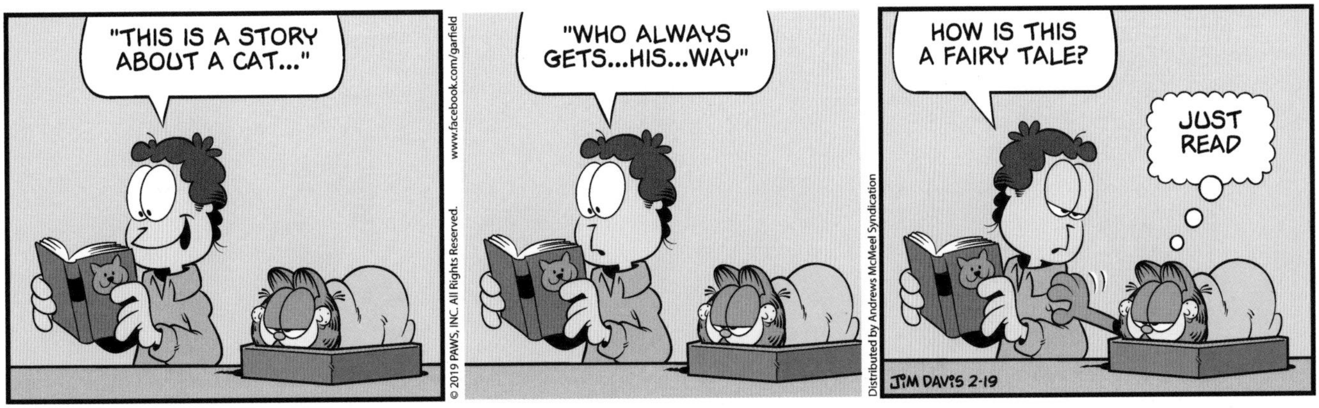
"THIS IS A STORY ABOUT A CAT..."
"WHO ALWAYS GETS...HIS...WAY"
HOW IS THIS A FAIRY TALE?
JUST READ
JIM DAVIS 2-19
© 2019 PAWS, INC. All Rights Reserved.
www.facebook.com/garfield
Distributed by Andrews McMeel Syndication

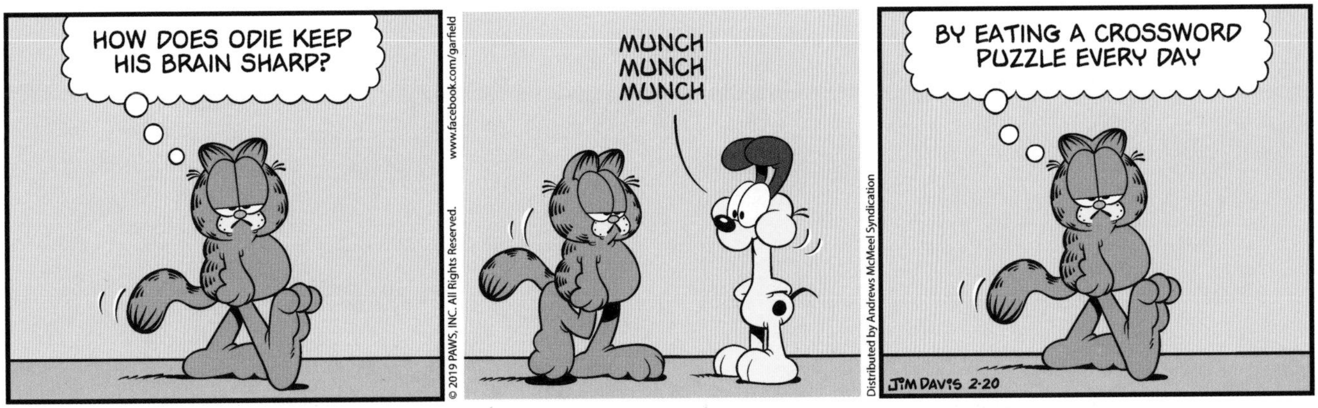
HOW DOES ODIE KEEP HIS BRAIN SHARP?
MUNCH MUNCH MUNCH
BY EATING A CROSSWORD PUZZLE EVERY DAY
JIM DAVIS 2-20
© 2019 PAWS, INC. All Rights Reserved.
www.facebook.com/garfield
Distributed by Andrews McMeel Syndication

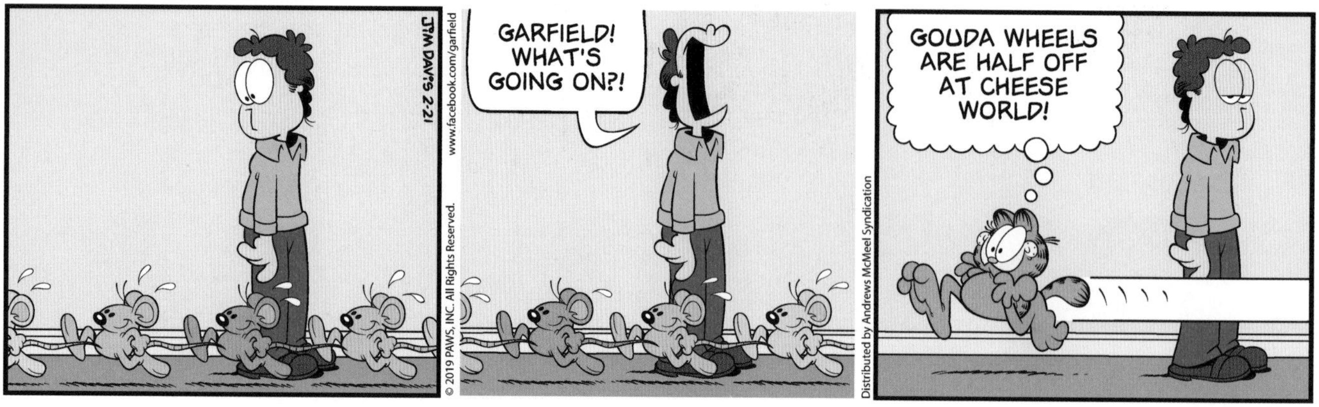
JIM DAVIS 2-21
GARFIELD! WHAT'S GOING ON?!
GOUDA WHEELS ARE HALF OFF AT CHEESE WORLD!
© 2019 PAWS, INC. All Rights Reserved. www.facebook.com/garfield
Distributed by Andrews McMeel Syndication

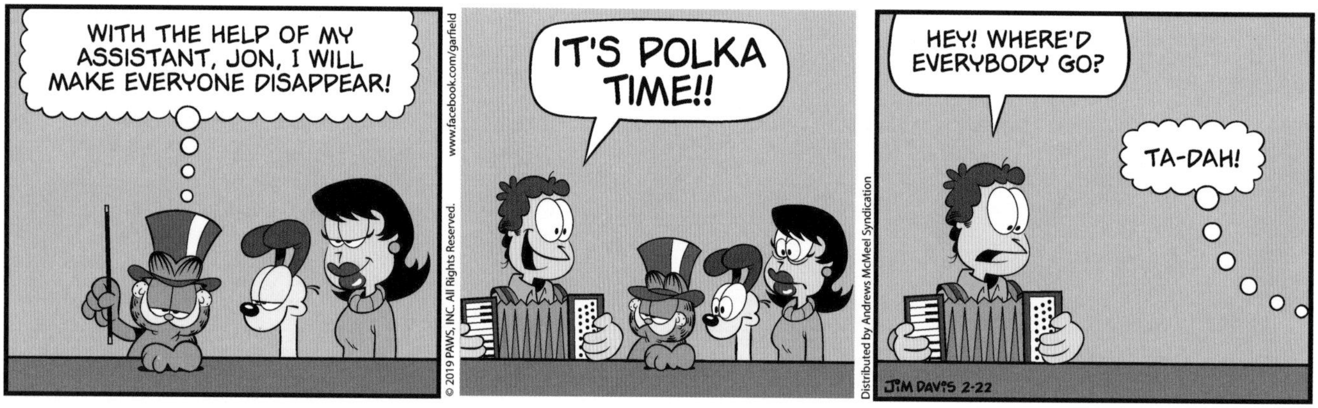
WITH THE HELP OF MY ASSISTANT, JON, I WILL MAKE EVERYONE DISAPPEAR!
IT'S POLKA TIME!!
HEY! WHERE'D EVERYBODY GO?
TA-DAH!
JIM DAVIS 2-22
© 2019 PAWS, INC. All Rights Reserved. www.facebook.com/garfield
Distributed by Andrews McMeel Syndication

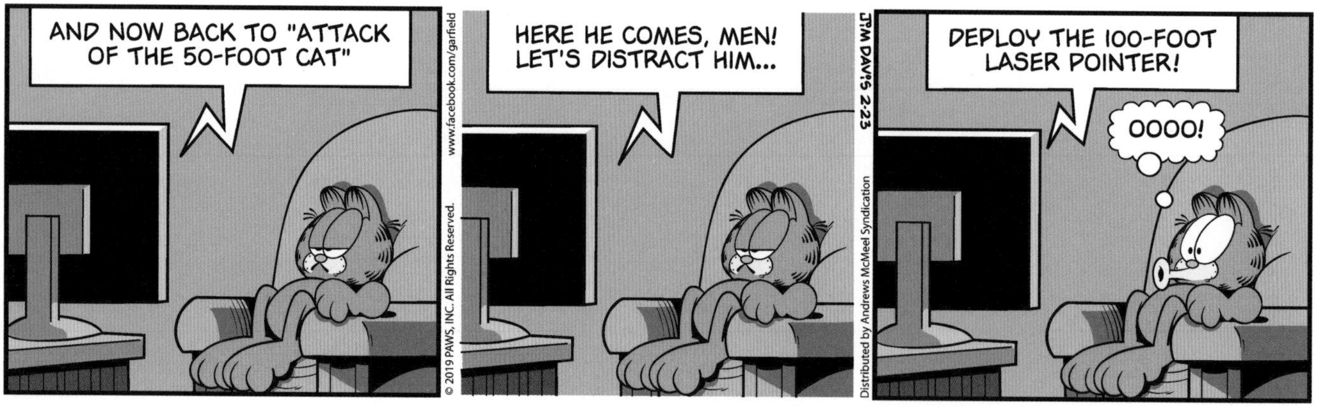
AND NOW BACK TO "ATTACK OF THE 50-FOOT CAT"
HERE HE COMES, MEN! LET'S DISTRACT HIM...
DEPLOY THE 100-FOOT LASER POINTER!
OOOO!
JIM DAVIS 2-23
© 2019 PAWS, INC. All Rights Reserved. www.facebook.com/garfield
Distributed by Andrews McMeel Syndication

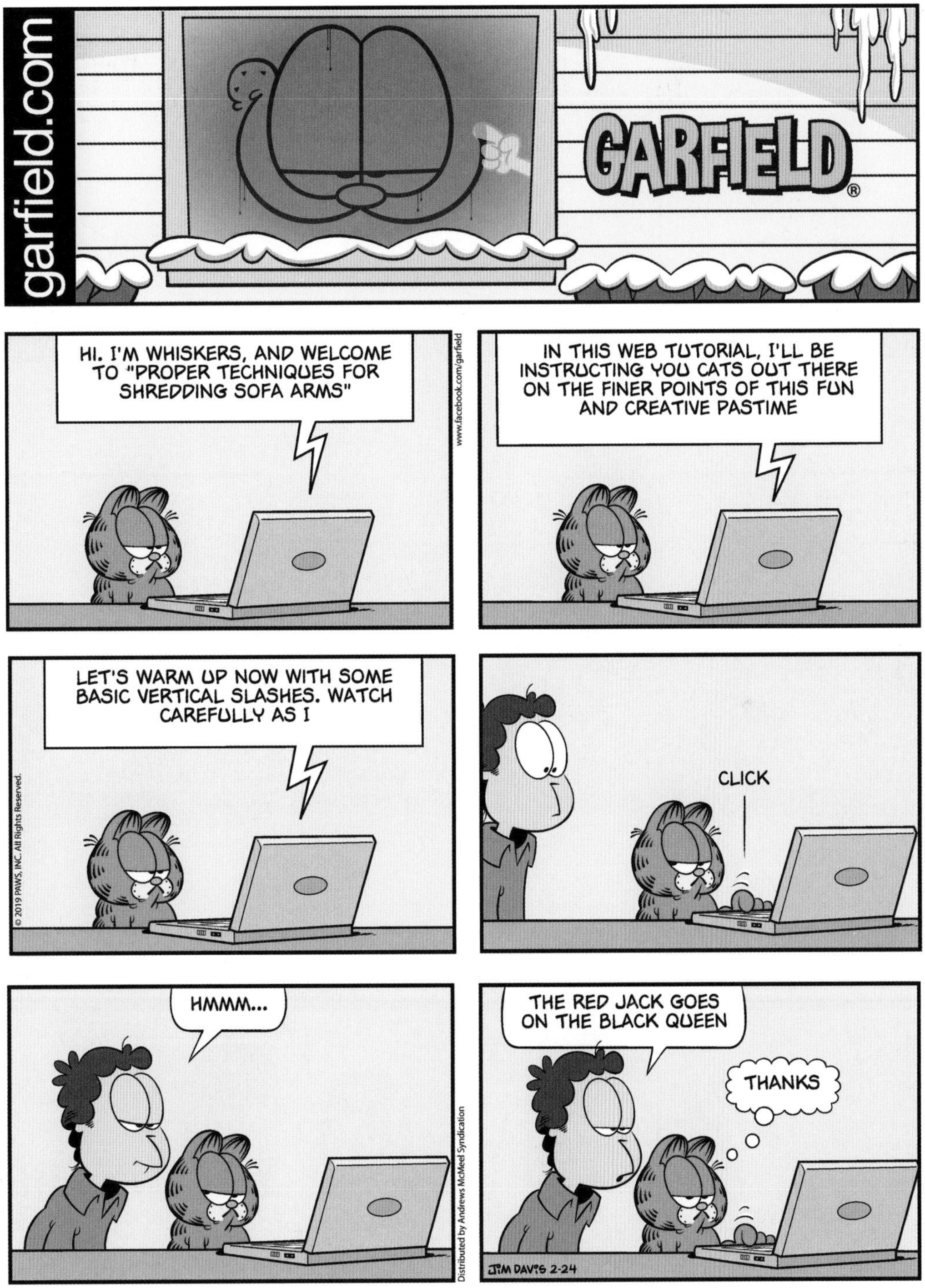
garfield.com
GARFIELD®
HI. I'M WHISKERS, AND WELCOME TO "PROPER TECHNIQUES FOR SHREDDING SOFA ARMS"
www.facebook.com/garfield
IN THIS WEB TUTORIAL, I'LL BE INSTRUCTING YOU CATS OUT THERE ON THE FINER POINTS OF THIS FUN AND CREATIVE PASTIME
LET'S WARM UP NOW WITH SOME BASIC VERTICAL SLASHES. WATCH CAREFULLY AS I
© 2019 PAWS, INC. All Rights Reserved.
CLICK
HMMM...
Distributed by Andrews McMeel Syndication
THE RED JACK GOES ON THE BLACK QUEEN
THANKS
JIM DAVIS 2-24

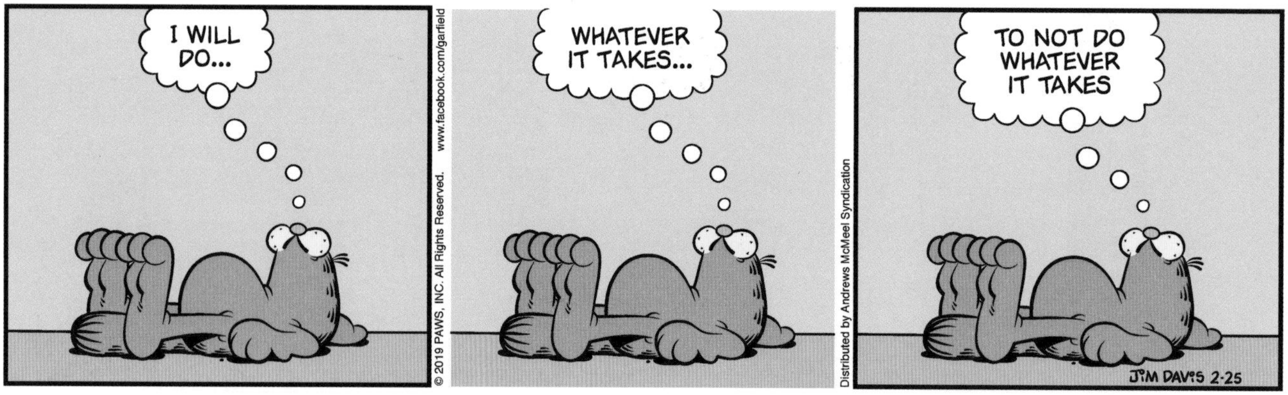
I WILL DO...
WHATEVER IT TAKES...
TO NOT DO WHATEVER IT TAKES
JIM DAVIS 2-25
© 2019 PAWS, INC. All Rights Reserved. www.facebook.com/garfield
Distributed by Andrews McMeel Syndication

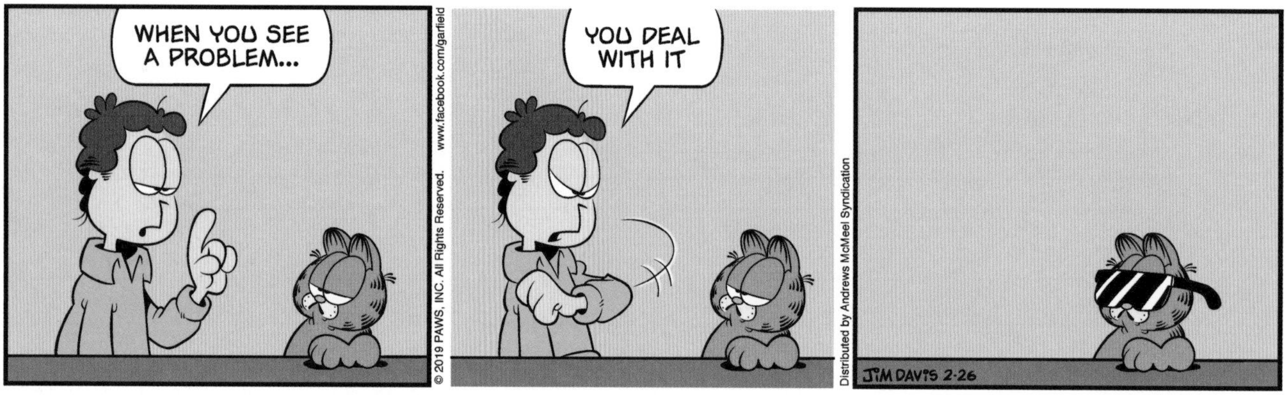
WHEN YOU SEE A PROBLEM...
YOU DEAL WITH IT
JIM DAVIS 2-26
© 2019 PAWS, INC. All Rights Reserved. www.facebook.com/garfield
Distributed by Andrews McMeel Syndication

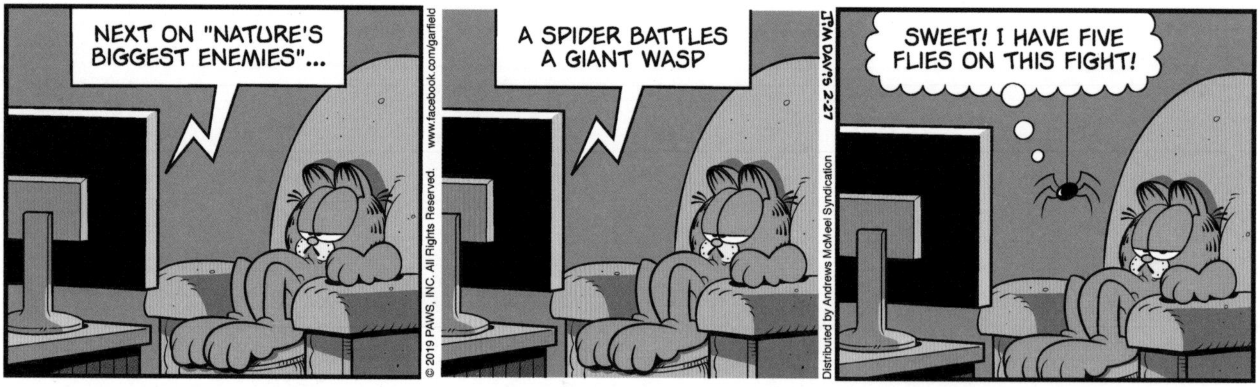
NEXT ON "NATURE'S BIGGEST ENEMIES"...
A SPIDER BATTLES A GIANT WASP
SWEET! I HAVE FIVE FLIES ON THIS FIGHT!
JIM DAVIS 2-27
© 2019 PAWS, INC. All Rights Reserved. www.facebook.com/garfield
Distributed by Andrews McMeel Syndication

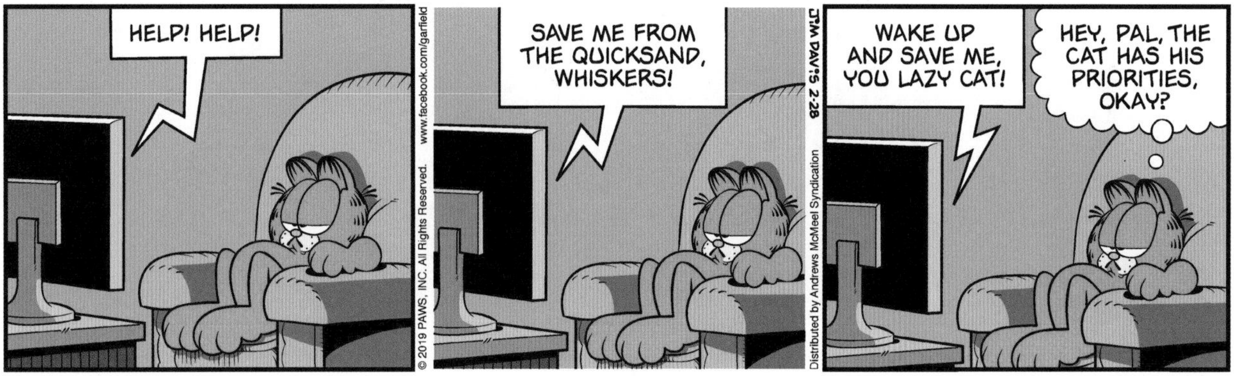
HELP! HELP!
SAVE ME FROM THE QUICKSAND, WHISKERS!
JIM DAVIS 2-28
WAKE UP AND SAVE ME, YOU LAZY CAT!
HEY, PAL, THE CAT HAS HIS PRIORITIES, OKAY?

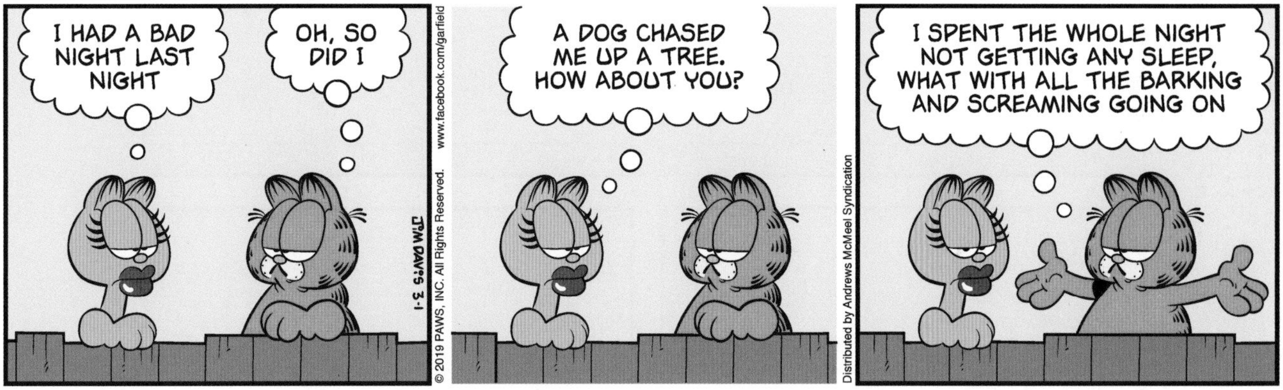
I HAD A BAD NIGHT LAST NIGHT
OH, SO DID I
JIM DAVIS 3-1
A DOG CHASED ME UP A TREE. HOW ABOUT YOU?
I SPENT THE WHOLE NIGHT NOT GETTING ANY SLEEP, WHAT WITH ALL THE BARKING AND SCREAMING GOING ON

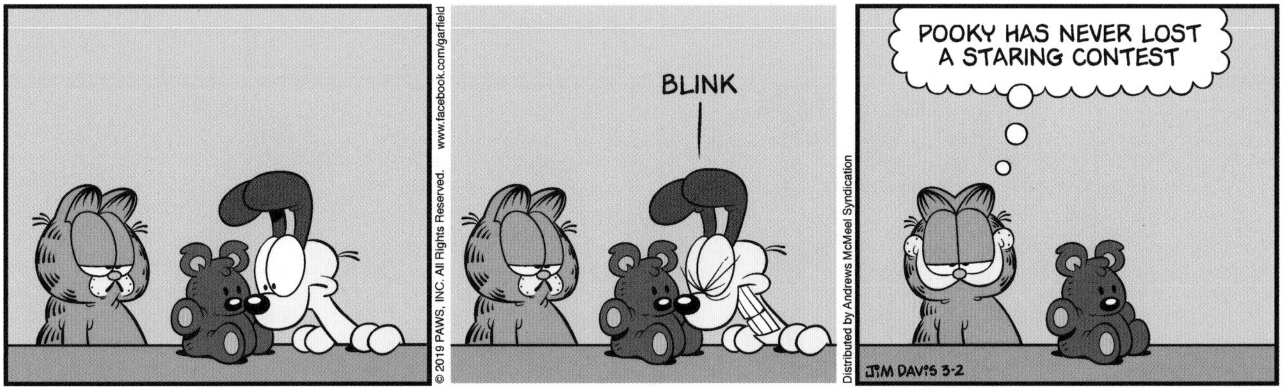
BLINK
POOKY HAS NEVER LOST A STARING CONTEST
JIM DAVIS 3-2

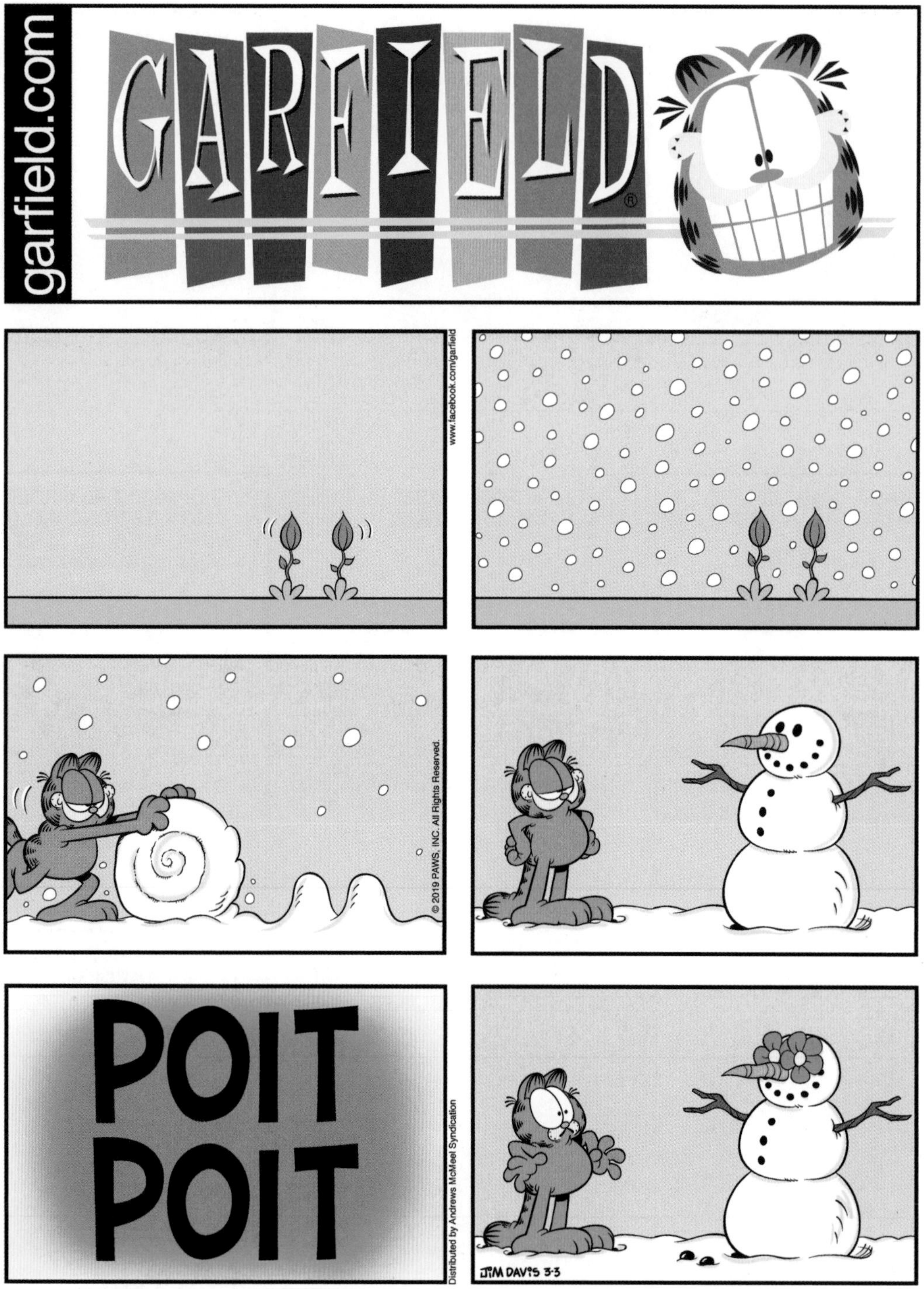
garfield.com
GARFIELD®
www.facebook.com/garfield
© 2019 PAWS, INC. All Rights Reserved.
POIT
POIT
Distributed by Andrews McMeel Syndication
JIM DAVIS 3-3

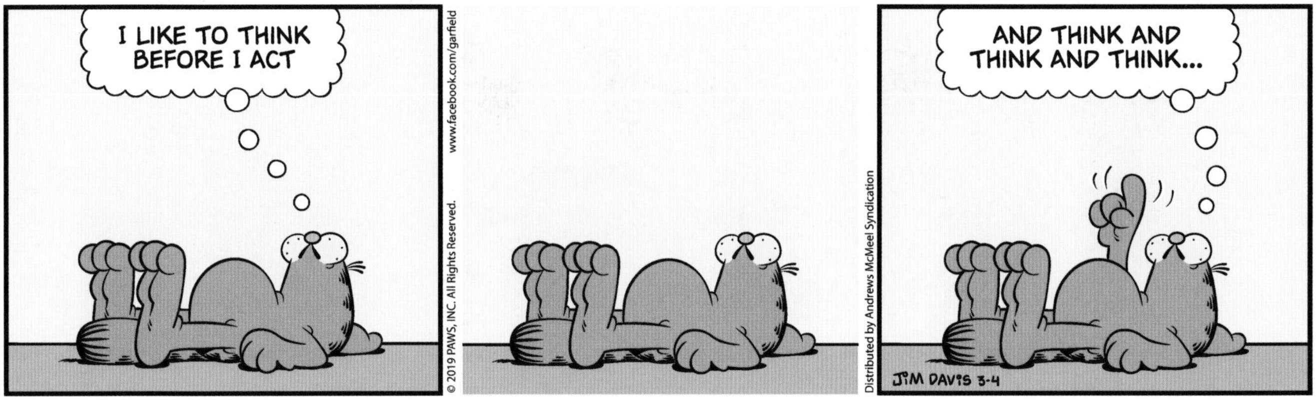
I LIKE TO THINK BEFORE I ACT
AND THINK AND THINK AND THINK...
JIM DAVIS 3-4
© 2019 PAWS, INC. All Rights Reserved. www.facebook.com/garfield
Distributed by Andrews McMeel Syndication

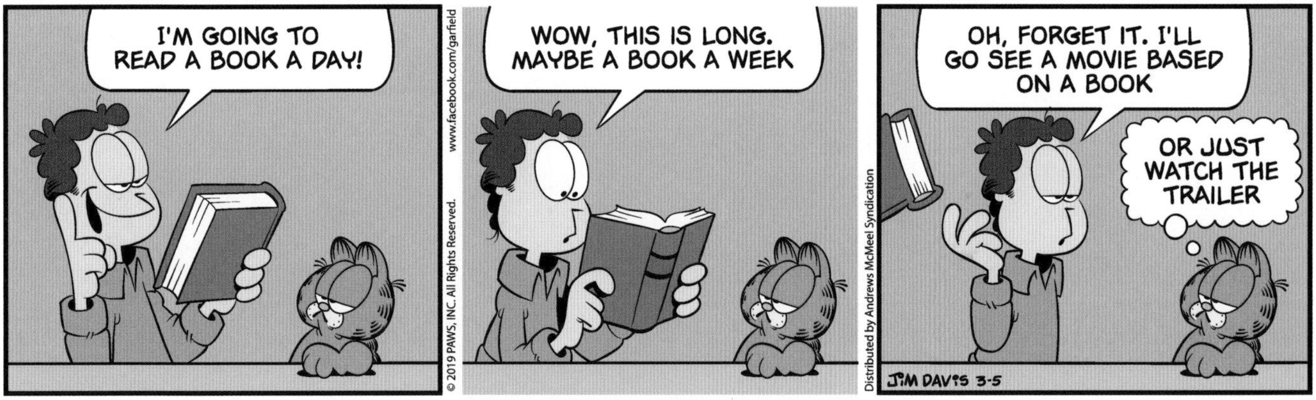
I'M GOING TO READ A BOOK A DAY!
WOW, THIS IS LONG. MAYBE A BOOK A WEEK
OH, FORGET IT. I'LL GO SEE A MOVIE BASED ON A BOOK
OR JUST WATCH THE TRAILER
JIM DAVIS 3-5
© 2019 PAWS, INC. All Rights Reserved. www.facebook.com/garfield
Distributed by Andrews McMeel Syndication

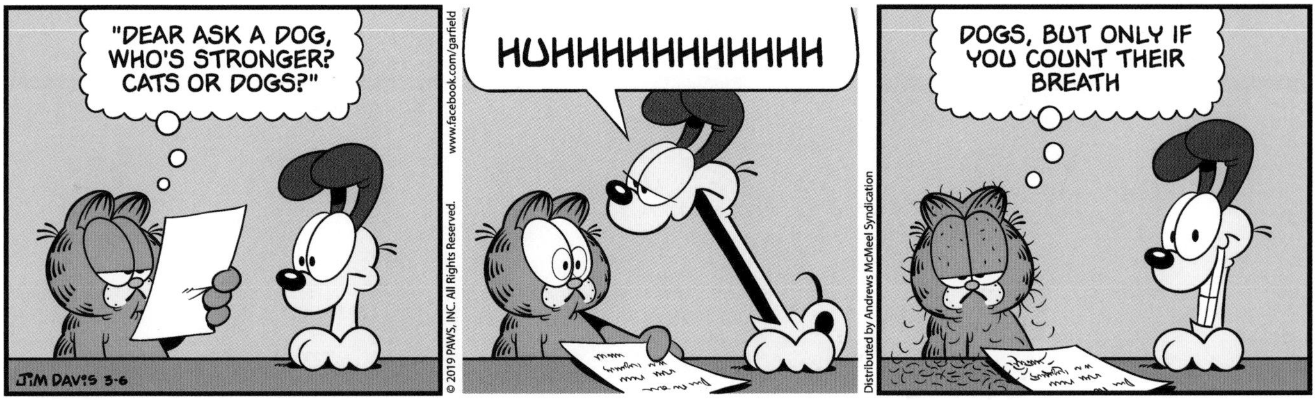
"DEAR ASK A DOG, WHO'S STRONGER? CATS OR DOGS?"
JIM DAVIS 3-6
HUHHHHHHHHHHH
DOGS, BUT ONLY IF YOU COUNT THEIR BREATH
© 2019 PAWS, INC. All Rights Reserved. www.facebook.com/garfield
Distributed by Andrews McMeel Syndication

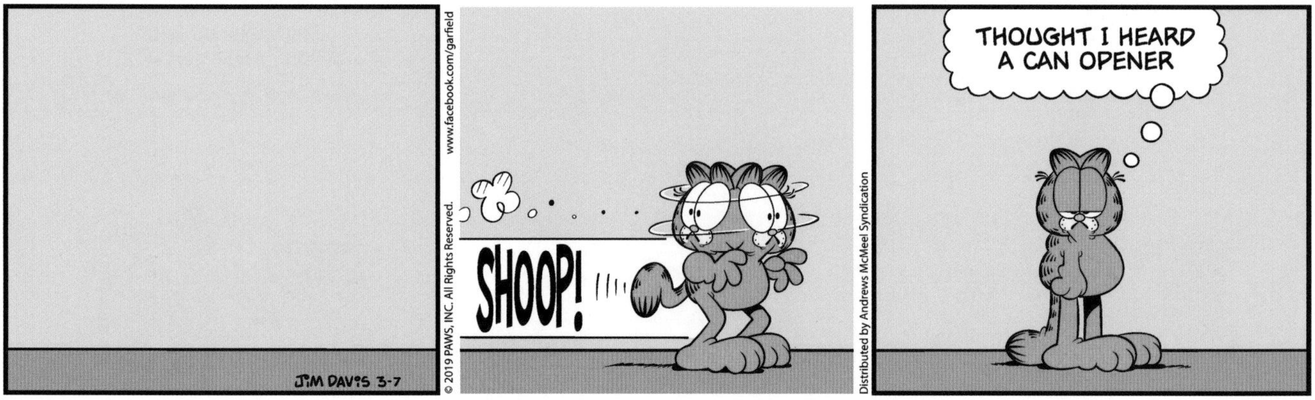
JIM DAVIS 3-7
© 2019 PAWS, INC. All Rights Reserved.
www.facebook.com/garfield
SHOOP!
Distributed by Andrews McMeel Syndication
THOUGHT I HEARD A CAN OPENER

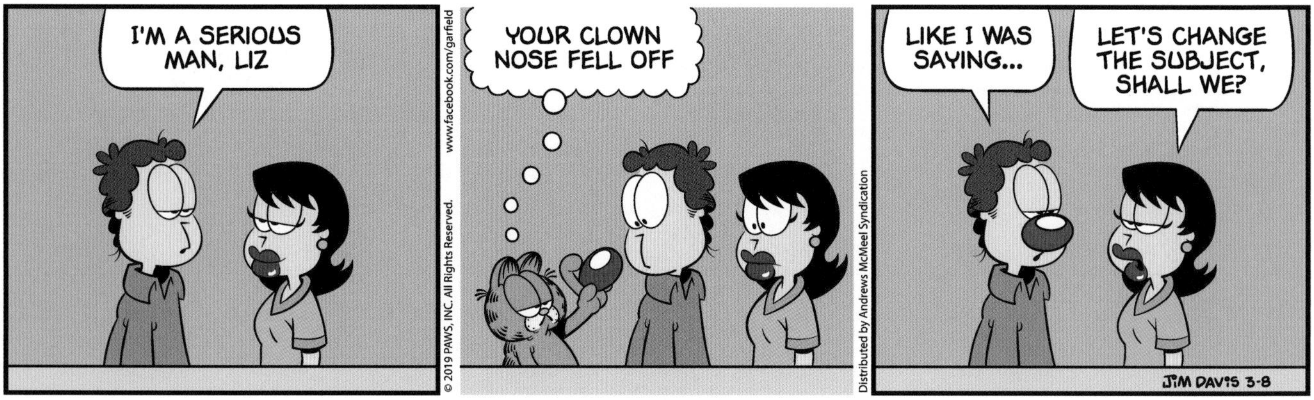
I'M A SERIOUS MAN, LIZ
© 2019 PAWS, INC. All Rights Reserved.
www.facebook.com/garfield
YOUR CLOWN NOSE FELL OFF
Distributed by Andrews McMeel Syndication
LIKE I WAS SAYING...
LET'S CHANGE THE SUBJECT, SHALL WE?
JIM DAVIS 3-8

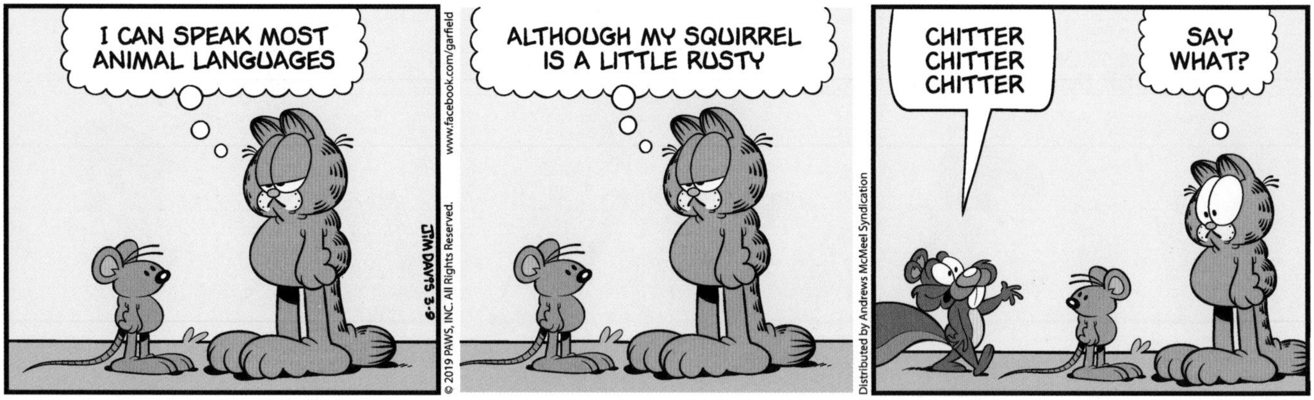
I CAN SPEAK MOST ANIMAL LANGUAGES
JIM DAVIS 3-9
© 2019 PAWS, INC. All Rights Reserved.
www.facebook.com/garfield
ALTHOUGH MY SQUIRREL IS A LITTLE RUSTY
Distributed by Andrews McMeel Syndication
CHITTER CHITTER CHITTER
SAY WHAT?

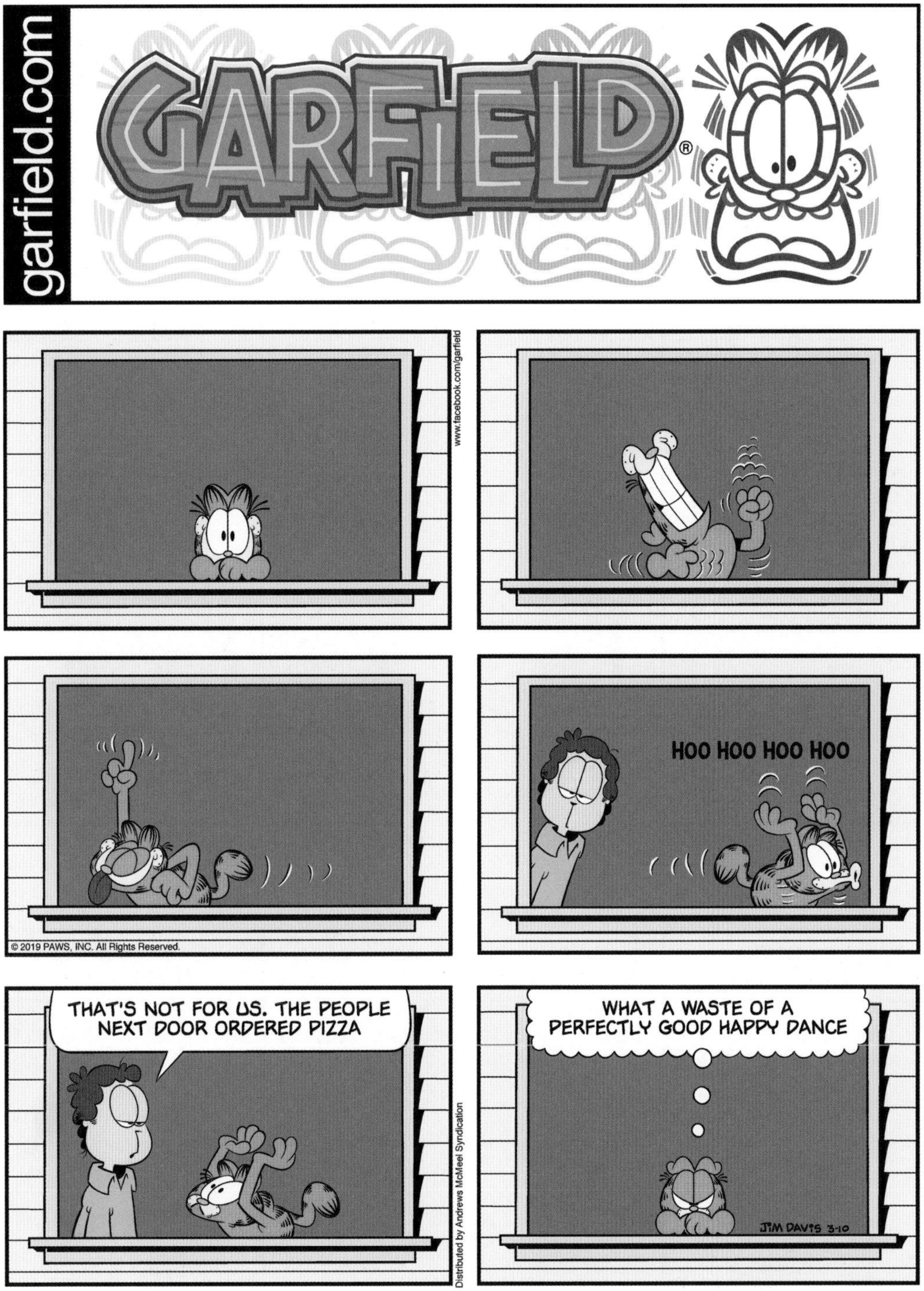
garfield.com
GARFIELD®
www.facebook.com/garfield
HOO HOO HOO HOO
© 2019 PAWS, INC. All Rights Reserved.
THAT'S NOT FOR US. THE PEOPLE NEXT DOOR ORDERED PIZZA
Distributed by Andrews McMeel Syndication
WHAT A WASTE OF A PERFECTLY GOOD HAPPY DANCE
JIM DAVIS 3-10

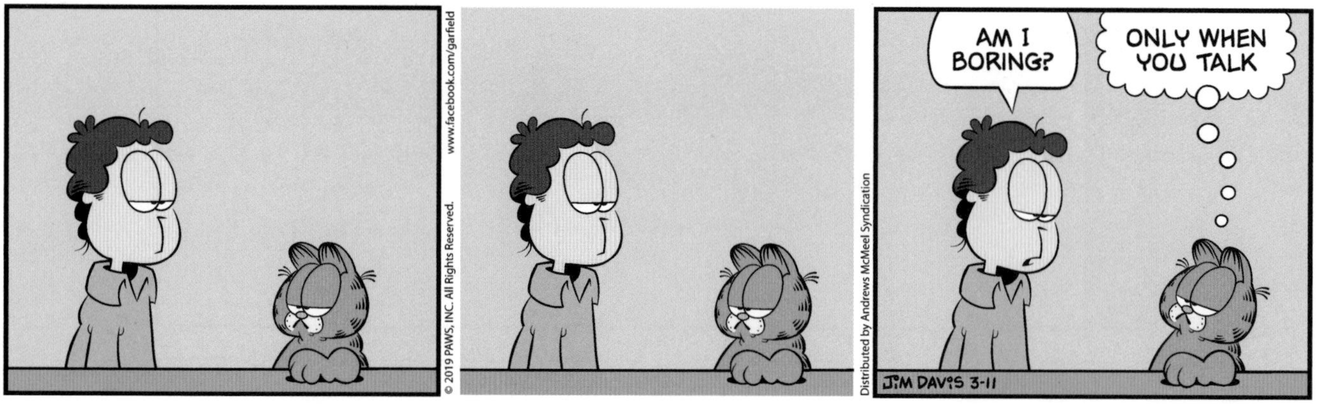
© 2019 PAWS, INC. All Rights Reserved.
www.facebook.com/garfield
Distributed by Andrews McMeel Syndication
AM I BORING?
ONLY WHEN YOU TALK
JIM DAVIS 3-11

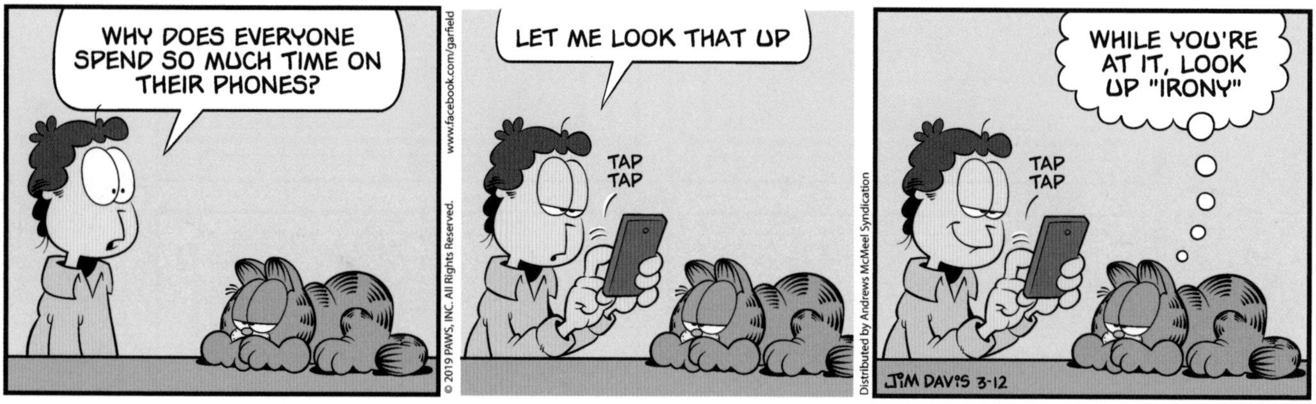
WHY DOES EVERYONE SPEND SO MUCH TIME ON THEIR PHONES?
© 2019 PAWS, INC. All Rights Reserved.
www.facebook.com/garfield
LET ME LOOK THAT UP
TAP TAP
Distributed by Andrews McMeel Syndication
WHILE YOU'RE AT IT, LOOK UP "IRONY"
TAP TAP
JIM DAVIS 3-12

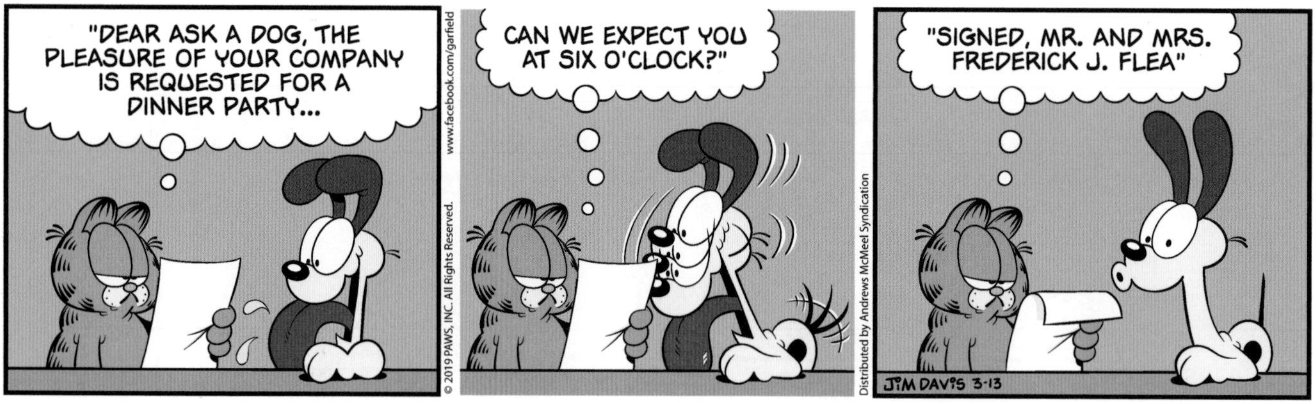
"DEAR ASK A DOG, THE PLEASURE OF YOUR COMPANY IS REQUESTED FOR A DINNER PARTY...
© 2019 PAWS, INC. All Rights Reserved.
www.facebook.com/garfield
CAN WE EXPECT YOU AT SIX O'CLOCK?"
Distributed by Andrews McMeel Syndication
"SIGNED, MR. AND MRS. FREDERICK J. FLEA"
JIM DAVIS 3-13

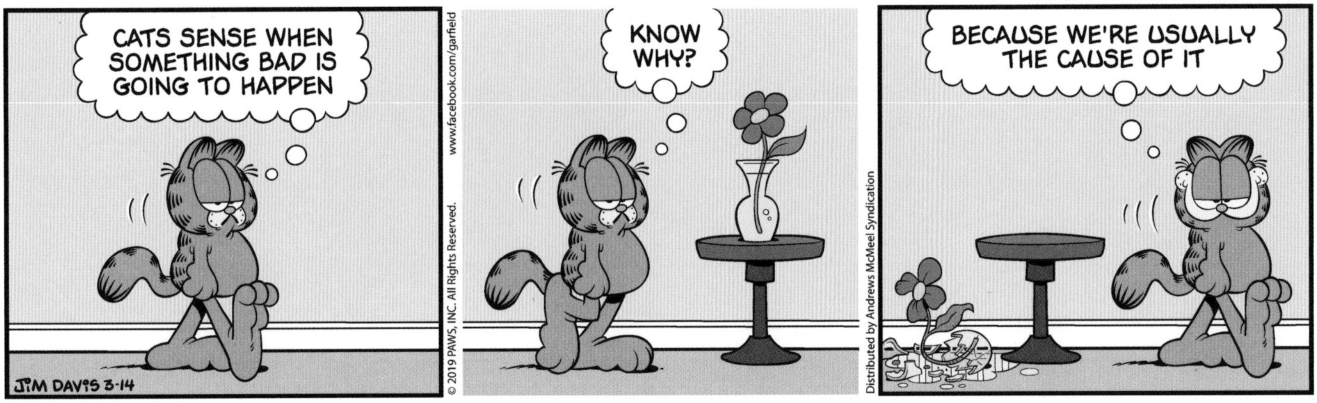
CATS SENSE WHEN SOMETHING BAD IS GOING TO HAPPEN
KNOW WHY?
BECAUSE WE'RE USUALLY THE CAUSE OF IT
JIM DAVIS 3-14
© 2019 PAWS, INC. All Rights Reserved. www.facebook.com/garfield
Distributed by Andrews McMeel Syndication

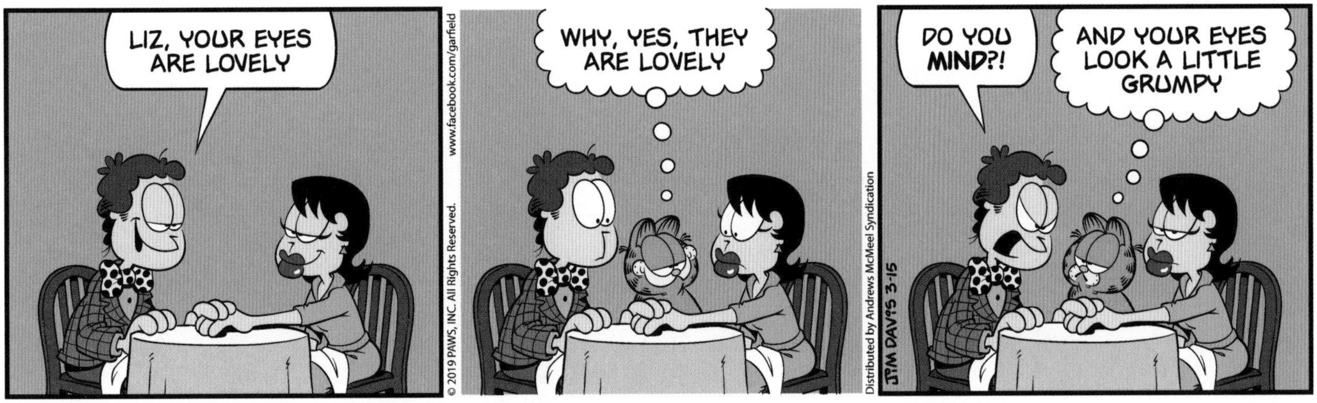
LIZ, YOUR EYES ARE LOVELY
WHY, YES, THEY ARE LOVELY
DO YOU **MIND**?!
AND YOUR EYES LOOK A LITTLE GRUMPY
JIM DAVIS 3-15
© 2019 PAWS, INC. All Rights Reserved. www.facebook.com/garfield
Distributed by Andrews McMeel Syndication

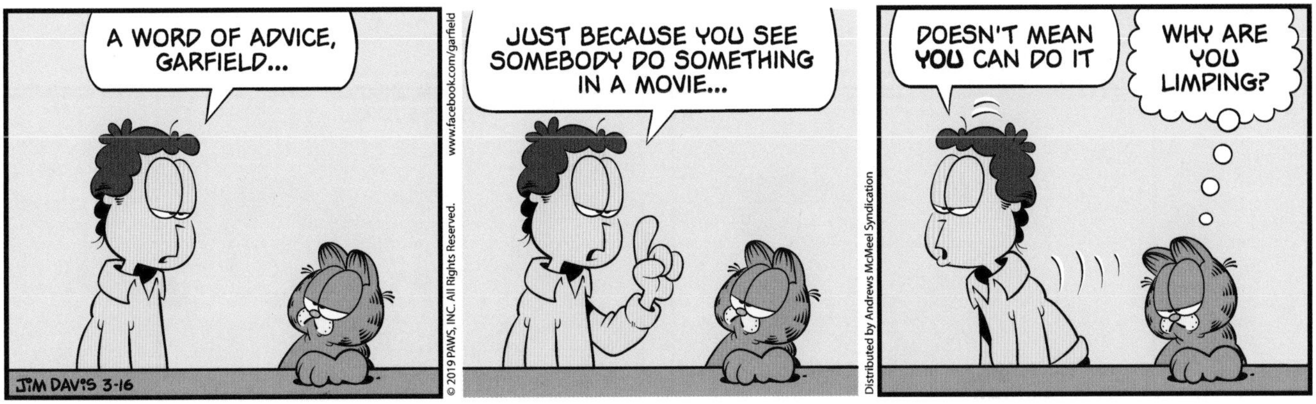
A WORD OF ADVICE, GARFIELD...
JUST BECAUSE YOU SEE SOMEBODY DO SOMETHING IN A MOVIE...
DOESN'T MEAN **YOU** CAN DO IT
WHY ARE YOU LIMPING?
JIM DAVIS 3-16
© 2019 PAWS, INC. All Rights Reserved. www.facebook.com/garfield
Distributed by Andrews McMeel Syndication

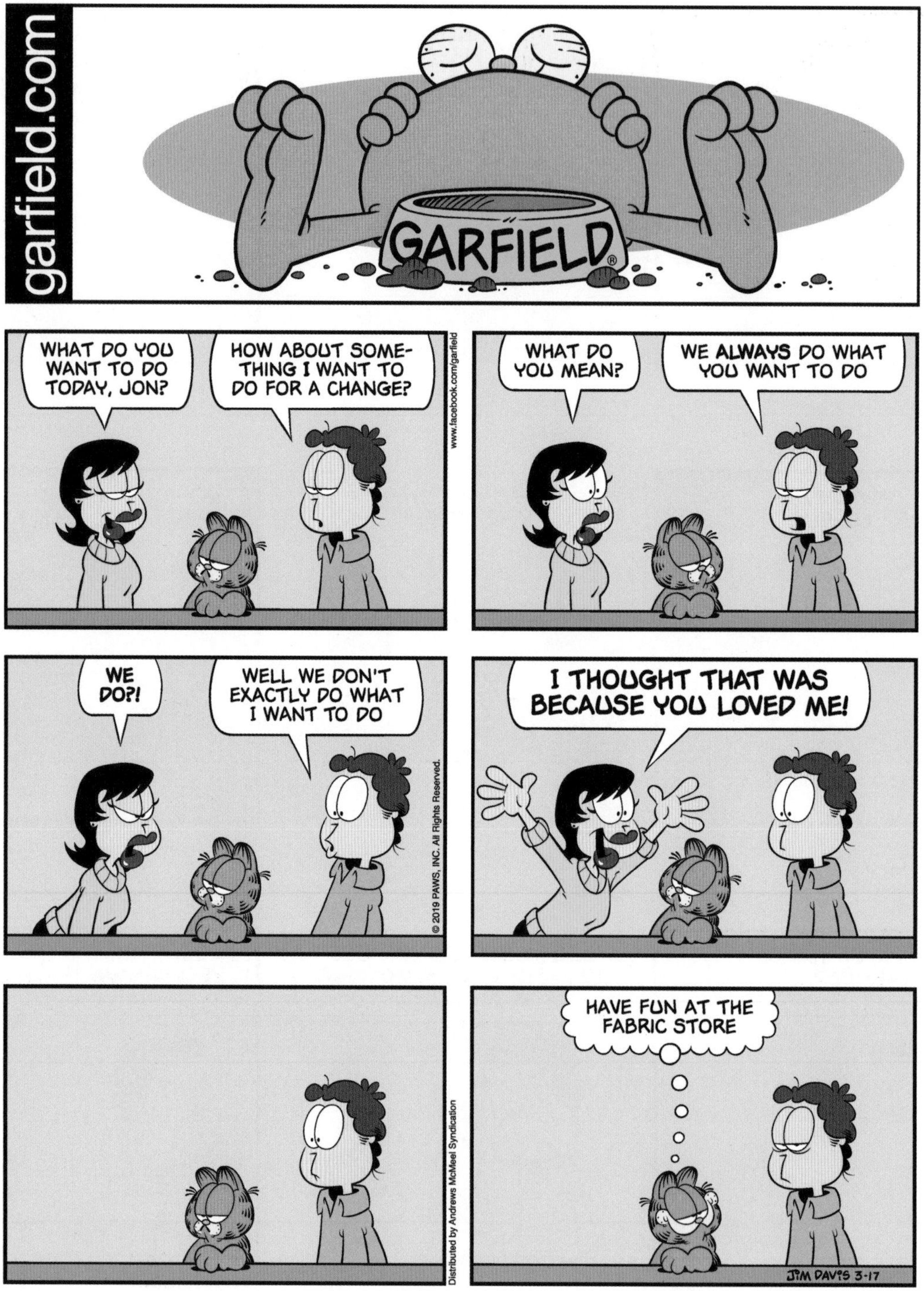
garfield.com
GARFIELD®
WHAT DO YOU WANT TO DO TODAY, JON?
HOW ABOUT SOME-THING I WANT TO DO FOR A CHANGE?
WHAT DO YOU MEAN?
WE ALWAYS DO WHAT YOU WANT TO DO
WE DO?!
WELL WE DON'T EXACTLY DO WHAT I WANT TO DO
I THOUGHT THAT WAS BECAUSE YOU LOVED ME!
HAVE FUN AT THE FABRIC STORE
JIM DAVIS 3-17
www.facebook.com/garfield
© 2019 PAWS, INC. All Rights Reserved.
Distributed by Andrews McMeel Syndication

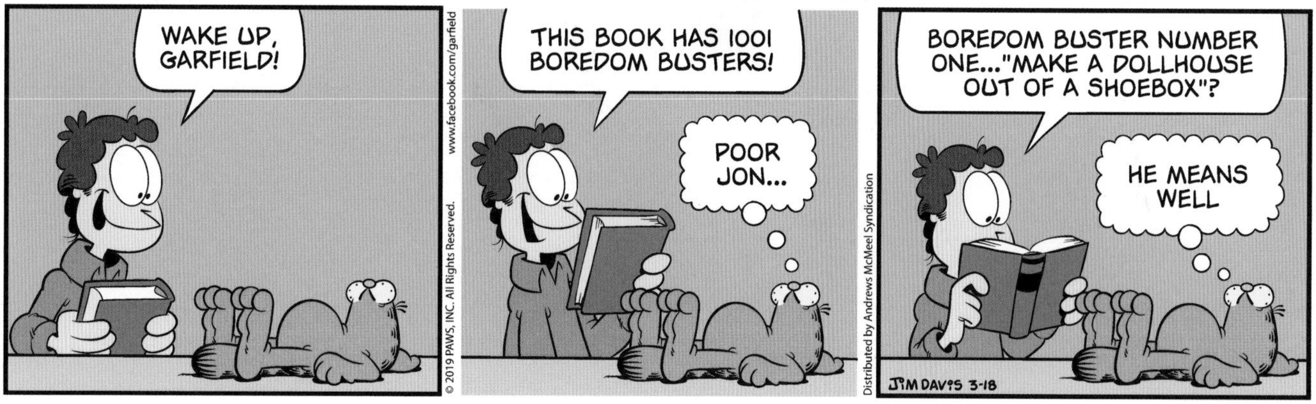
WAKE UP, GARFIELD!
THIS BOOK HAS 1001 BOREDOM BUSTERS!
POOR JON...
BOREDOM BUSTER NUMBER ONE..."MAKE A DOLLHOUSE OUT OF A SHOEBOX"?
HE MEANS WELL
JIM DAVIS 3-18
© 2019 PAWS, INC. All Rights Reserved. www.facebook.com/garfield
Distributed by Andrews McMeel Syndication

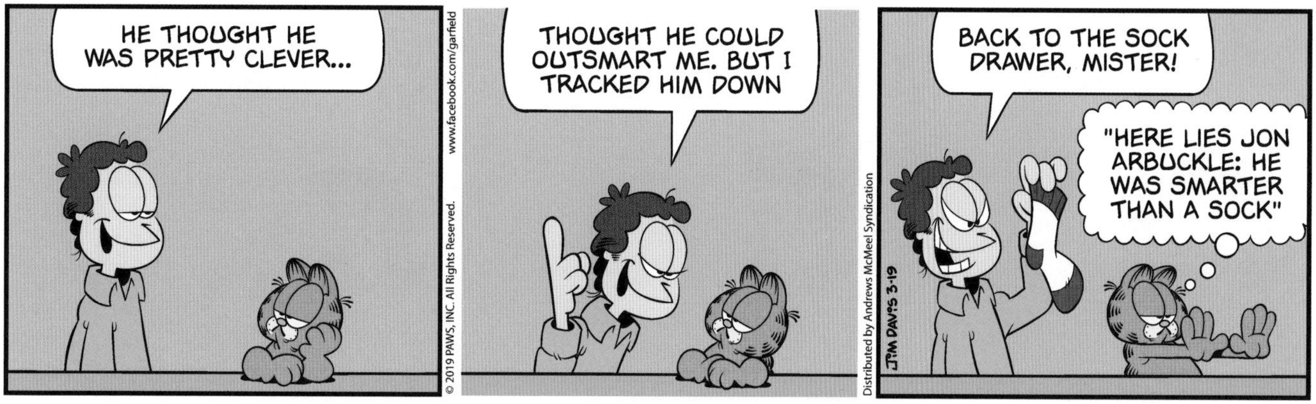
HE THOUGHT HE WAS PRETTY CLEVER...
THOUGHT HE COULD OUTSMART ME. BUT I TRACKED HIM DOWN
BACK TO THE SOCK DRAWER, MISTER!
"HERE LIES JON ARBUCKLE: HE WAS SMARTER THAN A SOCK"
JIM DAVIS 3-19
© 2019 PAWS, INC. All Rights Reserved. www.facebook.com/garfield
Distributed by Andrews McMeel Syndication

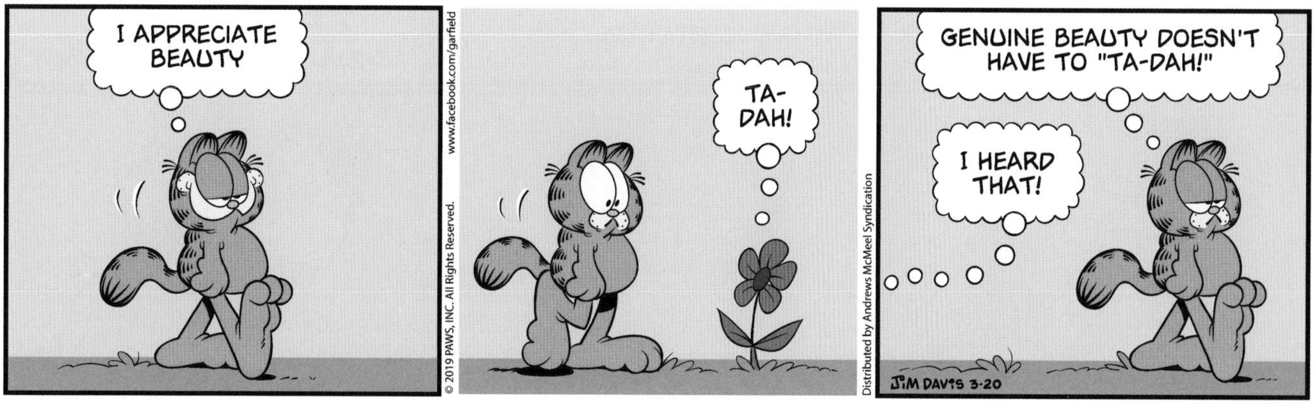
I APPRECIATE BEAUTY
TA-DAH!
GENUINE BEAUTY DOESN'T HAVE TO "TA-DAH!"
I HEARD THAT!
JIM DAVIS 3-20
© 2019 PAWS, INC. All Rights Reserved. www.facebook.com/garfield
Distributed by Andrews McMeel Syndication

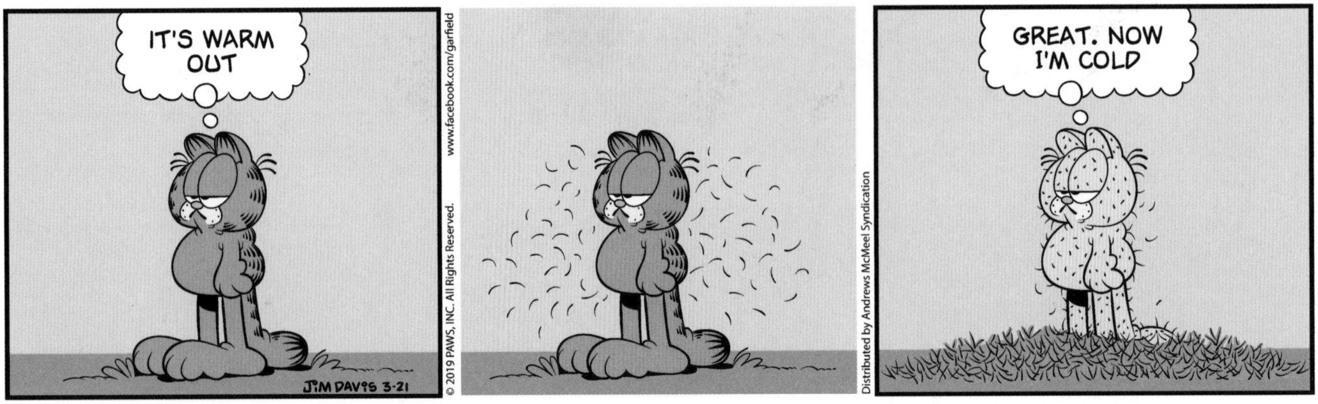
IT'S WARM OUT
GREAT. NOW I'M COLD
JIM DAVIS 3-21
© 2019 PAWS, INC. All Rights Reserved. www.facebook.com/garfield
Distributed by Andrews McMeel Syndication

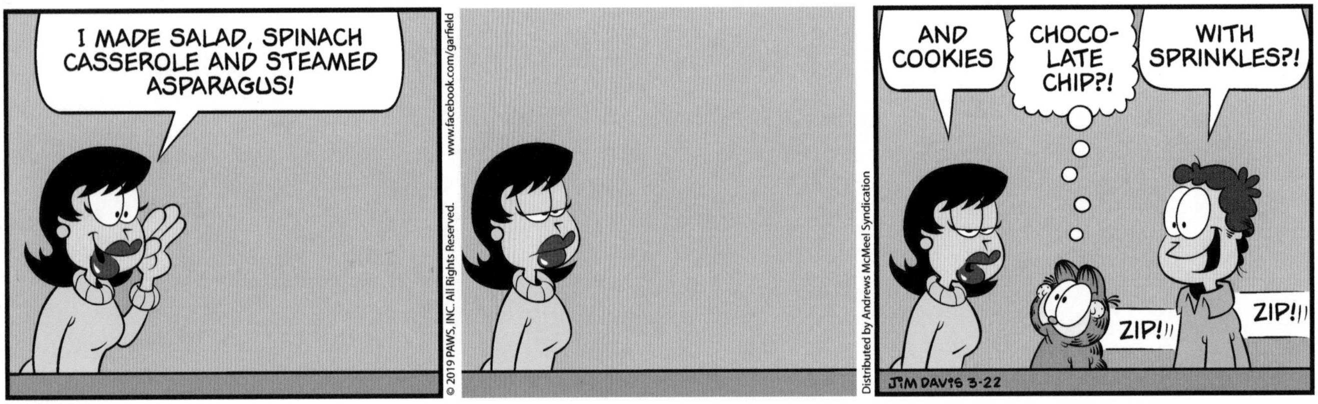
I MADE SALAD, SPINACH CASSEROLE AND STEAMED ASPARAGUS!
AND COOKIES
CHOCO-LATE CHIP?!
WITH SPRINKLES?!
ZIP!
ZIP!
JIM DAVIS 3-22
© 2019 PAWS, INC. All Rights Reserved. www.facebook.com/garfield
Distributed by Andrews McMeel Syndication

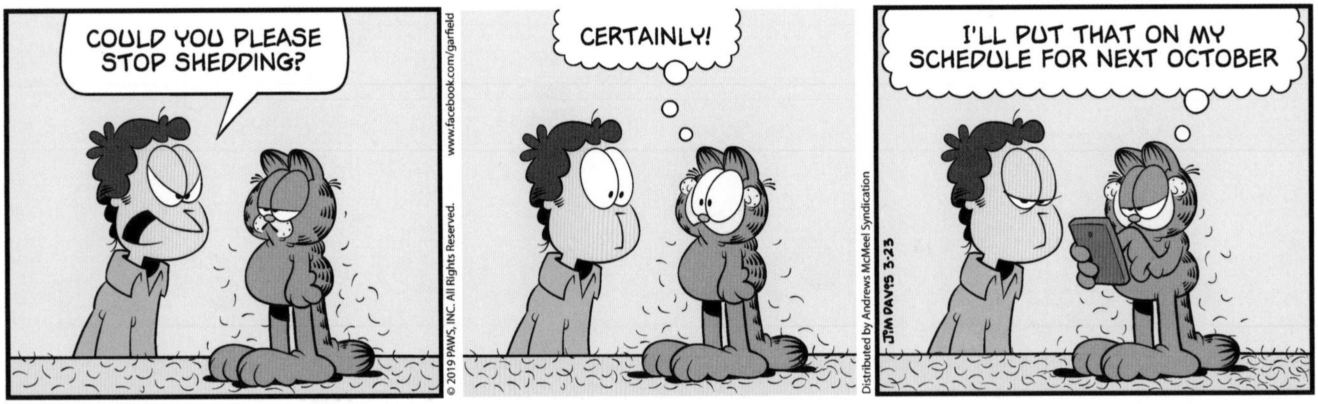
COULD YOU PLEASE STOP SHEDDING?
CERTAINLY!
I'LL PUT THAT ON MY SCHEDULE FOR NEXT OCTOBER
JIM DAVIS 3-23
© 2019 PAWS, INC. All Rights Reserved. www.facebook.com/garfield
Distributed by Andrews McMeel Syndication

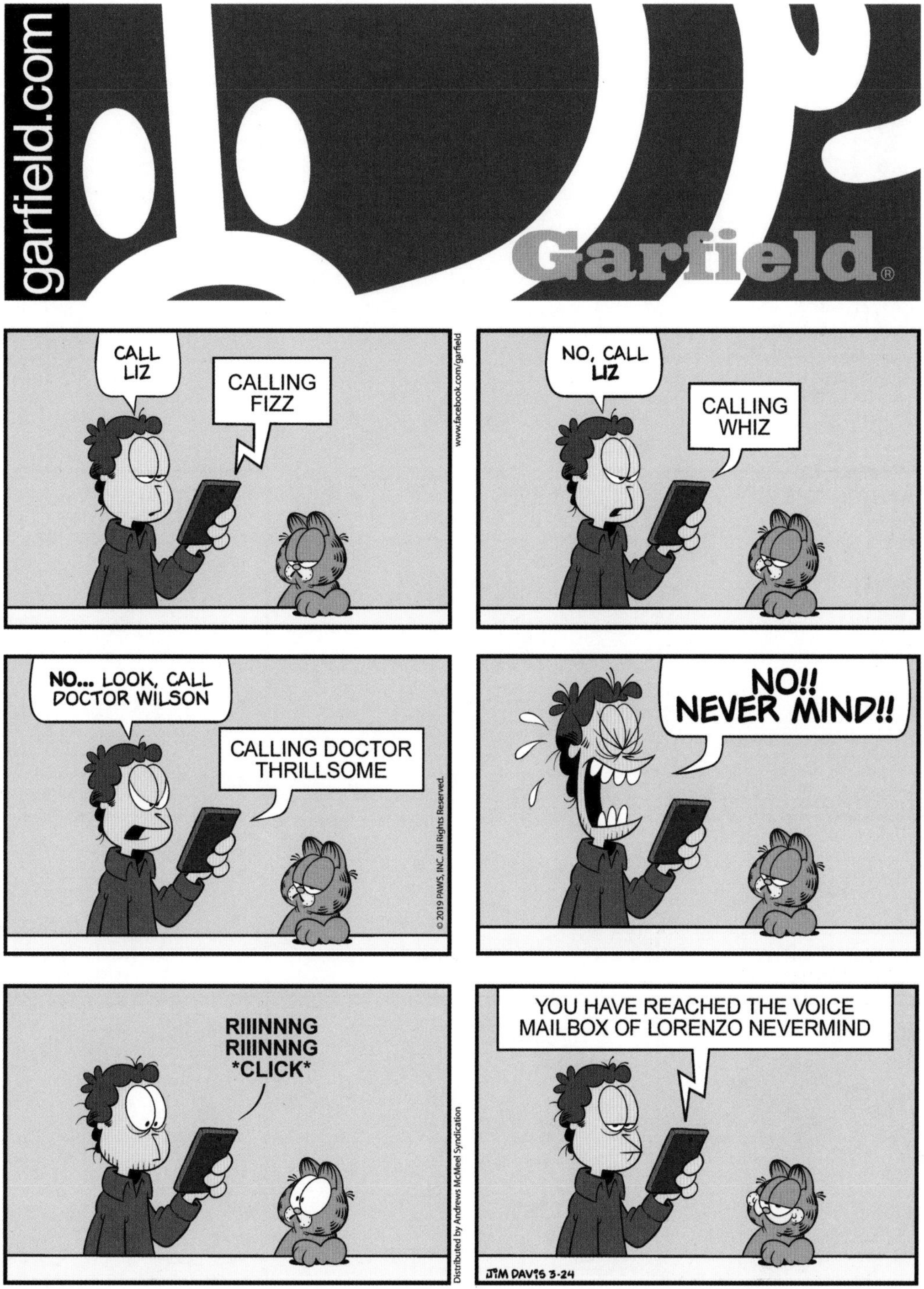
garfield.com
Garfield®
CALL LIZ
CALLING FIZZ
www.facebook.com/garfield
NO, CALL LIZ
CALLING WHIZ
NO... LOOK, CALL DOCTOR WILSON
CALLING DOCTOR THRILLSOME
© 2019 PAWS, INC. All Rights Reserved.
NO!! NEVER MIND!!
RIIINNNG
RIIINNNG
CLICK
Distributed by Andrews McMeel Syndication
YOU HAVE REACHED THE VOICE MAILBOX OF LORENZO NEVERMIND
JIM DAVIS 3-24

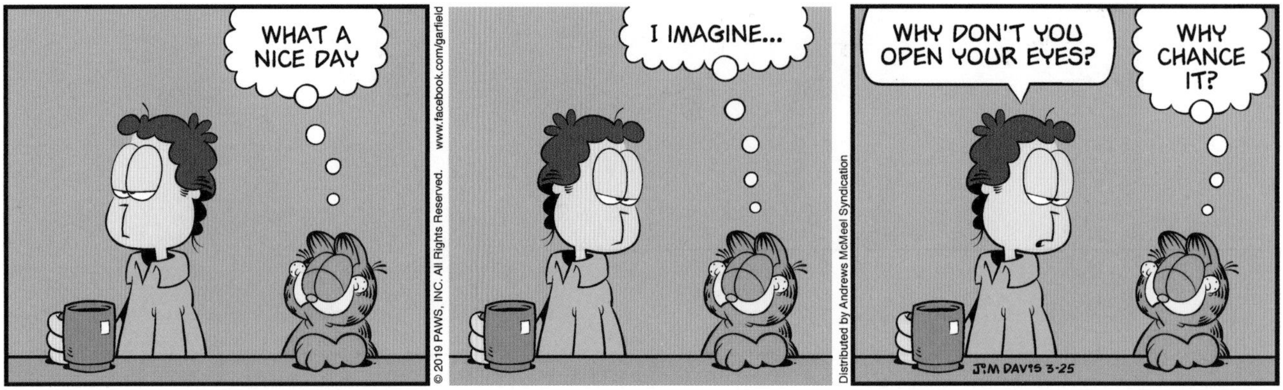
WHAT A NICE DAY
I IMAGINE...
WHY DON'T YOU OPEN YOUR EYES?
WHY CHANCE IT?
JIM DAVIS 3-25
© 2019 PAWS, INC. All Rights Reserved. www.facebook.com/garfield
Distributed by Andrews McMeel Syndication

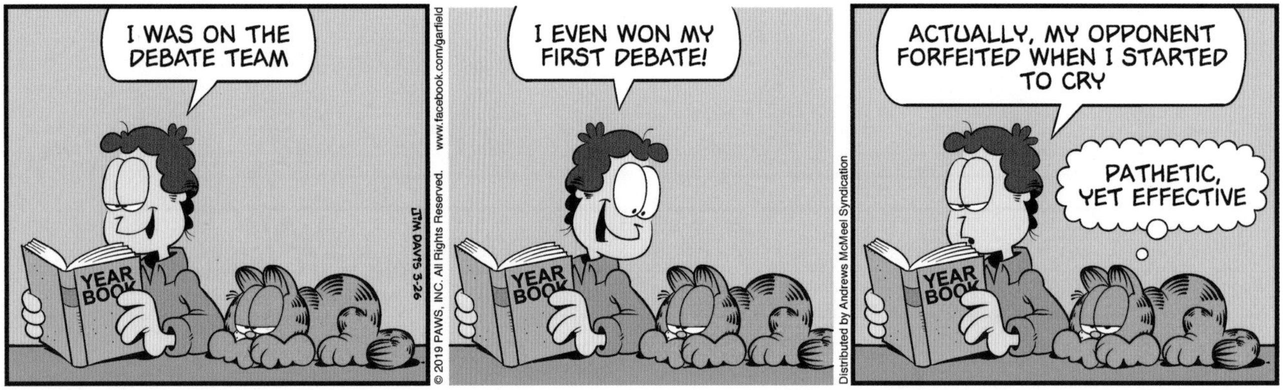
I WAS ON THE DEBATE TEAM
YEAR BOOK
JIM DAVIS 3-26
I EVEN WON MY FIRST DEBATE!
ACTUALLY, MY OPPONENT FORFEITED WHEN I STARTED TO CRY
PATHETIC, YET EFFECTIVE
© 2019 PAWS, INC. All Rights Reserved. www.facebook.com/garfield
Distributed by Andrews McMeel Syndication

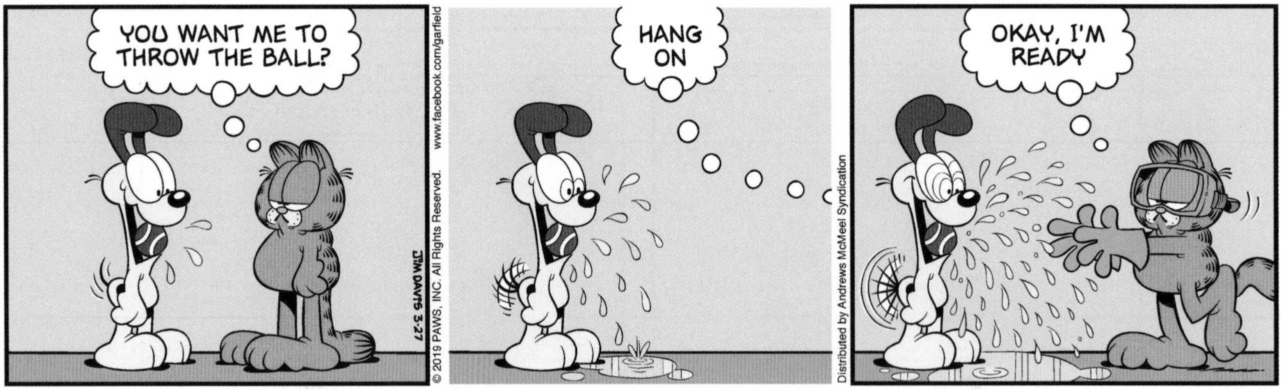
YOU WANT ME TO THROW THE BALL?
JIM DAVIS 3-27
HANG ON
OKAY, I'M READY
© 2019 PAWS, INC. All Rights Reserved. www.facebook.com/garfield
Distributed by Andrews McMeel Syndication

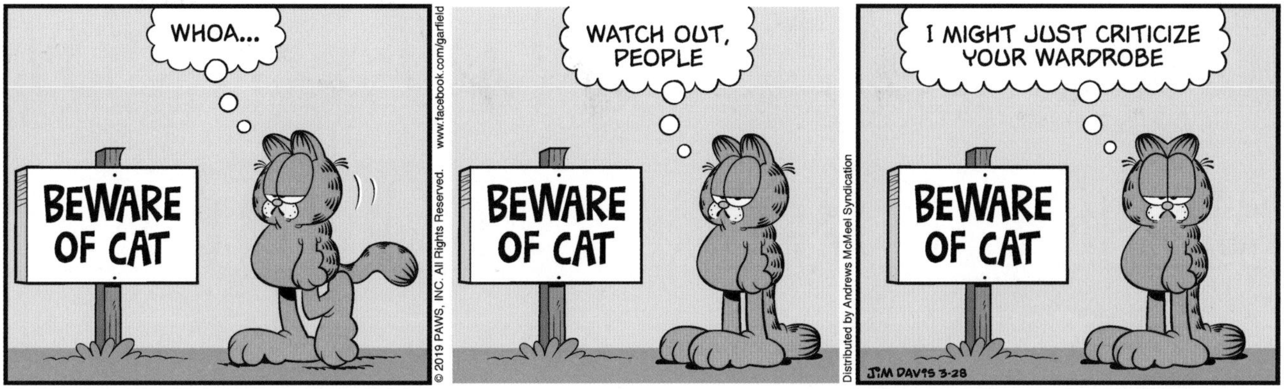
WHOA...
BEWARE OF CAT
© 2019 PAWS, INC. All Rights Reserved. www.facebook.com/garfield
WATCH OUT, PEOPLE
BEWARE OF CAT
Distributed by Andrews McMeel Syndication
I MIGHT JUST CRITICIZE YOUR WARDROBE
BEWARE OF CAT
JIM DAVIS 3-28

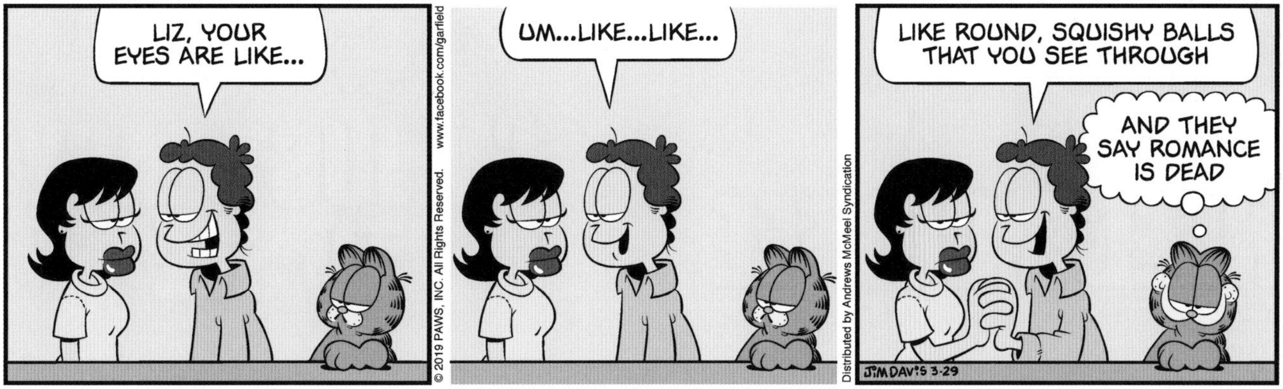
LIZ, YOUR EYES ARE LIKE...
© 2019 PAWS, INC. All Rights Reserved. www.facebook.com/garfield
UM...LIKE...LIKE...
Distributed by Andrews McMeel Syndication
LIKE ROUND, SQUISHY BALLS THAT YOU SEE THROUGH
AND THEY SAY ROMANCE IS DEAD
JIM DAVIS 3-29

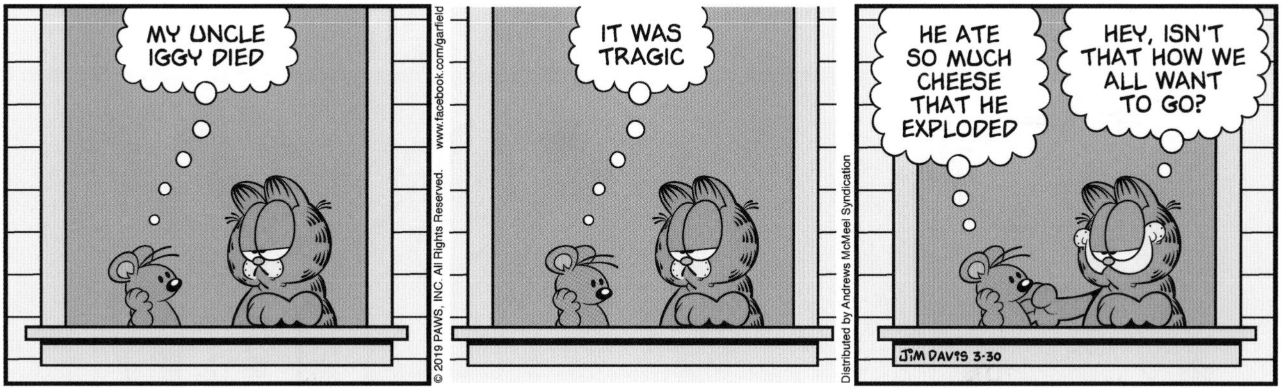
MY UNCLE IGGY DIED
© 2019 PAWS, INC. All Rights Reserved. www.facebook.com/garfield
IT WAS TRAGIC
Distributed by Andrews McMeel Syndication
HE ATE SO MUCH CHEESE THAT HE EXPLODED
HEY, ISN'T THAT HOW WE ALL WANT TO GO?
JIM DAVIS 3-30

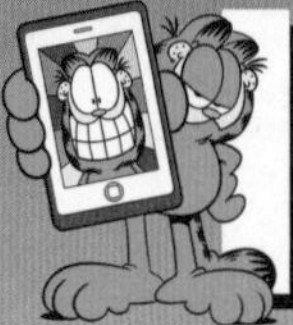

IT'S ALL ABOUT MEME

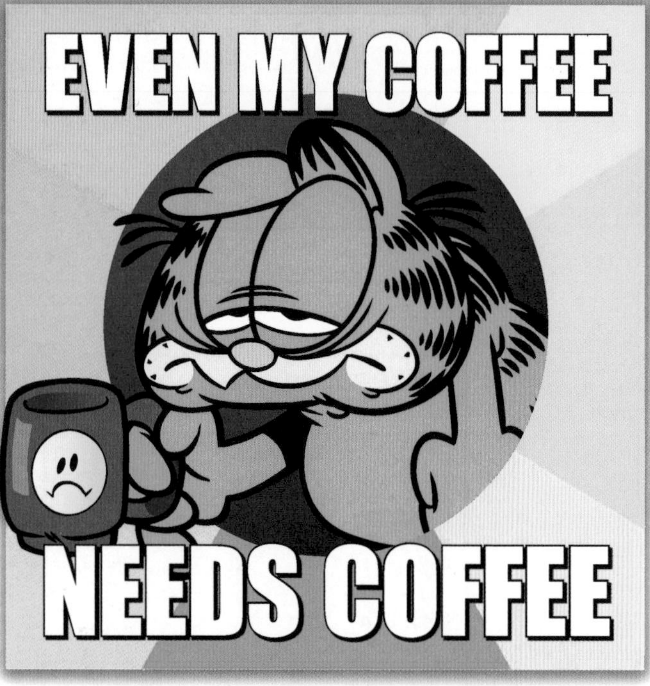
EVEN MY COFFEE
NEEDS COFFEE

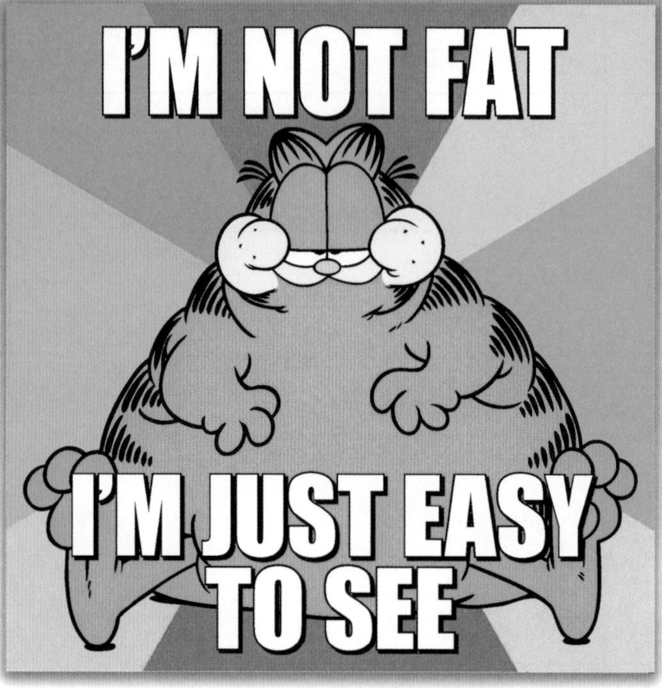
I'M NOT FAT
I'M JUST EASY TO SEE

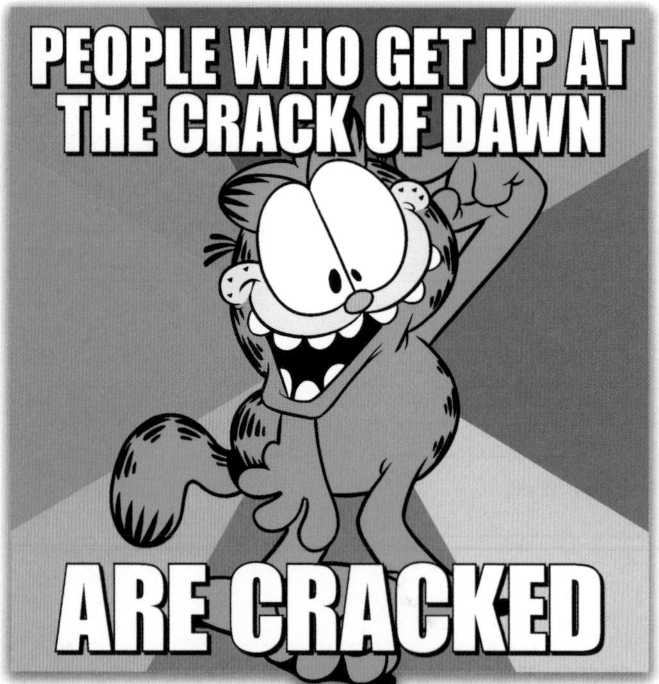
PEOPLE WHO GET UP AT THE CRACK OF DAWN
ARE CRACKED

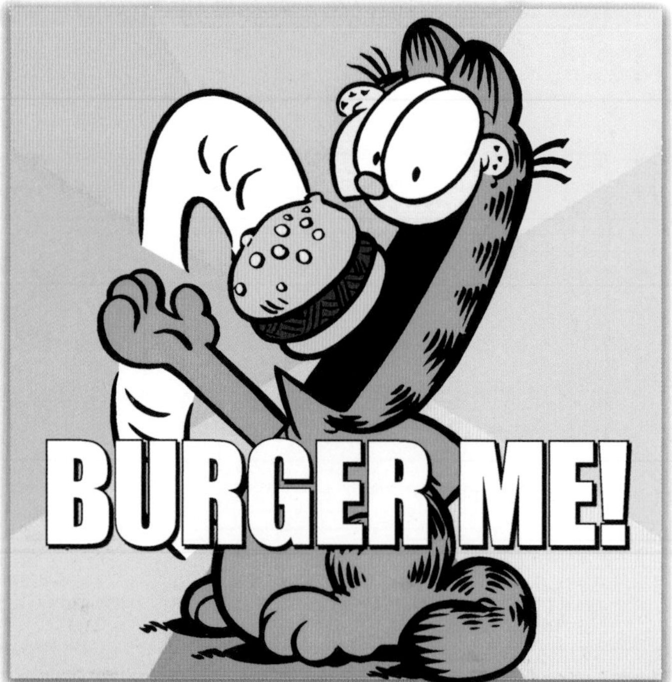
BURGER ME!

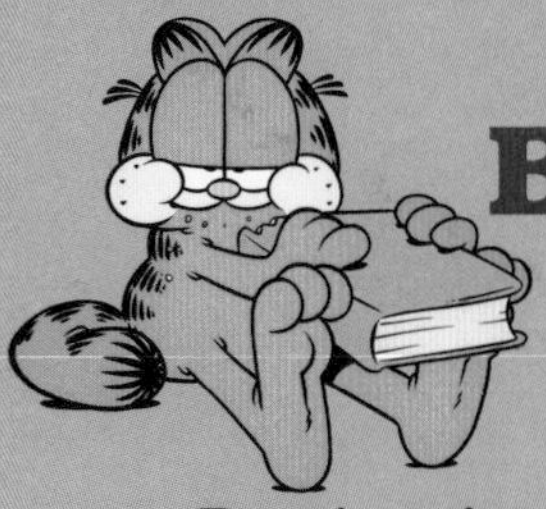

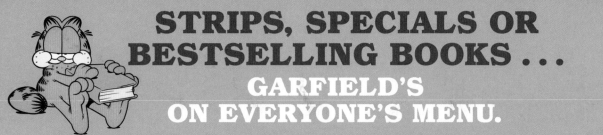

STRIPS, SPECIALS OR BESTSELLING BOOKS . . .

GARFIELD'S ON EVERYONE'S MENU.

Don't miss even one episode in the Tubby Tabby's hilarious series!

GARFIELD AT LARGE . . . (#1) 978-0-345-44382-3
GARFIELD GAINS WEIGHT . . . (#2) 978-0-345-44975-7
GARFIELD BIGGER THAN LIFE . . . (#3) 978-0-345-45027-2
GARFIELD WEIGHS IN . . . (#4) 978-0-345-45205-4
GARFIELD TAKES THE CAKE . . . (#5) 978-0-345-44978-8
GARFIELD EATS HIS HEART OUT . . . (#6) 978-0-345-46459-0
GARFIELD SITS AROUND THE HOUSE . . . (#7) 978-0-345-46463-7
GARFIELD TIPS THE SCALES . . . (#8) 978-0-345-46909-0
GARFIELD LOSES HIS FEET . . . (#9) 978-0-345-46467-5
GARFIELD MAKES IT BIG . . . (#10) 978-0-345-46468-2
GARFIELD ROLLS ON . . . (#11) 978-0-345-47561-9
GARFIELD OUT TO LUNCH . . . (#12) 978-0-345-47562-6
GARFIELD FOOD FOR THOUGHT . . . (#13) 978-0-345-47563-3
GARFIELD SWALLOWS HIS PRIDE . . . (#14) 978-0-345-91386-9
GARFIELD WORLDWIDE . . . (#15) 978-0-345-91754-6
GARFIELD ROUNDS OUT . . . (#16) 978-0-345-49169-5
GARFIELD CHEWS THE FAT . . . (#17) 978-0-345-49170-1
GARFIELD GOES TO WAIST . . . (#18) 978-0-345-49173-2
GARFIELD HANGS OUT . . . (#19) 978-0-345-49174-9
GARFIELD TAKES UP SPACE . . . (#20) 978-0-345-49178-7
GARFIELD SAYS A MOUTHFUL . . . (#21) 978-0-345-49179-4
GARFIELD BY THE POUND . . . (#22) 978-0-345-52558-1
GARFIELD KEEPS HIS CHINS UP . . . (#23) 978-0-345-52559-8
GARFIELD TAKES HIS LICKS . . . (#24) 978-0-345-52587-1
GARFIELD HITS THE BIG TIME . . . (#25) 978-0-345-52589-5
GARFIELD PULLS HIS WEIGHT . . . (#26) 978-0-345-52594-9
GARFIELD DISHES IT OUT . . . (#27) 978-0-345-52595-6
GARFIELD LIFE IN THE FAT LANE . . . (#28) 978-0-345-52600-7
GARFIELD TONS OF FUN . . . (#29) 978-0-345-52601-4
GARFIELD BIGGER AND BETTER . . . (#30) 978-0-345-52605-2
GARFIELD HAMS IT UP . . . (#31) 978-0-345-52606-9
GARFIELD THINKS BIG . . . (#32) 978-0-425-28516-9
GARFIELD THROWS HIS WEIGHT AROUND . . . (#33) 978-0-425-28559-6
GARFIELD LIFE TO THE FULLEST . . . (#34) 978-0-425-28564-0
GARFIELD FEEDS THE KITTY . . . (#35) 978-0-425-28569-5
GARFIELD HOGS THE SPOTLIGHT . . . (#36) 978-0-425-28574-9
GARFIELD BEEFS UP . . . (#37) 978-0-345-44109-6
GARFIELD GETS COOKIN' . . . (#38) 978-0-345-44582-7
GARFIELD EATS CROW . . . (#39) 978-0-345-45201-6
GARFIELD SURVIVAL OF THE FATTEST . . . (#40) 978-0-345-46458-3
GARFIELD OLDER AND WIDER . . . (#41) 978-0-345-46462-0
GARFIELD PIGS OUT . . . (#42) 978-0-345-46466-8
GARFIELD BLOTS OUT THE SUN . . . (#43) 978-0-345-46615-0
GARFIELD GOES BANANAS . . . (#44) 978-0-345-91346-3
GARFIELD LARGE & IN CHARGE . . . (#45) 978-0-345-49172-5
GARFIELD SPILLS THE BEANS . . . (#46) 978-0-345-49177-0
GARFIELD GETS HIS JUST DESSERTS . . . (#47) 978-0-345-91387-6
GARFIELD WILL EAT FOR FOOD . . . (#48) 978-0-345-49176-3
GARFIELD WEIGHS HIS OPTIONS . . . (#49) 978-0-345-49181-7
GARFIELD POTBELLY OF GOLD . . . (#50) 978-0-345-52244-3
GARFIELD SHOVELS IT IN . . . (#51) 978-0-345-52419-5
GARFIELD LARD OF THE JUNGLE . . . (#52) 978-0-345-52584-0
GARFIELD BRINGS HOME THE BACON . . . (#53) 978-0-345-52586-4
GARFIELD GETS IN A PICKLE . . . (#54) 978-0-345-52590-1
GARFIELD SINGS FOR HIS SUPPER . . . (#55) 978-0-345-52593-2
GARFIELD CAUTION: WIDE LOAD . . . (#56) 978-0-345-52596-3
GARFIELD SOUPED UP . . . (#57) 978-0-345-52598-7
GARFIELD GOES TO HIS HAPPY PLACE . . . (#58) 978-0-345-52602-1
GARFIELD THE BIG CHEESE . . . (#59) 978-0-345-52604-5
GARFIELD CLEANS HIS PLATE . . . (#60) 978-0-345-52608-3
GARFIELD CHICKENS OUT . . . (#61) 978-0-425-28515-2
GARFIELD LISTENS TO HIS GUT . . . (#62) 978-0-425-28557-2
GARFIELD COOKS UP TROUBLE . . . (#63) 978-0-425-28562-6
GARFIELD FEEDS HIS FACE . . . (#64) 978-0-425-28567-1
GARFIELD EATS AND RUNS . . . (#65) 978-0-425-28572-5
GARFIELD NUTTY AS A FRUITCAKE . . . (#66) 978-0-425-28576-3
GARFIELD SLURPS AND BURPS . . . (#67) 978-1-9848-1773-0
GARFIELD BELLY LAUGHS . . . (#68) 978-1-9848-1777-8
GARFIELD EASY AS PIE . . . (#69) 978-0-593-15640-7

DVD TIE-INS

GARFIELD AS HIMSELF . . . 978-0-345-47805-4
GARFIELD HOLIDAY CELEBRATIONS . . . 978-0-345-47930-3
GARFIELD TRAVEL ADVENTURES . . . 978-0-345-48087-3

AND DON'T MISS . . .

GARFIELD AT 25: IN DOG YEARS I'D BE DEAD . . . 978-0-345-45204-7
GARFIELD'S JOKE ZONE/INSULTS . . . 978-0-345-46263-3
GARFIELD FAT CAT 3-PACK/ VOL. 1 . . . 978-0-345-46455-2
GARFIELD FAT CAT 3-PACK/ VOL. 2 . . . 978-0-345-46465-1
GARFIELD FAT CAT 3-PACK/ VOL. 3 . . . 978-0-345-48088-0
GARFIELD FAT CAT 3-PACK/ VOL. 4 . . . 978-0-345-49171-8
GARFIELD FAT CAT 3-PACK/ VOL. 5 . . . 978-0-345-49180-8
GARFIELD FAT CAT 3-PACK/ VOL. 6 . . . 978-0-345-52420-1
GARFIELD FAT CAT 3-PACK/ VOL. 7 . . . 978-0-345-52588-8
GARFIELD FAT CAT 3-PACK/ VOL. 8 . . . 978-0-345-52599-4
GARFIELD FAT CAT 3-PACK/ VOL. 9 . . . 978-0-345-52607-6
GARFIELD FAT CAT 3-PACK/ VOL. 10 . . . 978-0-425-28558-9
GARFIELD FAT CAT 3-PACK/ VOL. 11 . . . 978-0-425-28566-4
GARFIELD FAT CAT 3-PACK/ VOL. 12 . . . 978-0-425-28578-7
GARFIELD FAT CAT 3-PACK/ VOL. 13 . . . 978-0-345-46460-6
GARFIELD FAT CAT 3-PACK/ VOL. 14 . . . 978-0-345-49175-6
GARFIELD FAT CAT 3-PACK/ VOL. 15 . . . 978-0-345-52585-7
GARFIELD FAT CAT 3-PACK/ VOL. 16 . . . 978-0-345-52592-5
GARFIELD FAT CAT 3-PACK/ VOL. 17 . . . 978-0-345-52603-8
GARFIELD FAT CAT 3-PACK/ VOL. 18 . . . 978-0-399-59440-3
GARFIELD FAT CAT 3-PACK/ VOL. 19 . . . 978-0-425-28561-9
GARFIELD FAT CAT 3-PACK/ VOL. 20 . . . 978-0-425-28571-8
GARFIELD FAT CAT 3-PACK/ VOL. 21 . . . 978-1-9848-1775-4
GARFIELD FAT CAT 3-PACK/ VOL. 22 . . . 978-0-593-15638-4
GARFIELD'S 20TH ANNIVERSARY COLLECTION . . . 978-0-345-42126-5
SEASON'S EATINGS: A VERY MERRY GARFIELD CHRISTMAS . . . 978-0-345-47560-2
GARFIELD'S GUIDE TO EVERYTHING . . . 978-0-345-46461-3
ODIE UNLEASHED! . . . 978-0-345-46464-4
GARFIELD'S BOOK OF CAT NAMES . . . 978-0-345-48516-8
THE GARFIELD JOURNAL . . . 978-0-345-46469-9
LIGHTS, CAMERA, HAIRBALLS!: GARFIELD AT THE MOVIES . . . 978-0-345-49134-3
30 YEARS OF LAUGHS AND LASAGNA . . . 978-0-345-50379-4
GARFIELD MINUS GARFIELD . . . 978-0-345-51387-8
GARFIELD FROM THE TRASH BIN . . . 978-0-345-51881-1
GARFIELD LEFT SPEECHLESS . . . 978-0-345-53058-5
MY LAUGHABLE LIFE WITH GARFIELD . . . 978-0-345-52591-8
GARFIELD'S SUNDAY FINEST . . . 978-0-345-52597-0
AGE HAPPENS: GARFIELD HITS THE BIG 4-0 . . . 978-0-345-52609-0
GARFIELD COMPLETE WORKS: VOLUME ONE: 1978 & 1979 . . . 978-0-425-28712-5
GARFIELD COMPLETE WORKS: VOLUME TWO: 1980 & 1981 . . . 978-0-425-28713-2

New larger, full-color format!

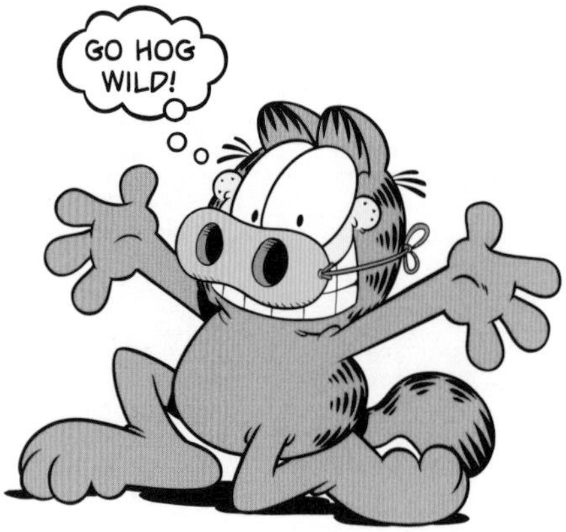
GO HOG WILD!